THAT UNEARTHLY VALLEY

A Donegal Childhood

Patrick McGinley

NEW ISLAND

THAT UNEARTHLY VALLEY
First published 2011
by New Island
2 Brookside
Dundrum Road
Dublin 14
www.newisland.ie

ISBN 978-1- 8484-0119-8

Cover Image "Kent Rockwell. Dan Ward's Stack"
© The State Hermitage Museum / photo by Vladimir Terebenin,
Leonard Kheifets, Yuri Molodkovets
And by kind permission of The Plattsburgh State Art Museum

Typeset by Mariel Deegan.
Printed by SPRINT-print Ltd.

New Island received financial assistance from
The Arts Council (An Comhairle Ealaíon), Dublin, Ireland

10 9 8 7 6 5 4 3 2 1

*For Kathleen
wife and companion*

Foreword

This memoir is not merely my story. It also tells the story of the changes that have taken place in the Donegal glen where I was born. I left Glen to go to boarding school in 1950 when I was 13, and since that time I have been home only on holiday. Nevertheless, Glen is the most important place in my life. I think of it every day, and now and again I dream about it as well. Kathleen, my wife of over forty years, tells me that for all practical purposes I still live there, and in a sense that is true. Glen is a magical place that remains firmly rooted in the memory of all of us who were born there. To get to know Glen and to come to possess it, one must go away, because its riches in all their fullness can be apprehended only in the imagination and after much unavailing travel in search of a substitute home.

Paradoxically, those who go away and stay away for many years come back with a dream that is destined to be shattered. That, I regret to say, has happened to me. Glen has changed, and so have I. Living and working in a large, amorphous city has transformed my habits of thought and perception, while the Glen of my imagination has remained unchanged. In reality, of course, the place I left behind has also been transformed. It may have changed less noticeably than London, but it has changed in more fundamental ways. No wonder the returning emigrant often finds his birthplace more alien than the foreign city he has left. No wonder his response is often one of incomprehension. I have striven to make sense of this conundrum, to try to work out which of us has undergone the greater change, Glen or myself. And I have come to the conclusion that even if I had remained as I was, I'd still think Glen had undergone a metamorphosis beyond my wildest imaginings. However, there is one thing about which I am adamant: I would not wish to have been born and brought up anywhere else. By that I mean the Glen of the 1940s and 1950s, before television and its attendant fripperies did for the old traditional culture.

Glen at that time was a homogeneous and organic community. For centuries it had been a little-known enclave, rarely touched by the preoccupations of the wider world. Now and again an emigrant might return and tell stories of happenings in strange places, but people's knowledge of life was derived largely from their own personal experience and from observing the lives of their neighbours. The culture that emerged from these conditions may have been inbred and inward-looking, but it was rich in imagination and, above all, courteous and humane. One of its distinguishing qualities was a generosity of spirit that buttressed a belief in the common humanity of every living man and woman. Tramps, tinkers, tourists and returned emigrants, all were made welcome with the same undesigning hospitality. Though their 'funny' ways might provide occasion for humorous gossip, they were willingly accepted as a manifestation of life's unending diversity.

Any reservations about a visitor would remain unspoken until after his or her departure. In the discussion that inevitably followed, everything that had passed would be analysed with appreciative humour, and original or amusing comments stored in the memory for future reference. A clever turn of phrase in either Irish or English would become part of the living folklore, forevermore linked with the phrase-maker's name. From having listened to my parents and neighbours I can still recall the names of men and women who lived and died in the nineteenth century, and left a legacy of wit and humour that survived in the local folklore for more than three generations.

Nearly everyone in the Glen of my boyhood was bilingual in Irish and English, and everyone was steeped in the local history and folklore. There were no organised forms of entertainment. Folk music and story provided the basis for amusement. There were no luxuries, nothing in excess of life's daily requirements. Cupidity and worldly ambition were almost unknown. It was a hard life, a life of enforced asceticism that bred its own stoical philosophy and sense of shared experience with your equally hard-pressed neighbour. It was a matter of keeping your head above water and your self-respect as a member of the tribe. A man who had been brought up in Glen in the early years of the twentieth century could have endured any hardship known even in the most primitive societies. He would have felt at home in the desert with the nomadic and tent-dwelling Bedouin of Arabia. And he would certainly have understood their sense of community, not to mention their ancestral pride.

The last quarter of the twentieth century transformed Glen out of all recognition. Now people have more money to spend, and with money has come the opportunity to savour ways of life unknown to previous generations. While my father and his neighbours rarely travelled outside the county, many young people today go abroad for their holidays. Increased mobility has brought an intensified awareness of other ways of living and thinking, accompanied by a tendency to assimilate the forms of speech heard on radio and television. All that has had an impoverishing effect on the local dialect, traditionally made up of words and idioms from the Irish language and the dialects of Scotland and northern England.

Of course these cultural and economic changes are not unique to Glen. They can be seen in a thousand villages all over Ireland, but I think it fair to say that in Glen the changes have been more rapid and more fundamental than elsewhere. What will be left of Ireland? I fondly ask myself. And will what still remains last my time? While on holiday in Glen in the early 1980s, I went into John Oweneen's pub (now The Glen Head Tavern) in the hope of enjoying an evening's yarning with my former neighbours. I remembered the pub from the 1950s when there was only one small bar and when everyone present joined in the same conversation. Now there were two bars, and the drinkers were no longer standing at the counter. Instead they were all seated at tables watching 'Hurricane' Higgins proving yet again his invincibility at snooker. The new television had become the centre of all interest. There was no conversation, only shouts of awe and approbation whenever the hero potted a ball. I tried talking to the man next to me but he was absorbed in the match on the screen. I realised then that I could have been in any nondescript pub in Donegal Town, Bundoran or even London. The inventive and humorous style of conversation that for me gave Glen its special flavour was a thing of the past. For one Glen man at least, Glen had lost its quiddity.

While Glen may now be a less distinctive community, it is no less desirable as a place in which to live. For one thing it is livelier, especially if you are young with a wad of euros in your pocket. There is an air of swagger and prosperity about, and more in the way of organised entertainment. The old thatch-roofed cottages have been replaced by bungalows with big picture windows, and everyone who can work enjoys a disposable income. There is no doubting the value of these developments. It is just a pity that they have been accompanied by a dilution of traditional patterns of speech and the indigenous way of looking at things, a loss that cannot be measured in monetary terms.

I have lived the best years of my life in and around London, during which few days passed without my thoughts returning to Glen. Celts seem to miss their homeland more keenly than any other people. The Welsh call the longing for the homeland *hiraeth*. We Irish have another word for it, *cumha* or *cumhaidh*, though a Welshman would probably claim that his *hiraeth* is a different thing altogether. I know nothing about *hiraeth* but I have experienced *cumhaidh*, a knot of emotions involving longing for a place and a people in the knowledge that the time longed for can never return. More than likely the people remembered with such affection will have departed, and the place itself will have changed. All that will remain of the past perhaps is an empty house, an overgrown garden, or an indomitable cliff facing out to sea. *Cumhaidh* is not a simple emotion. It is a wistful longing coloured with memories of a time of happiness now lost; it embraces the pleasure of remembrance and the pain of incompleteness that refuses to be assuaged.

This memoir is an attempt to resurrect facets of one man's past, to make a time and a place come alive again — however briefly — before they finally recede from living memory.

PART I

The Glen

1

The View from Cashel Hill

The Donegal glen in which I first opened my eyes was a small, self-contained world, far removed from the great events and conflicts that shaped Europe in the first half of the twentieth century. My people had lived in the glen for generations, eking out a living on a small farm and fishing lobsters during the summer season. It was a life of severely limited prospects. The most a family man could hope for was to keep himself, his wife and children in food and clothing, and perhaps enjoy a pipe of tobacco when the day's work was done. The business of making ends meet was so demanding that few people had either the time or inclination to cultivate an interest in the greater world. Few took a daily newspaper or had access to a wireless. For news from the other side of the hill people relied on the occasional visitor or the local newspaper, which by its nature reflected the world they already knew.

The ancient name for this special place where I was born was *Sean Ghleann*, meaning Old Glen. After St Colmcille reputedly paid us a flying visit in the sixth century, it came to be known as *Gleanncholmcille*, or Glencolmcille.

Like everyone else who has ever been born in the place, I find Glencolmcille something of a mouthful. We simply call it Glen: a satisfying name because it implies that there is but one glen, the one in which we were born.

Glen is a broad-based valley with a stony river running through it. Surrounded by hills to the east, north and south, it is open to Atlantic winds in the west and frequent rain from above. Seen from a distance the landscape is one of freakish contrasts. On closer inspection it becomes a hard, unyielding place of uneven fields, rocks and ditches with here and there a few stunted trees providing shelter for a cottage and its outbuildings. There are few fruit trees apart from an occasional cherry or crab apple. The branches of sycamores, ash, alder and blackthorn reach out to the east, as if in supplication, seeking escape from the salty west wind that in winter burns all it touches. On the hillsides rushes grow in clumps and narrow streams bite into the thin soil. The roads run aimlessly here and there, as if seeking the longest way home. Most are without hedges, apart from occasional bursts of wild fuchsia in sheltered hollows.

Few families were burdened with a plethora of worldly goods, but what people lacked in possessions they made up for in a rich oral heritage. Everyone had his or her fund of sayings and stories, and these could vary from family to family and from one townland to another. Growing up, I noticed that the stories I'd had from my parents differed from those my school friends had from theirs. Now I realise that the world I got to know as a boy had been coloured by the indigenous oral culture and enriched through reinterpretation over generations whose most treasured possession was an active and creative imagination. It was a good place for an aspirant writer to get to know.

As a returning emigrant, I always treasure the slow approach to Glen as you leave Carrick behind and travel through Loughunsha with its bleached brown moorland. For the last few miles of the journey the only sign of human settlement are the black bog-cuttings, the heaps of turf along the roadside, and the limekiln on the right which was built by the old Musgrave landlords. I always think of these last few precious miles as a kind of spiritual preparation, a relinquishing of the great world for something less fractured, something more solid and true. As you turn the corner above Curreen Bridge the valley suddenly opens up before you — bursting upon you with the force of a revelation, a spread that is almost impossible to take in at a glance. In fact I once met a perfectionist who went back on his tracks and made the approach a second time, just to ensure that he was mentally prepared and his eye properly focused.

After the quiet browns of the surrounding moorland the scene gives an impression of quirky variety. The fields and ditches run crazily here and there, defying logic and expectation. In the west the glimmering Atlantic seems to provide the only escape route for someone who is not prepared to go back on his tracks. Though the scene is etched on my memory, it invariably comes each time as a surprise because there is always something that evokes a thought I've not had before. Today the glen is dotted with tile-roofed bungalows, but in the days of thatched cottages the scene was even more striking. Then the houses looked as if they had grown naturally out of the landscape, the yellow-gold thatch and the whitewashed walls standing out in glorious contrast to the green fields, grey rocks, and purple hills, and the roads and lanes that ran between like the veins in a sycamore leaf. For me, Glen is a place that encircles and embraces. From it there is no going forward: it is always the end of the journey. It grips the imagination and holds it captive in a way that a place on the road to somewhere else cannot.

Local folklore gives Glen a romantic history. In blessing the island of Ireland, St Patrick omitted to include Glen in his benediction. To add insult to injury, when he was banishing the demons from Ireland, he sent them all to this secluded haven at the south-western extremity of Donegal. Here they lived in crowded contentment for over a hundred years until the arrival of St Colmcille, a Donegal man of princely stock who took it upon himself to rectify the national apostle's inexplicable oversight.

The demons had raised a fog over the glen to discourage inquisitive travellers from entering their stronghold, and had turned the river into a fiery stream so that anyone who touched its water or tried to cross it would die instantly. When Colmcille and his followers reached the spot, the demons flung a holly rod out of the fog, killing Colmcille's servant. The saint, who was not to be deterred, flung the holly rod back across the stream, extinguishing the fire and clearing the fog. Then he crossed the stream while the demons fled before him. They gathered their forces on Glen Head but Colmcille raised his right arm and hurled them down the cliff into the sea below, where they were turned into dogfish.

Scholars who are great demolishers of folk tradition have cast doubt on Colmcille's association with the glen to which he gave his name. There is a theory that a strong cult of Colmcille in the years following his death took over the traditions associated with local saints, replacing them with legends of Colmcille. In Glen this folk revisionism may have also happened with the local St Fanad, who gave his name to the townland of Killaned where I was born. The last time I was home I had a look at St Fanad's well on a neighbour's farm. My neighbour said that it went dry many years ago, when a tinker woman washed her clothes in it. Then he told me what modern scholars think. Scholars may say what they will but local folklore goes its own way and creates its own intrinsic interest. Given time, one scholarly theory will spawn another, but the roots of folklore run deeper. There is no telling how many scholarly tomes it would take to supplant a good story or extinguish local tradition and the ancestral pride it inspires.

2

'That Unearthly Valley'

Not so long ago 'the back of beyond' was a common enough description of Glen, which was too remote from so-called civilisation to be seen as a desirable place of residence. All that has changed. Nowadays people who have lived all their lives in cities are seeking out quiet nooks in the country in which to spend their weekends or their retirement years. Glen is no exception. Increasingly, those who emigrated in the 1950s and 1960s are returning and building new houses in places where their ancestors never imagined a house would stand. Rocky patches on hillsides have been cleared for building and rough places made into fertile gardens. Slowly but surely Glen is beginning to look domesticated, less wild, like a place where house building takes precedence over farming. If St Colmcille were around these days, he would have to go out to Glen Lough to find a quiet place to make his stone bed.

The early Irish saints sought out Glen for its remoteness, but I like to think that they stayed because of the sense of spirituality conveyed by the landscape. That it was a place in which they could feel alone with God because the terrain itself suggested the peace and mystery of an Otherworld. This is nowhere more apparent than in seldom-visited coves beneath the sea cliffs. There among the twisted black rocks you can find yourself overtaken by a sense of otherness, of a self that is not the one you know, of a being who is in touch with a rhythm or music that goes back to a time before humanity. The feeling may come from the eerie shapes of rock and reef, from the seemingly regular, yet erratic, slap and suck of the waves, or the empty cries of seagulls and cormorants. Whatever its source, it jolts you out of the rut of everyday perception with a cleansing sense of renewal and release. Glen is a place where, if you are receptive, you may catch an echo of a prehistoric world, of a life beyond the bourn of what is consciously known.

Strangers are more sharply aware of this quality of antiquity than those who have lived in Glen all their lives and for whom hill, cliff and sea are a ubiquitous backdrop to the round of common tasks. Most people who have written about Glen or portrayed it in their art see in it what they bring to it, making it into a mirror reflecting their own personalities and preoccupations. They show us many different Glens, or rather many shadows of the same immemorial Glen. I have come to feel that the truest and most sensitive reflection of the place is to be found in the writings of the English composer and lover of all things Celtic, Arnold Bax, who lived for extended periods in Glen in the early decades of the twentieth century.

Bax got to know the place and its people intimately, and he saw both with the eye of a poet. Some of his short stories and poems, written under the pseudonym Dermot O'Byrne, draw directly on this experience. In his autobiography *Farewell, My Youth* he gives a memorable account of the people he knew in the village of Cashel. That he was steeped in the early poems of Yeats and the writers of the Celtic Twilight is evident even in his vocabulary. For him Glen was 'that unearthly valley', a place which encompassed the fury of the Atlantic in winter, the serene glow of summer sunsets, and the spectacle of the aurora borealis above Glen Head on a clear winter night. He even hoped that he might return to it, if only in memory, before finally departing this world:

> I like to fancy that on my deathbed my last vision in this life will be the scene from my window on the upper floor at Glencolumcille, of the still, brooding, dove-grey mystery of the Atlantic at twilight; the last glow of sunset behind Glen Head in the north, with its ruined watch-tower built in 1812 at the time of the scare of a Napoleonic invasion; and east of it the calm slope of Scraig Beefan, its glittering many-coloured surface of rock, bracken, and heather, now one uniform purple glow.

In 1926 the American artist and writer Rockwell Kent and his wife spent four months in Glen. Kent was a man in search of elemental experience. Spurning cities, he lived for long periods in Labrador, Alaska, Greenland, and Tierra del Fuego, and many of his paintings show his fascination with the landscapes of the wilderness and life in the raw. While in the parish of Glen, he was not attracted by the relative comforts of Cashel. Instead he made straight for Glen Lough to the north of Port, a place of rock, bog and heather then inhabited by Dan Ward and his wife. There was no road into Glen Lough, not even a path over the mountain. Kent rented a ruined house that was being used as a byre by Ward, and with much heavy labour converted it to a habitable state. As an artist he was not idle either, and he made several well-known paintings during his stay. Some of these show coastal landscapes with stark outlines lit by a mysterious back-glow, giving familiar scenes an exotic and unfamiliar quality. Simple living suited his purpose. He got on well with the people of the neighbouring townlands, and above all he enjoyed drinking their poteen. Kent himself says that he loved even the smell of turf smoke. The paintings for which he is best known in Glen are *Dan Ward's Stack* and *Annie McGinley*, which shows a local girl lying on a cliff top on a summer day looking out to sea. The Glen people took to him and still talked about him and recounted his exploits many years after he'd left.

Glen owes its distinctive scenery to its geological formation, but equally telling is the influence of the wide Atlantic, which most of the time brings the weather, especially the rain. Unlike Teelin Bay, Glen Bay is a place of little or no shelter, as generations of fishermen have found to their cost. It is open to wind and storm. For most of the winter it is impossible to put out in a small boat, as the sea is a boiling cauldron, rising up over the rocks and thickening the air with spume. In summer the opposite is often true. On a fine evening there is nothing more peaceful than hand-lining from a boat along the coast, enjoying the cliff scenery and the play of sunlight on the water. However, to see Glen only in summer is to enjoy but one facet of its personality. The locals will tell you that it needs to be experienced in all weathers, in rain and mist, on cloudy days and sunny days, on calm days and on days when the wind threatens to blow you away. The Atlantic gives Glen its bleak austerity. If it were situated in the Mediterranean, it might attract more tourists but it would lose more than half its fascination.

Like most Glen people, I always enjoy hearing what strangers make of the place. Browsing in the London

Library one afternoon, I came across a reference to Glen in a nineteenth-century topographical dictionary. At the end of a short paragraph of rather prosaic fact there was a sentence that made me stop and think: 'There is a remarkable echo in the mountains.' I had to admit to myself that if there is, I hadn't noticed it, and I wondered if the author had imagined it or meant it metaphorically, referring not to an actual echo but to something that keeps reverberating in the memory. Shortly afterwards I came across an article by the poet Geoffrey Grigson in an old issue of *The London Magazine*, which confirmed beyond doubt that the echo was real.

Grigson and Dylan Thomas spent part of the summer of 1935 in Glen Lough, living in the house belonging to Dan Ward that Rockwell Kent had made habitable some years before. Grigson writes:

> From the cliffs he [Dylan] watched gannets drop and fleck the Atlantic; or climbing steeply to the lakes at the back of the farm and the converted stable, we shouted up to the surrounding, ringing mountains *We are the Dead*, for the multiple echo to reply in sequence *We are the Dead, the Dead, the Dead, the Dead*. We shouted to these mountains above the lake one evening till we frightened ourselves, stumbling down afterwards through heather and fern and bog to the comfort of the cottage, where Dylan stretched stained white feet, Swansea feet, to the warm turf, alongside the brown, huge feet of the farmer Dan Ward.

Sadly, Dylan Thomas was to leave behind a discordant echo in the mountains. Geoffrey Grigson went home after a few weeks, having settled up with Dan Ward and given money to Dylan to pay for his keep and other necessaries. Unlike Grigson, Thomas was less than impressed by the landscape and the people. In a letter to a friend he referred to this 'wild, unlettered and unfrenchlettered country, too far from Ardara, a village you can't be too far from'. In spite of that, he stayed on until the end of August, being looked after by Dan Ward and his wife. Then one morning he left suddenly without saying goodbye and without paying a penny of the agreed sum for his food and lodging. More than likely, he had spent the money that Grigson had given him on poteen. I like to think that Dan Ward was not all that surprised. As a young man, he worked for several years on a sheep farm in New Zealand and had seen something of the world. Perhaps he had already learnt that poetry and the word of a poet are not necessarily the same thing. When Dylan's London friends heard about the incident, they were furious. They gave Thomas a roasting, and one of them, the poet Norman Cameron, sent Dan Ward the money that was owed him.

Over the generations many young people have left Glen to seek work in Scotland, England, America, Australia, and indeed wherever they could find it. A few returned in middle age to end their days where they had begun. Most never came back. My father's uncles went to Scotland and never once wrote home. They hadn't forgotten Glen, though. Locals who ran into them in Scotland said that they talked of nothing else. Remembering from a distance is the fate of most exiles, if only because they know that there is no going back. The man who returns is not the man who went away, and the place he finds is no longer the place he left. For the exile the homeland must remain a place of the imagination. Like Hemingway's Paris, it is a movable feast. You carry it with you. You can revisit it no matter where you are. It is a case of love in absence, or, as we say in Irish, *grá éagmaise, grá i gcéin.*

All exiles have memories that keep returning. We may remember a particular day, or even an incident of little significance, which somehow symbolises our experience of home and all that we feel about it. I have three recurring recollections of Glen: the eerie feeling I had as a boy on first seeing Port with its deserted village and beach of white stones presided over by the black obelisk known to the locals as Bod a' Diabhail, the Devil's Penis; my sense of wonder at the soaring majesty of Glen Head viewed from a small boat on a summer evening between Tor a' Chreasaigh and Carraig na nIolar; and my sense of incongruity on seeing the Tower rise over the curve of the land as I climbed Beefan hill for the first time. On the one hand it seemed out of place; on the other it lent a noble distinction to a bleak and windswept scene.

However, the memory that best sums up my unfulfilled relationship with Glen is that of a late September evening in Skelpoona, with the wind from the north and a dark rack of cloud in the west edged by the deepening red of a setting sun. Further out there's a jabble on the water. I am fishing from Leic na Mágach, and from where I stand, I can hear the thump of the waves at the mouth of Úig a' Chogaidh and the furroo of the wind coming round the shoulder of Glen Head. It is towards the end of harvest. The hay is in tramp-cocks, the fields behind me are bare. In November the glassan or saithe will come in for a few precious weeks before winter and the water around the Clúidín will be thick with them. I am saddened at the thought of having to go back to university. I shall miss the best fishing of the year.

Overlooking Skelpoona is Screig Beefan, a solid, sloping, flat-topped crag clad below with green ferns in summer that turn to reddish bracken in winter. Between the patches of fern are areas of naked rock and scree that give the mountain its stern face and personality. For me

Screig Beefan is central to any delineation of Glen as Bax's 'unearthly valley', symbolising as it does the Glen of the early anchorites, a place of hallowed power and austere spirituality. No matter how much the rest of the Glen is tamed and commercialised, Screig Beefan will remain itself. In its noble solidity it is proof against the servile scurrying of would-be entrepreneurs and indeed all who live hurried lives. It is simply there morning, noon and night, in all weathers and in all seasons, and best contemplated in silence.

3

Living on the Wind

My earliest memories are of the war years in Glen, the
years of the so-called Emergency. While some local
families had sons serving in the British army, for most
people the events that were taking place in Europe and
the wider world seemed far away. I once asked an old man
what the Second World War had meant to him. He said,
'No tea, no tobacco. They were the only luxuries in my
life.' Elderly people still remember the war years as a time
of misery. There was little or no employment and little or
no money to go round. We lived in an enclave, cut off
almost entirely from the rest of the county and the rest
of the country, which, by virtue of De Valera's policy of
neutrality, was itself cut off from the rest of the world.

Throughout the 1940s few strangers came to see us
except the occasional tourist from Scotland or Northern
Ireland. Some of them were middle-aged couples who
had been in the habit of coming year after year. Unlike the
modern tourist, they didn't come in cars. They walked
everywhere, they enjoyed talking to the locals, and they
took a civilised interest in the place and what went on in

it. I suppose they thought the glen itself was lovely but that the life of the people was one of unrelieved hardship. They wouldn't have known the things that made life possible and sometimes even rich in interest. As all they would have seen was the work in the fields, they could be forgiven for wondering how anyone managed to wrest a living from a few wet patches of rocky ground.

'What do you live on here?' one of them asked a neighbour of mine who was mowing in a field by the road.

'The wind,' came the serious but unenlightening reply.

'You won't go hungry, then,' the tourist smiled sympathetically.

'And we won't go thirsty either. The rain and the wind, they're our manna from heaven.'

My neighbour was neither joking nor complaining. At that time people's expectations were simple and for the most part achievable. Provided they enjoyed good health and had enough to eat, they were content. The purpose of life was not the pursuit of pleasure. Indeed, they had been schooled by their priests not to expect fulfilment in this world, and to find solace in the parable of the rich man and Lazarus in Luke's gospel. Good things came the way of the rich man in this life. He feasted sumptuously every day while Lazarus, a poor man, lay at his gate, desiring nothing more than to be fed the crumbs that fell from the rich man's table. In the afterlife the rich man found himself suffering the torments of hell while the once-destitute Lazarus rested in Abraham's bosom in heaven. It was the kind of parable that would make any God-fearing person pray for someone who was unfortunate enough to dine sumptuously every day. It meant that justice was not to be found here, that money could not buy eternal bliss.

Perhaps it was just as well that the teachings of religion encouraged people not to lust after luxuries and wealth. What little money there was went on food and clothing. For that reason the shopkeepers were probably better off than anyone else. Only teachers, lighthouse keepers, civic guards and the postman enjoyed the privilege of a regular income. Most people depended for their livelihood on farming and the dole.

During the war years Charlie Murrin came in from Killybegs in his lorry once a week with necessary provisions, mainly flour, bread, butter, jam, tea and tobacco. As Glen was at the very end of the run, his load was light by the time he reached Cashel. On one memorable occasion he arrived with only one loaf. Lacking the gift of miraculous multiplication, and finding himself surrounded by a crowd of angry shoppers who had been waiting several hours for his arrival, he did what he thought was the sensible thing: he threw the loaf in the air, and the story has it that it was caught by a local footballer noted for his skill in high fielding. No doubt it was a time for the agile and the strong rather than the lame and the weak. Furthermore, shopkeepers had their pets. Those who paid their bills on time got preference over those who were a credit risk. For that reason there was much underhand or secret shopping in the kitchen, since shopkeepers felt they must not be seen to favour one customer over another. People who have lived through those terrible years now say that it is a time best forgotten.

Farms were small, no more than six or seven acres. Most households kept two cows to provide milk and sometimes butter, and a flock of chickens to provide eggs and now and again a good dinner on Sunday. For food, people grew potatoes and some vegetables, mainly turnips, cabbage and carrots. As there were no cash crops, money had to be found to buy flour, tea, sugar, jam, and items of clothing from the shop. Luckily, with each farm went a fairly large expanse of mountain pasture, which the householders of each townland held in common. This acreage provided grazing for cattle during the summer and for sheep throughout the year. Sheep and lambs were sold at Carrick or Ardara fair once or twice a year, and jobbers came round in their lorries from time to time to buy calves. During spring, summer and autumn, lobster, mackerel, herring and cod fishing provided a source of income for a few families along the shore. The season was short, however, extending only from May to October. During the rest of the year, the sea was often too rough to put out in a small rowing boat.

Handloom weaving was another useful source of income. To the casual observer with an eye for the romance of rural living, it was the cottage industry par excellence. The sheep from which the wool came could be seen grazing the hillsides. They were clipped every summer and the wool cleaned, teased, carded and spun into yarn by the women of the family. The crotal or lichen used in wool-dyeing grew on the rocks all around. The yarn produced by women on their spinning wheels by the fireside could be made into cloth by the weaver in his thatched loom-house. Thus the whole operation appeared to rest within the control of each individual family. However, for most weavers the reality was somewhat different. They worked for Gaeltarra Éireann, a government-sponsored agency for the development of Gaeltacht enterprises. The yarn came from the factory in Kilcar. Weavers collected it from Cashel once a week and returned the finished web the following week. On web day you could see a line of weavers approaching the Lace House in Cashel from north, south, east and west, each carrying his web on his back. Web day was a social occasion when weavers met other weavers and, after receiving payment for the previous week's web, discussed their work over a drink before going home.

As a boy I loved going into a loom-house to watch the weaver at work. He worked with both hands and both feet, and there was so much movement, so much going on simultaneously, that I found it difficult to understand how it was all accomplished. The sley was moving back and forth, the shuttle was flying from left to right and from right to left, and the heddles were going up and down as the weaver pressed the treadles. To cap it all, the metal-tipped shuttle made a hollow 'clock-clocking' sound as it travelled, but in spite of all the noise and movement the web did not seem to be getting any longer. My uncle explained it all to me by putting a piece of coloured thread between the strands of warp so that I could watch it travel and see for myself the rate of progress.

Filling bobbins for the shuttle was another fascinating business. The bobbin-winder was a makeshift contraption consisting of a wooden frame and an old bicycle wheel without its inner tube or tyre, which looked like a simple version of a spinning wheel complete with treadle. Sometimes the weaver himself filled the bobbins, but more often than not this work was done by his wife or a younger member of the family so that he could devote his time to the more skilled business of weaving.

Few weavers devoted all their time to weaving. Most worked their farms as well, cutting and 'saving' their turf in the spring and hay in the summer and autumn. Likewise, fishermen kept up their farm work. During the lobster-fishing season my father got up at five every morning in order to reach Log na dTruán slip by six. He came back shortly after nine and did a day's work on the farm before going back to the slip again at six in the evening. Sometimes he would do more jobs about the house after finally returning at nine. He seldom got to bed before twelve. During the summer he worked for as long as daylight lasted. His work was his life. He did not complain, though now and again he would say that all he had to show for his efforts was the certainty of a sound night's sleep. As I look back now, I can't help envying his quiet stoicism. If I'd had half his gift for dogged application, I might have made more of my life.

The food we ate was plain but healthy. I don't think anyone died of obesity-related disease. Housewives were expert at making a little go a long way. A good cook was one who could rustle up a tasty meal from next to nothing. Most people lived on cereal foods and potatoes. In every kitchen there was a ten-stone bag of flour and a smaller bag of oatmeal. The flour was used for making soda bread and the oatmeal for porridge and oatcakes, which we called oatmeal farls. Between them they accounted for at least fifty per cent of the diet of the average household. The other fifty per cent was made up largely of potatoes in one form or another. A working man would eat from seven to ten pounds of potatoes for dinner. They were eaten mainly with fish, and if there was no fish, with milk and salt. Sometimes colcannon or champ, which we called *brúitín*, was eaten for supper. It was made from potatoes mashed with onions, milk and butter, and was greatly appreciated by us children. Another treat was potato cake, which we called 'boxty'. Raw potatoes were peeled and grated and placed in a linen cloth so that the water could be wrung from them. A little flour was used to bind them, and the resulting mixture was made into flat cakes and fried on a pan and eaten hot with melting butter. Housewives in a hurry sometimes made cakes from potatoes that had been boiled first and then mashed, but these would never qualify as the real thing in the eyes of a boxty connoisseur.

The importance of the potato as an item of diet is reflected in the number of Irish words to describe potatoes that were too small for human consumption. Among these are *sceoidín*, *scidín*, *póirín*, and *sceoirín*, which were boiled mainly for fowl and animal feed. I have heard serious-minded farmers debate the relative sizes of these and disagree about which of them could be eaten with a pinch of salt in a time of need. However, everyone seemed to agree that a *sceoirín*, which is no bigger than a marble, is even too small to boil for farmyard fowl.

Generally, the aim was to allow no potato to go to waste. In the spring, when seed potatoes were being split or cut for planting, the leftover parts (*tónóga*) were used to make colcannon or potato cakes. During the spring digging, the spade would uncover potatoes that had been overlooked during harvesting and had remained in the ground over the winter. These, called *atochailt*, were watery and tasteless. In spite of that, we children gathered them diligently so that they could be boiled for farmyard use.

Breakfast consisted of a boiled egg and plenty of homemade soda bread and butter. During the summer we had potatoes and fresh fish for dinner, and during the winter salt cod, mackerel or herring. We had bread and jam for tea and porridge for supper, which was taken an hour or so before bedtime. The porridge, or stirabout, was made in the family skillet-pot over the turf fire, which gave the porridge its memorably smoky flavour. Sometimes the leftovers, what we called 'the scrapings of the pot,' were eaten with hot milk for breakfast the following morning. The scrapings had a burnt taste that was not to everyone's liking. As a boy, I loved the scrapings, which I saw as a delicacy that not everyone was capable of appreciating.

Oatcakes were cooked on a wire griddle in front of the turf fire. The cake was made into four quarters called farls and eaten at teatime with plenty of butter. Oatmeal farls were hard as timber. You needed good strong teeth to deal with them. There was a story about a nineteenth-century traveller who came to Glen to study the life of the people. He entered a house one day, and as he looked pale and in need of sustenance, the woman of the house gave him a buttered farl with a mug of milk. He had never seen an oatmeal farl before and he did not quite know what to do with it. Reluctant to give offence, he drank the milk and licked the butter off the farl. Then he handed back the farl to the astonished housewife and said, 'Thank you for the butter, Ma'am. I'm returning the board.'

Porridge was a staple food for the Donegal seasonal labourers who went to Scotland every autumn for the potato digging or 'tattie-hoking'. My father used to tell us that six or seven tattie-hokers would sit round a big communal porridge pot in the middle of a barn floor. Each of them would be given a noggin of milk and a wooden spoon, and each would make a hollow in the porridge with his spoon and pour a little of the milk into it. The hollow would widen and deepen as he ate, and he would have to take great care to ensure that his ration of milk did not leak into the hollows made by his neighbours. It was not an ideal way to eat porridge, and listening to that story as a boy, I often felt grateful that I could eat my porridge from a bowl in peace.

Tea was rationed during the war. Instead, we drank a black, unpalatable concoction that disgraced the name of coffee. Even oatmeal was scarce, and we often had to make do with porridge made from Indian meal or maize, which was unpleasantly grainy in texture and almost uneatable except with generous lashings of milk.

One day I pushed my plate aside and said that I didn't like Indian meal porridge.

'You should count your lucky stars it isn't sowens,' my father said.

'What's sowens?' I asked.

He told me that it was a kind of stirabout made from the husks of oats. The husks were steeped in water for five or six days till they fermented. Then the water was drained off and what was left at the bottom of the tub was cooked to make a kind of porridge. 'I had it once as a boy,' he said. 'Maybe you'd eat your Indian meal porridge, if it was either that or sowens.' It was cold comfort but I've never forgotten it. Now, whenever I'm confronted with an unpleasant choice, I think of my father and the Sowens Principle.

On Saturday the local butcher did his rounds with bicycle and basket. Most of the time his basket contained only mutton, though he might kill a bullock once or twice a year. Not everyone bought meat from the butcher. For Sunday dinner many people had rashers and sausages from the shop. It was a common practice to run up bills at the shop and settle up two or three times a year, when a heifer or bullock or year-old wethers were sold at the fair. Taking animals to the fair wasn't easy. There was no means of transport. They had to be driven six miles to Carrick or nine miles to Ardara, and when markets were slack, farmers often suffered the frustration of having to drive them home again.

Wives contributed to the family exchequer by spinning, knitting and needlework. The money they earned may have been meagre, but it helped to eke out the family income. The quality of life enjoyed by each family depended not only on whether the husband was a good provider but also on the domestic skills of his wife. The best wives kept their homes spick and span. They churned regularly and made good country butter. They made blackberry and rhubarb jam in season, and they were good cooks within the limits that circumstances had imposed on them. It was an axiom among men that a good wife was worth her weight in gold.

The ideal was to be as self-sufficient as possible, and to buy as little as possible from the shop. My father used to tell us about a mountain man who was out at heel. He clipped one of his sheep on Thursday and went to Mass the following Sunday wearing a new pair of socks knitted by his wife from thread she had spun from the wool of the newly clipped sheep. This feat attracted general admiration as the very acme of good housekeeping.

One result of my upbringing is that I am still fond of fish, preferring it to meat or any other food. My favourite fish was cod, which my father caught in the spring. These were North Atlantic cod, greenish-brown in colour with a whitish belly and yellow dots on the back and flanks. Cod live in deep water and can't be fished from a rock. The fishermen rowed from Log na dTruán slip to the Sound in Malinmore, which was a noted place for cod. They fished with a hand-line bearing a baited hook and sink. Not everyone had the required expertise to be a good cod fisher. My uncle used to tell a story about a young man who thought he might try his luck for a day. After a while the seasoned fishermen couldn't understand why he wasn't catching anything and began making fun of him. At the end of the day he pulled in his line only to find a dead cod at the end of it.

Cod is a fish that loses its flavour quickly. The cod we ate came straight from the sea and my mother cooked it while it was absolutely fresh, certainly within six hours of being caught. Whenever I have cod for dinner now, I ask myself if it tastes like the cod I remember, and more often than not it doesn't for the simple reason that it has lain too long on the fishmonger's slab or in a freezer.

Glassan, the local name for saithe, was an important part of the diet in townlands by the shore. Young glassan are about nine inches to a foot in length. They have their own distinctive flavour, quite different from cod or pollock. Shoals of them came in every autumn. They were fished from the rocks with rod and line and a fly made from sheep's wool. They were split and salted and then hung up from the rafters in the kitchen to dry.

Some men were noted for their skill in fishing sand-eels, which came into the strand in plentiful numbers every November. Living as they did in the sand, they were fished in shallow water at low tide in the evening or on moonlit nights. Each fisherman carried a sack tied round his waist and used a special hook while standing in the sea with the water up to his knees. He would draw the hook through the sand with one hand until he felt a sand-eel wriggling on it. He would then lift the sand-eel from the water with his free hand and put it in the bag. Here speed was of the essence. A good fisherman might catch as many as 10 score sand-eels in an evening. The biggest catch I've heard of was 34 score caught by Jamie Cannon of Dooey in one night, quite possibly a record. Needless to say, it doesn't appear in any reference book. Sand-eels were hung up from the rafters to cure, and then eaten with potatoes for dinner or supper.

During the winter months, when there was no fresh fish, we had salt cod or ling for dinner. Salt fish from the shop was known simply as 'big fish', a direct translation of the Irish *iasc mór*. It was as hard as a piece of wood and had to be soaked overnight and the water changed three or four times before cooking. Once, while on holiday in Lisbon, I was interested to discover that the Portuguese are so fond of salt cod or *bacalhau* that they eat it at Christmas. I had it for dinner one evening for old times' sake and was delighted to find that it tasted exactly like the 'big fish' of my boyhood. It was one flavour that had not changed.

Another 'delicacy' was crab claws, which we called crab toes. As there was no market for crab at that time, fishermen used the body of the crab for lobster bait and kept the claws for home consumption. Again, they arrived fresh from the sea and were roasted over the coals of a turf fire, spilling their juice as they cooked. As a result the cooked flesh was dry and firm, quite different from that of crab claws that have been boiled in water. Now and again we had fresh lobster but that was a rare treat. Unlike crab, lobsters were for the market. They weren't plentiful, and those that were caught were precious.

There was little of what you might call 'organised social life', and what social life there was centred on the home and the pub. Housewives visited each other and exchanged the latest gossip over tea. Men went 'raking' to neighbours' houses during the long winter nights and there enjoyed their own brand of gossip. Once or twice a year they might take their wives to an old-time dance in the Spink Hall, a rough-and-ready building of tin and wood that got its name from a nearby pinnacle of rock, but otherwise husbands and wives seldom went out together. Men spent most of their time working with other men, and whenever they went to the pub for a drink they met only other men. Women seldom went into pubs, and the few who did had their drink in the kitchen or in the privacy of the snug where they could enjoy a glass of sherry or port wine without everyone in the parish getting to know about it.

Men who went to the pub regularly were in a minority. When I was growing up, my father went to the pub about three or four times a year, at Christmas and New Year, on St Patrick's Day and on sports day, the 15th of August. Most men could not afford to drink regularly and only those with a steady income could afford to drink spirits. For most men the preferred drink was bottled stout or beer, since draught did not come to Glen until the 1960s. In those days, before the advent of television lounges, pubs were small and intimate, and everyone knew every-one else. A good pub was one that was 'as good as any raking house', where everyone could take part in the same conversation, if that was the general inclination.

Pub talk had its own characteristics. It was more imaginative than ordinary talk, and it roamed more freely and amusingly, at least in the first few hours while the drinkers' faculties were still keen. Not everyone could make good pub talk, which was a matter of keeping the conversational balloon aloft without pricking it. Only those who were 'good crack' had this most cherished of creative gifts, the ability to enlarge the subject, revealing new and unsuspected facets of interest, without pushing the conversation out of shape. People who were 'good crack' were described as 'antic', which in the local dialect did not mean 'grotesque' or 'absurd' but 'droll' or 'amusing'.

In the absence of organised entertainment, most people found their only amusement in the contemplation and discussion of other lives. Good gossips had analytical skills to match those of the most gifted novelist. They knew their neighbours' every psychological quirk. They knew everyone's family history going back several generations, and they knew who had taken after whom. They knew who was harmless and who was 'cute as a fox'. Given such knowledge, it is small wonder that there were so many experts in character analysis — and even character assassination when the occasion demanded.

Nowhere was the pursuit of knowledge about other lives more evident than in pubs, where 'fishing for information' had become something of an art form. Listening to an expert fisher was 'as good as a circus'. An expert fisher would never ask a direct question; he would always go the long way round so as to confound his interlocutor. The real fun arose when the person who was the object of interest realised what was afoot. If he himself was an antic man, he would keep his neighbour in suspense with infuriating hints that were deliberately wide of the mark, if not positively misleading. To tell a bare-faced lie would have been an admission of defeat, showing an unforgivable lack of imagination and conversational resource.

The most enjoyable pub conversations had a competitive edge that defined the characters of the participants. Two men would begin a conversation, ostensibly about someone who was absent while directing their oblique barbs at a third person who was present. The beauty of it was that no one could accuse them of 'ribbing', certainly not the person at whom the ribbing was directed. More often than not he would join in the fun, as if totally unaware of any personal reference. To do otherwise would be an admission that the cap fitted to the great delight of his neighbours.

Presiding over the never-ending drama was the pub landlord, who, as master of the revels, knew when to put his oar in and when to say nothing. The best landlords were good listeners and as such were repositories of all sorts of news and scandal. They knew how to tell a story when the occasion demanded, and they knew better than to take inordinate pleasure in the sound of their own voice or parade their superior knowledge in case it might snap the thread of a promising conversation. Some landlords were characters in their own right. Their customers didn't come in just for a drink but to hear what they had to say and how they said it. Their anecdotes and witty rejoinders were quoted freely in the fields the following day. These landlords did more than just run a business. They were protagonists in the local drama, enjoying two lives in one, living on both sides of the counter simultaneously.

The tolling of the church bell the day the war ended signalled a profound sense of relief. Later, people talked about how Mussolini had died and wondered what had become of Hitler, and if they'd heard the last of him. Talking about his death was like talking about the death of Satan. People had lived with the hardships occasioned by his works for so long that they could hardly believe his reign had ended.

'What will happen now?' I asked my father.

'Nothing, I hope,' was his reply. 'Far too much has happened already.'

Some time in the following year I tasted my first orange. The first bananas arrived later. The war years were truly over but things remained more or less the same. The changes that transformed Glen beyond recognition did not begin until the 1950s.

One of the things that enriched life in Glen was the culture of sharing, which is often found among hard-pressed communities. If a fisherman caught more pollock, glassan or mackerel than served the immediate needs of his family, he would give some of the catch to his neighbours. Likewise, given an opportunity, his neighbour would do the same for him or at least help out in an hour of need.

A farmer or fisherman with a wife and young family to support depended entirely on his strength of limb and stamina. A man who had lost his health and strength, even temporarily, had little or nothing to fall back on. When I was about ten, my father took to his bed with an illness the doctor could not put a name to. It was early summer, the beginning of the lobster season and after he had just cut his supply of turf for the following winter. For six weeks or more he lay in the kitchen bed, eating next to nothing, while my mother did her best not to look worried. Dr Byrne came, took his temperature, and put him on a diet of oranges. I still do not know what was wrong with him, nor what the oranges were meant to do for him. What I remember most clearly is going from shop to shop with my mother in search of them, as they were a scarce commodity in Glen in 1947.

The weeks went by. The house was unusually quiet. I began to wonder if my father would ever get up. In July the neighbours gathered one day with their scythes and cut our hay. It was my first experience of a *meitheal*, a party of voluntary workers who give their work for a day in return for nothing more than food and hospitality. The *meitheal* did wonders for my father's spirits. Shortly afterwards, he got out of bed and spent a week or so walking about, surveying what needed to be done when his strength returned. Before long he was making hand-cocks and tramp-cocks. I knew that he was feeling better when he sent me to the shop for plug tobacco and lit his pipe again.

4

Old Beliefs and Practices

Frank Boyle, our primary teacher, used to say that our parents, who were born in the early years of the twentieth century, had seen the twilight of the superstitions that had haunted the lives of previous generations. I am not altogether sure that he was right. Though belief in superstition as such was not widely evident when I was growing up, it had not died out entirely. No one would consciously admit to being superstitious but an awareness of past beliefs and customs still coloured people's thoughts and attitudes.

My father often spoke dismissively of 'the old people with their old stories and pishrogues'. A pishrogue was a charm or spell, a superstitious belief or practice. He would tell us about old women who were believed to have *fios* or occult knowledge. People with *fios* could foretell the future; could actually see things happening before the event, and they were much feared and even respected for their ambivalent gift, which could be used for either good or evil. Though my father did not believe in any of this, he had an innate respect for past beliefs and practices.

Behind one of the roof-couples in our house were the hooves of a bullock or heifer that had died from disease or a fall off a cliff. My father told me that the old people had preserved them in the belief that they would ward off further calamity. Apparently, they had remained behind the roof-couple for several generations and no one had any inclination to remove them.

'Will you ever get rid of them?' I asked.

'They're doing no harm where they are,' was his reply. Like his forebears, he was a man who would neither make nor break a custom. The hooves remained behind the roof-couple until he had the house renovated in the 1970s. I suppose I mustn't criticise him for that. Our house in Kent has a horseshoe nailed to the garage door. It was there when we bought the house twenty years ago, and there it will remain for the simple reason that removing it would make a statement I have no wish to make.

Some superstitions had been modified or transformed in the light of subsequent religious belief. The coals or embers from the bonfire on St John's Eve, June 23rd, which were scattered on the fields to ensure a good yield or harvest, may originally have been part of a fertility rite linked to the festival of the summer solstice. Churning was still surrounded by a hint of superstition, even when I was a boy. The quality of the cream varied, with the result that from time to time butter would be slow in forming, or might not form at all. In such cases the much-maligned 'old people', lacking a scientific or even practical explanation, believed that a neighbour had worked a spell and transferred the butter to her own churn. My mother used to laugh at these beliefs, but I noticed that she always made the sign of the cross before starting the churning. Perhaps it was a true expression of religious belief and a form of insurance both, invoking the aid of a Christian God against possible intervention by the powers of evil.

Though everyone dismissed the old pishrogues, I could never be sure whether the dismissal was absolutely genuine. Superstitions were frequently evoked in conversation, possibly because they were part of the very language. If a puff of wind raised a cloud of dust along a road, someone might refer to it as a *seideán sí*, a fairy gust, not because he believed in fairies but because that was the Irish name for it. Similarly, if someone lost his way on the hill, he might be said to be suffering from *seachrán sí*, straying under fairy influence. In both cases the use of the Irish name would be accompanied by the phrase, 'As the old people used to say…'.

Some places were described as 'gentle' because, according to tradition, they were inhabited by 'the gentle folk' or fairies. It was said that a man who mowed a gentle place would lose his 'edge' or his ability to sharpen his scythe. Worse still, he might never again have a day's luck as long as he lived. People also talked of *féar gorta* (hunger grass), claiming that if you trod on a patch of it while out on the mountain, you would experience such debilitating hunger that you might never manage to reach home. *Glas ailt* (cliff lock) was a psychological condition, a kind of mental paralysis, experienced by people while climbing cliffs in order to rescue sheep or search for sea birds' eggs. If you were overtaken by an attack of *glas ailt* on a cliff ledge, you would be incapable of escaping from the danger. You might even hurl yourself down the cliff onto the rocks below. Certain places could induce *glas ailt*, which was a more mysterious condition than simple vertigo. Some places were said to be ghostly or eerie (*uaigneach*) and to induce feelings of loneliness or even fear, especially at twilight. These beliefs are indicative of the influence of landscape on the human spirit and the quasi-mystical relationship people had with certain distinctive landscape features. Yet if you asked most people whether they believed in either *glas ailt* or *seachrán sí*, they would simply laugh at you and say, 'Just old pishrogues'.

From a child's point of view, stories about old superstitions were a godsend. There were stories about fairy boats warning fishermen of an imminent drowning or an approaching storm. There were lovely stories about mermaids, including one about a fisherman who captured a beautiful young mermaid and tricked her into marrying him by removing her fishy tail and hiding it so that she could not return to the sea. They raised a family and were very happy together, but after several years she discovered where he had hidden her tail. She took it and returned to the sea and he saw neither hide nor hair of her again.

In some of the best stories the natural world is often invested with supernatural power or seen as the physical embodiment of a supernatural agent. Fishermen used to talk about the *tonn bháite*, a 'drowning wave' or beachcomber, as if there was no escaping its powers of destruction. One of my favourite stories concerns a man from Port called Paddy Byrne who was out fishing in a rowing boat one day with four or five neighbours. While they were lifting lobster creels, a violent storm blew up out of nowhere, forcing them to make for land. As they rowed for all they were worth, they were horrified to see the first of three drowning waves about to overtake them. The skipper said, 'Men, we're done for. All we can do is say a wee prayer and hope it works.' Paddy Byrne, who was in the bows of the boat, got up and went back to the stern where he stood facing the three approaching waves with a knife in his outstretched hand. Just as the first wave was about to break over them, he flung the knife at it. The knife split the wave in two and it passed by harmlessly on either side of the boat. Barely able to believe their eyes, they all bent over the oars and pulled and pulled while the second and third waves pursued them. But luck was with them, and as they reached the safety of the slip the two waves spent themselves harmlessly on the beach.

That evening after supper Paddy Byrne set out to visit a sick cousin in Leargain na Saortha, which was a fair walk from Port. Before long he was overtaken by a stranger on horseback, who asked him where he was going and told him to jump up behind him as he was heading in the same direction. However, just as they approached Leargain na Saortha, the stranger asked him to come home with him. He said that his daughter was very ill, and that only Byrne could cure her. Byrne was reluctant to go, as neither he nor anyone in his family was skilled in the art of healing, but finally he consented. The horseman turned off the road onto a little path between tall rocks and there in a hollow was the loveliest house that Byrne had ever seen. As they dismounted, a heavy oak door opened before them. They entered a vast hall lit by a thousand candles. 'She's in there and she's dying,' the stranger said, pointing to a closed door. Byrne went in and saw before him a beautiful young woman twisting in agony on a bed.

'I'm glad you've come,' she said. 'I'm dying and no one but you can cure me.'

With that she flung off the bedclothes and lifted up her nightdress, revealing a comely white body with a big knife stuck in the flesh between the ribs. Byrne took a backward step. It was the knife he had thrown at the drowning wave that morning.

'Don't be afraid,' she said. 'Pull it out.'

Byrne did as he was told. The girl breathed a sigh of relief and got up off the bed smiling.

'You've done me a good turn and now I'll do you one. I'll give you anything you like this minute, including the longest kiss in the history of Glen and more,' she said.

Byrne was a shy man, particularly with women he fancied. 'I'm parched,' he stammered. 'I'd like a drink of fresh milk.'

'You can have it from my breast,' she said, lifting her left breast with her hand.

Byrne didn't know where to look. 'Milk from a cup will do me fine,' he managed to mumble.

The door opened and in came the horseman with a cup of milk. Byrne drank it but still the cup was full. Pretending not to notice, he handed back the cup and thanked him, saying that it was the sweetest milk he'd ever tasted.

'It should be sweet,' the horseman said. 'It is the richest of the milk from the best cows in the Four Provinces of Ireland.'

Then Byrne knew for sure that he had found himself in the dwelling place of the fairies because, as everyone knows, they skim off the best of the milk at milking time and steal the best of the butter at every churning. He thanked both of them again and said he must be going. He knew better than to tarry even another minute.

The story of Byrne and the fairy woman was one of those stories that captured the folk imagination; it aroused more comment and discussion than any other fairytale. Some said that Byrne was lucky to have escaped with his life; that if he'd kissed her even skimmingly, he'd have been her prisoner forever. Others questioned his unmanly lack of courage in turning his back on such a challenging offer, while a few amateur psychologists wondered if he later came to regret his timidity. Local legend had it that he never married. Had he fallen in love with the fairy woman in retrospect? Had the memory of her comely white body possessed him to such a degree than no earthly woman could ever fill his eye again? Everyone was agreed, however, that it was a good story. You did not have to believe in fairies to appreciate a story that retained its magic no matter how often retold. As one old man said, 'It makes you think. A wave of the sea could be

Death itself or a lovely young woman in disguise. When faced with Death, Byrne had courage; faced with a woman, he turned his back. He failed the simplest and the hardest test of all.'

Luckily for me as a boy, the older generation were only too willing to tell stories about ghosts and fairies. What is interesting is that the stories survived long after overt belief in the superstitions that informed them had faded. Superstitious belief originally created the stories, and later perhaps the stories played some part in the survival of those beliefs. Of course, the best stories may have survived simply because people enjoyed telling them. Whatever the reason for their survival, I am pleased to have had the opportunity to hear them. As children we didn't have television or a library of picture books for our amusement. In many ways what we had was more precious, the well-worn words of the storyteller and the pictures created by our own overactive imagination.

5

Visitors

Cocooned among hills, Glen was a place apart, and for that reason perhaps, visitors inspired both excitement and curiosity. Visitors had their own way with words, they had seen something of the world, and they brought with them new ideas and new topics of conversation. They would talk about things I'd never heard mentioned before, and they often gave me sixpence or a shilling as they said goodbye. A house that attracted its fair share of visitors was held in some esteem. Every family had relatives in England, Scotland or America, but not all relatives were 'active'. Only those who had made good in their adoptive country and could afford to travel, or those with a strong sense of familial obligation, came back. Some families had large 'connections', and in clannish families the connection could extend as far as second cousinship.

The McGinleys weren't particularly noted for their connection. My father's mother's people the Lyonses always came to see us, and my mother's people turned up from time to time, but I don't ever remember a McGinley coming to our house. When I mentioned this odd fact to my father, he said that his McGinley uncles left for Scotland because they had to and were too sensible to come back. Now it is a matter of regret to me to have lost all trace of them. All I know of them is that in their homesickness they talked endlessly in Glasgow of the place names on our farm. It is a sad fact but it is the only trace of their lives left to me. As an exile myself, I have at least a vague idea of how they must have felt, and I would dearly love to know what they had to say about Carraig na Sían and Garraí na hEorna.

Our next door neighbour James McGlinchey was a tailor. He often employed journeymen who would stay for a month or two and sometimes longer. These men were great sources of new information. They had travelled the length and breadth of the county and were full of stories about places and events. McGlinchey, an easy-going and philosophical man, listened to their stories in amused silence, having heard them all before. He might sum up a discussion from time to time but I never once heard him tell a story of his own. Something of a diplomat, his usual stance was to smile knowingly and keep his own counsel. Much later he told me that he once employed a tailor who was a stickler for accuracy and insisted on calling the two big goose-irons 'gooses' rather than geese. McGlinchey found that amusing, especially since the stickler for verbal accuracy, when it came to sewing a button, was not the most accurate of tailors.

I always enjoyed visiting McGlinchey's workshop, where the tailors would be sitting cross-legged on the L-shaped bench, sporting one thimble and sometimes two, and McGlinchey himself would be busy doing the cutting-out with paper patterns, rule and chalk. The low wooden bench was marked at the edges with black streaks where cigarettes had been left burning. The workshop had its own unforgettable smell, the smell of good worsted cloth at its most distinctive when sprinkled with water which rose in steam under the heat of the gooses.

McGlinchey was a reader in his leisure time. He subscribed to *The Tailor and Cutter* for professional reasons, and to *The Reader's Digest* which provided the kind of facts that often served as a useful antidote to the more dubious 'facts' imparted by the journeymen he employed. He used to lend me old copies of the *Digest*, which was a change from the books in our house, something from the great world 'out the hill' with titbits like 'It Pays to Increase Your Word Power', 'Quotable Quotes' and 'Laughter, the Best Medicine'. The *Digest* also always seemed to have at least one article on health matters. In the early 1950s it carried a series of articles linking cigarette smoking to lung cancer, something that was not generally appreciated then. McGlinchey, like his journeymen, was a smoker but he did not allow the *Digest* to interfere with his pleasure. He used to say that nothing enjoyed in moderation can be bad for a moderate man.

The tailors he employed had their own personal idiosyncrasies. One was a great walker, possibly as a means of getting sea air and exercise as a change from the tailor's sedentary life. After Mass on Sunday he would head into the hills with a sandwich in his pocket and not return until nightfall no matter what the weather. He aroused the interest of the neighbours who did so much unavoidable walking during the week that they couldn't conceive of anyone walking for pleasure on Sunday.

Another tailor was so determined to win the money prize crossword in *The Sunday Press* that he subscribed to the *Competitors' Journal*, which each week listed the most likely answers, making an infuriatingly cogent case for each. Every Monday there would be heated discussions in the workshop about the previous day's crossword clues and all the possible answers. McGlinchey listened patiently to these futile discussions, taking the view that all answers were equally valid and that the only difference was in the deluded minds of the judges. Whenever anyone questioned this radical view of things, he would say that even the judges did not have the last word because 'the decision of the editor is final'. None of us came anywhere near winning the coveted prize, but it must be said that the prize crosswords fed our dreams of immediate wealth and provided an evergreen topic in discussions that could never be resolved because, as McGlinchey had said, there was no such thing as an indubitably correct answer.

Meanwhile, the tinkers, as we called them, came and went without leaving anyone any the wiser. They travelled in families in their painted caravans drawn by a wind-broken horse or pony. They would park the caravan in a quarry or at the side of a disused road and let their animals loose to graze in someone's field or lane. The men folk kept to themselves, spending their days making tin mugs, cans and saucepans, which their women hawked from house to house with a baby on their arm and a child or two in tow. They might ask for 'a few coppers' or a cup of milk for the baby, and they were rarely refused, if only because a tinker woman's curse was something to be avoided. However, I don't think they contributed much to the local culture or to the fund of outside information reaching the glen. A law unto themselves, they spoke their own lingo, and most of them appeared sullen and unapproachable. They were seen as a harmless nuisance, vagrants who would arrive out of the blue and depart again when it suited them.

What we called travellers (*fir siúil*) were a different breed. They weren't tinsmiths. They didn't live in caravans or tents. They walked everywhere, and all they had between them and the inclement heavens was the sack they carried on their backs. They went from house to house and ate wherever they were given food. If they were offered a shakedown for the night they gratefully accepted it. If not, they slept in a barn or, failing that, under the open sky. Travellers, unlike the tinkers, were great bearers of news. They would warm their hands over the fire and tell of their escapades, where they had come from and what they had seen or heard on the way. Their conversation was different from that of other visitors. It was more eccentric, at times so mysterious that it was difficult to follow. Some of the travellers I remember were well-known in the area. They had been coming periodically since they were young men, and over the years they had earned a fund of goodwill that always ensured a welcome and a meal or a few pence.

Another source of outside information was the travelling salesmen who went from house to house with a suitcase containing articles of clothing or small household utensils. They weren't strangers in any real sense. They were known throughout the parish, and they would receive a welcome and a cup of tea before they turned to the serious business of opening the suitcase and displaying their wares. It was a precarious way of earning a living. A suitcase could hold only a limited number of articles, and not everyone could afford to buy. I often watched these salesmen holding up dresses, pullovers and shirts, and then folding them neatly and returning them to the suitcase. I could not help marvelling at their patience; at the way they never showed the slightest sign of disappointment or discouragement. It was as if they were resigned to refusal and were going from house to house merely to pass the time. I remember saying to myself as a boy that I wouldn't be a travelling salesman for all the tea in China. When I told that to my father, he said that he'd rather row up and down the bay in the rain even if he knew there wasn't one lobster this side of Aranmore.

6

Bilinguists

For centuries Glen was more or less cut off from the great world 'out the hill'. Roads and communications were poor. Until the 1950s few people from beyond Carrick, apart from the occasional intrepid traveller, came to trouble us. Consequently, we were free to develop our own richly distinctive culture without exposure to outside influences. Apart from priests, schoolteachers, coastguards, lighthouse keepers, policemen and the odd returning emigrant, there was no one to introduce a foreign thought or fashion. Few people had access to radio and no more than twelve people in the whole Glen bought a daily newspaper. We depended on ourselves for entertainment, and the dialect we spoke had evolved from the close juxtaposition and interaction of the Irish and English languages. It differed significantly from that spoken in, say, Killybegs, which is only seventeen miles away.

In the Glen valley most people spoke English as their everyday language, but they could also converse reasonably competently in Irish, and they certainly could follow a conversation between two Irish speakers. In the mountain

townlands, including Lougheraherk, Straboy and Kilty-
fanned, Irish was the spoken language in the home. Like
many Glen people of my generation, I grew up reasonably
fluent in both languages. My aunt was a practised Irish
speaker and she conversed with me in Irish most of the
time. My father and mother spoke English in the house,
though they both had a good passive knowledge of Irish.
The English we spoke was far from standard. Many of the
idioms in use were direct translations from the Irish, and
the vocabulary was a mixture of English, Irish and Scots.
'The big *spágaí*, he fell into the whins and couldn't thole
the pain', a sentence you might have heard in the Glen of
the 1940s, shows evidence of Irish, English, Scots, and
Anglo-Saxon. In Irish a *spágaí* is a clumsy-footed person.
Whins, a word that came to us from Scotland, was used
instead of furze or gorse, and *thole*, derived from Anglo-
Saxon, means 'suffer' or 'endure'. We didn't think that
there was anything strange or unusual about our rich linguistic mix. When we used an Irish word in an English
sentence, we pronounced it as we would in an Irish sentence. This sleight of tongue gave rise to a complex and
interesting range of phonemes.

We used Irish words in English sentences when there
was no English word for what we wished to say. For
example, we used the Irish *praistéal* to describe a handful
of potatoes baked in the embers of a turf fire. Potatoes
cooked in this way were very tasty and much appreciated
by us children. We used the word *corrchoigilt* to describe the
green and blue lights that appear in the embers of a turf
fire when a line is made through them with a stick or
tongs. These lights resembled glow-worms and were said
to be a sign of rain. Likewise, we used the Irish *spadar* for
sodden turf that had been 'killed' by frost. *Spadar* was
almost useless as it produced no flame and gave off next
to no heat.

Sometimes we used an Irish word simply because we did not know the English equivalent. For example, we used the word *fúog* rather than 'thrum' to refer to the thread ends in weaving. Similarly, the word *doirnín* referred to one of the two grips or handles on a scythe pole. We did not even use the word 'shaft' or 'pole'; we preferred the Anglo-Saxon word 'snead' which we pronounced 'snid'. The word *bogóg* indicated an egg that had been laid without its shell. For some other things we used both their Irish and English names indiscriminately. An ant was sometimes called a *seangán*, an earthworm a *cuiteog*, and a limpet a *bairneach*. Most of the Irish words we used were nouns, and, curiously, we gave them English plurals. Thus, we said 'cuiteogs' instead of *cuiteoga*, 'seangans' instead of *seangáin*, and 'bairneachs' instead of *bairnigh*. All this, I am sure, must have made life a nightmare for our teachers, who were trying to teach us proper English and proper Irish and keep them in two separate compartments.

Now and again we used an Irish word or expression just because it sounded more amusing or because it had the ring of *le mot juste*. Referring to a youth who had just begun to take an interest in girls, we would say, 'He has a *soc suirí* on him already.' *Soc* in Irish means a snout and *suirí* is the word for courting or courtship. Somehow it seemed funnier and perhaps more dismissive to say that a young fellow has developed a courting snout than to say that he is looking a bit frisky for his age.

Sometimes an Irish phrase might be used simply because it was more expressive than its English equivalent. The phrase *bruth toinne* describes the churned yellow scum and debris left floating on the waves after a storm. It evokes an image of a boiling or seething mass, which is an accurate representation of the thing in question. No one would say 'an east wind with good drying'. Instead they would use the phrase *gal phiútair*, which has the advantage of being both concise and onomatopoeic.

However, the general attitude to Irish was at best ambivalent. While most people regretted its decline as a spoken language, they made no effort to preserve it in practice. They were content to see it as an already lost heritage that had once enshrined the essence of pithy expression, superior to the brand of vernacular English they used in everyday transactions. An English speaker would frequently quote an Irish proverb to make a point, just as an educated Englishman of the nineteenth century might quote Horace or Virgil in support of his opinion. My father was particularly prone to this habit, though his knowledge of Irish was far from perfect. *Éist mórán is can beagán* (Listen a lot and say little) and *Is binn béal ina thost* (Silence is golden) were among his favourite sayings.

The vocabulary of contempt and vituperation was mercilessly rich. A guldy or a gulpin was an ignorant or ill-bred fellow. A *gámaí* was an awkward and foolish-looking person. A haverel was a talkative halfwit, and a secretive or deceitful person was dismissed as a snool or *snámhaí*. Even women did not escape the local genius for invective. A bold young girl, however chaste, could be called a strumpet, and an awkward, untidy woman a *cuachán*. The word 'strap' could be used as a general term of abuse for either a girl or a woman, as in 'useless strap'. The words for beating and punishment were legion. Unruly children were threatened with thrashing, trouncing, leenging, paiking, larruping and loodering. The above might lead one to believe that we lived in fear of our lives, but it must be acknowledged that there was no shortage of terms of endearment, whenever the occasion for them arose.

A variety of Scots words survived in everyday use, even though the English synonym was widely known. A field of braird was a field of young corn with the shoots having just appeared above the ground. A drackie day was a day of mist and drizzle, and if you didn't know the airt the wind was blowing from, you could be accused of having no sense of direction. If you were seen to be scheming or in league with someone, you could be described as colloguing. To walk lamely or with difficulty was to hochle and to walk with long strides was to spang. To duck or keep out of sight was to jouk and to trudge along slowly was to dodge. A gap or opening in a ditch, meaning a stone wall, was often called a slap and a wooden pestle for mashing potatoes was called a beetle. These words are still in use among the older generation, though they are heard less frequently among the young, who are more amenable to the influence of television and radio and what they read in the popular press.

The culture of the older generation was primarily oral. Stories told in Irish were at its very centre, stories about actual people, particularly stories about people who had a way with language and knew how to coin a pithy phrase. Some people went down in local history for one of their favourite sayings. Others were remembered for a witty rejoinder or for something they said in unusual circumstances. The circumstances would be described in English and the frequently ribald punch line given in Irish, the speaker switching readily from one language to the other, while his hearers took pleasure from the linguistic *legerdemain*.

Men or women who were fond of retelling the same story earned a special place in the local *Táin*. Their favourite story became an extension of their personality, encouraging much mimicry and ribald humour when their back was turned. I well remember a man who was fond of recounting the same story about a former neighbour no matter what the occasion. Whenever two people saw him approach, one might say to the other, 'I'll bet you sixpence I'll be the first to get him to tell the story about the woman who couldn't say no.'

Some of these stories were extremely simple, but they survived in the folk memory because they were seen to be droll, witty or unconsciously amusing. My mother used to tell us about an old woman from Garveross who was noted for her readiness to speak her mind. One Sunday, as the priest preached a thundering sermon against poteen-making, she got so carried away by his eloquence that she stood up in church and said, '*Dheamhan smid bhréige, a athair, is fearr braon tae*' (Not a word of lie, Father, a drop of tea is better!).

Another frequently told story concerned a local man who was worried on his wedding night in case he might do his petite wife an injury. '*Kitty, 'bhfuil mé trom,*' (Kitty, am I heavy?) he enquired. '*Oibir leat, a Bhrínigh,*' (Work away, Briney!) was her appreciative reply. A man who thought the world of himself is commemorated in local history with one of his favourite sayings: '*Bhail, amach uaim féin, ba ag Roibeard Ribeach a bhí an bod ba mhó da bhfaca mé ariamh...*' (Well, apart from myself, Hairy Robert had the biggest penis I've ever seen...). No one ever told either of those stories from beginning to end. Simply to say, '*Bhail, amach uaim féin...*' (Well, apart from myself...) was enough to arouse ribald laughter, especially among a group of men outside the church on Sunday or coming up to closing time in a pub.

Triads were often quoted in Irish as a means of clinching an argument or for the sake of amusement. The best Irish triads have the conciseness of an aphorism in which folk wisdom and homely humour combine. The language in which they are couched frequently takes on the rhythm and lilt of poetry with now and again an ingenious rhyme or figure of speech that does not easily translate into felicitous English. Examples include the three coldest things, which are the head of a hammer, the snout of a dog, and an old woman's bottom. The three most frolicsome things are a kitten, a month-old kid, and a widow not too old to remarry. The three best hands are the hand of a good carpenter, the hand of a good blacksmith, and the hand of a good woman. When I was growing up sixty years ago, most people could reel off a dozen or more triads in Irish. I just wonder how many of them have survived in the folklore of today.

Living folklore depends on accurate oral transmission. Many of the older generation had extraordinarily retentive memories. They could even remember clearly things they had been taught at school seventy years before. An old man once said to me as he looked up at the sky, 'It will be rain tonight.' When I replied, 'The forecast is good,' he was most disappointed, having expected me to echo the First Murderer's reply to Banquo in *Macbeth*, 'Let it come down!'

'The scholars don't read Shakespeare at school any more,' he complained. 'We all read *Macbeth* in old Master Byrne's time', and he proceeded to quote the speech that begins, 'Doubtful it stood / As two spent swimmers that do cling together / And choke their art.' Obviously he enjoyed *Macbeth* in the way that he enjoyed recounting old stories. Yet the capacity to remember oral history in the detail in which it was originally transmitted is dying out. Television and radio are gradually destroying it. As my elderly neighbour put it, 'The young people would only laugh at you now if you tried to tell them a story.'

7

The New Curate

The priests we had in Glen over the years were quiet, reflective men who lived private and prayerful lives and did not meddle much in worldly affairs. In December 1951, however, a new curate arrived who broke the mould of the past, turning centuries of tradition on its head. Glen was never to be the same again. The new priest was tall and dark-featured and, unlike his predecessor, he was physically strong. On his first Sunday he looked more like a farmer than a priest. As he came out of the sacristy to say Mass, he moved with a headlong drive as if prepared to make smithereens of anything that might get in his way. On the road home one of my neighbours said, 'I wouldn't like to meet him in a lonely place on a dark night.'

I got my first glimpse of Father James McDyer during the Christmas holidays from boarding school. I saw immediately that he had little in common with the priests I'd served Mass for in Glen as a boy. For a start he seemed to walk on springs. He was busy and brisk, very much like the priests who ran my school. You couldn't imagine any of these men spending a quiet evening alone in prayer.

They were professionals who saw themselves as teachers, businessmen or politicians first of all — and as priests merely as a means to an end. Impatient of anything that did not serve their immediate purpose, they were not the kind of men who would find much time for the writings of Thomas á Kempis or the poetry of St John of the Cross.

McDyer saw the Glen as a prime example of rural decay, a place that lacked electricity, piped water, and the gainful employment that would keep young people from emigrating to England, Scotland and America. From the beginning he set himself the task of transforming the local economy. He had spent ten years in England and did not much care for the English; he saw London and Birmingham as cities of sin and depravity, unfit places for a good Irish Catholic to live in. Young men and women must be kept at home to create a healthy community, sheltered from the excesses and frivolities of twentieth-century urban culture. And so he set himself the task of developing the local tourist trade and introducing light industries that would provide jobs for young men and women who would otherwise have been forced to emigrate. To achieve this he saw that he must inculcate in people the will to change ingrained habits, attitudes towards work, and indeed their whole purpose of living.

His sermons were different from those of other priests. At Mass on Sunday he had a captive audience, and he used it as an occasion to preach the gospel that work is prayer, quoting the motto of the Benedictines, *Laborare est orare*. He saw the Glen people as lazy and shiftless, lacking will and ambition and the desire to change things for the better. In his own words, the enemies he had to destroy were 'indolence, emigration, cynicism, greed and individualism'. Nothing displeased him more than the sight of a strapping young man leaning on his scythe, chatting over a ditch to a neighbour. 'Go out into the fields and die with your boots on,' he would thunder from the altar. Needless to say, men who'd spent their lives working hard for little return on land and sea did not think much of this injunction. At times it seemed that the good priest lacked an appreciation of the subtleties of the indigenous culture with its wry humour, healthy scepticism, and firm determination to be neither hurried nor deceived.

One Sunday in late November, as he was telling his congregation what work they should be doing at that time of year, an old man who was hard of hearing was straining every nerve at the back of the church to catch what he was saying.

'Is he talking about God or the Devil?' he asked the man next to him.

'Neither,' came the reply. 'He's talking about idlers who still have their hay in hand-cocks at the end of November with aftergrass growing up through them.'

It seemed that there was no escaping the workaday world, no rest for the wicked, not even at Mass on Sunday. As one perplexed parishioner put it, 'We used to come to Mass to hear the word of God. Now it's the word of Mammon.'

In order to set change in motion, he spent much time in his Volkswagen on the road up and down to Dublin to lobby government ministers, civil servants, and businessmen with capital to invest. He had boundless energy for the task and such single-mindedness that one local wag wondered if he ever found time to say a prayer at all. He spawned new ideas with unrivalled fecundity, and in his unbridled enthusiasm for his many schemes he often appeared fanatical and high-handed. He had an opinion on everything, and he preached with authority on everything from archaeology to ladies' fashions. In his sermon one Sunday he held up to ridicule a local girl who'd come home from England in trousers. As we listened in dumb-struck disbelief, he told us that a woman in trousers was like a potato with two matchsticks stuck in it for legs.

Mercifully, most people saw the funny side of his obsessions. One summer morning as he left for Dublin, he waved to two of his neighbours who were leaning over the bridge by the parochial house, exchanging weather forecasts. After a while each of them went his way, one to do a day's work on the bog and the other to fish lobsters. Towards dusk, they met again by the bridge and were busy exchanging tales of the day as McDyer returned from Dublin. Rolling down the car window, he exclaimed, 'Under God are you still here?' 'We are,' said one of them, omitting to enlighten him further. It was too good a joke to spoil, and they enjoyed it all the more when they merited a none-too-honourable mention in the following Sunday's sermon. A work ethic that was foreign to the local culture had invaded the house of God. Now it seemed that the only sin, apart from sex, was idleness.

Understandably, people were sceptical at first. A not uncommon attitude was that the last thing we needed was a man from Glenties telling us how to cut turf. Gradually, however, attitudes began to change. His appeal was to the worldly instincts of his flock, and even his most persistent critic had to admit that he was a man who got things done. Within five years of his arrival we had piped water and electricity, and in the wake of electricity came all the known conveniences of the twentieth century.

Soon people had come to realise that they were blessed with a very special priest. While other priests might try to twist God's arm on your behalf, McDyer's skill lay in twisting the arms of businessmen and govern-ment ministers. If you wished to apply for a grant to modernise your house or farm outbuildings, he would pull the appropriate strings. In seeking to be both priest and businessman simultaneously, he succeeded above all in demystifying the priestly function. After twenty years of his ministry people's idea of the qualities required of a 'good priest' had changed forever.

Understandably, the fulfilment of conflicting roles left him open to the criticism of purists. One local sage said that as a priest he was a very fine businessman, and as a businessman a very fine priest. As a businessman he did many things over the years that didn't make much business sense, but hard-nosed businessmen who had dealings with him found that he was no pushover. Some were more than surprised to find their costs exceeding their revenue. One entrepreneur, more philosophical perhaps than his fellows, wrote off his losses not as an act of McDyer but as 'an act of God'. Yet another, who'd just had his fingers burnt, jokingly advised me to equip myself with a long spoon if ever McDyer should invite me to sup with him.

I suppose McDyer could be described as one of the first of the modern clerics. A man of the world as opposed to a man of prayer, he believed that God was on the side of the strong — and that it was his divine mission to make his parishioners strong. For strength, you need bread rather than Hail Marys, and bread was what he set out to provide. During his curacy, the pulpit became a platform for censure and exhortation. No one escaped unscathed; everyone was made to realise that he wasn't pulling his weight. There were only two sins, laziness and impurity, and they both went hand in hand.

What's more, he had a nose for a good story, which endeared him to journalists. An inveterate egotist, he fondly imagined that his personal history was the history of Glencolmcille. A determined mythmaker, the hero of the myth he created was predictably himself. He painted a picture of Glen before his arrival as a backwater of idleness and decay, and pointed to the prosperous community of ambitious young men and women he had nurtured. Journalists in search of ready-made copy were only too eager to propagate the legend, and if the legend exceeded the plain, unadorned truth, it did not much matter, as it was all good clean fun.

Now as I look back, I believe that McDyer saw the priesthood as a straitjacket from which he was determined to burst forth in splendour. Not content with the clerical round of Mass, confessions and sick calls, he sought personal fulfilment in a dozen other spheres. One day he would be a businessman, the next a politician, and on the third a great actor or a leader of men. Though skilled in all those roles, he particularly excelled as an actor; in fact he excelled to such an extent that it was difficult to know when he was being sincere and when he was indulging in the kind of humbug that created the legend.

Possibly, the role that gave him most satisfaction was that of ladies' man. He was only forty-one when he first came to Glen. Dangerously handsome, he was the best-looking man in Glen at that time. Naturally, the Glen women fell head over heels in love with him. By enlisting the nubile among them in the Children of Mary, he ensured that they remained safely under his wing. Soon they were in thrall to such a degree that no other man could get a look-in. Those of us who were coming into manhood at the time could only envy his knack of putting young women at ease and allaying their natural suspicions by addressing them as 'My child', a salutation that was not open to us lesser mortals.

Another weapon in his armoury was a plentiful supply of Old Spice aftershave lotion, which we simple country lads could not afford. Understandably, we felt that we were up against impossible odds. Taking the only revenge open to us, we nicknamed our tormentor Father McSpice, but that was only cold comfort for any red-blooded young man. As we danced with the local girls in McDyer's new hall, we could tell from the faraway look in their eyes that their hearts were set on pleasures more ethereal than any we Glen boys could offer. The grip that McDyer had on the objects of our dreams was the cause of many a disappointed love affair. Some young men emigrated in desperation. A friend of mine said sorrowfully that the only other solution was to buy a clerical suit complete with Roman collar and pretend that we could forgive any sin a girl might care to commit with us. Sadly, he did not have the courage of his imagination, and shortly afterwards he, too, left to seek adventure in other pastures.

Whatever one may think of his methods, McDyer succeeded in his ambition to change the face of the Glen. Gainful employment put money in people's pockets. Before long there was a television set in every living room and a car outside every house. He took the view that money earned in Glen should be spent in Glen, and that any money left over would be best spent on the entertainments he provided in the new parish hall which he had built for the purpose. Gradually, tile-roofed bungalows with big picture windows replaced the old thatched cottages. With the television came soap operas, chat shows, razzle-dazzle, and the dilution of the old culture with its distinctive way of looking at things. Belatedly but irresistibly, the twentieth century had come to Glen. As you might expect, the gains were material, the losses both spiritual and cultural.

'It would have happened anyway, it's happened all over Ireland,' an old friend said to me on one of my visits home. 'What you could say is that it happened too quickly here. In one generation we've gone from the early nineteenth to the late twentieth century.'

'It's rather ironic that it was all hurried along by a man who never stopped preaching the spiritual values of the old Irish culture,' I said.

'Let no one hear you say that,' he replied. 'He put money in our pockets. It would be a rash man who'd criticise him for that in a pub.'

I couldn't help smiling, as I had always seen McDyer as a restless activist marooned in the wrong age and in the wrong country. Perhaps in seventeenth-century France he would have found worldly fulfilment as a minor Richelieu, assuaging his itch for power over men and women without hindrance from what he himself called 'begrudgers and nay-sayers'.

Yet in his wisdom McDyer foresaw that with the coming of the twentieth century to Glen the old culture would shrivel and vanish. Lest it be forgotten entirely, he founded a folk museum consisting of traditional thatched cottages, in which are displayed the farming implements and domestic utensils used by our ancestors. Visiting the folk museum one wet day while on holiday, I experienced an eerie sense of dislocation, which I am sure was not shared by the German tourists who were also sheltering from the rain. Here I was in a museum less than half a mile from where I was born, looking at a replica of the type of cottage in which I grew up, and at farming implements I had seen in our barn as a boy. I felt as if I had come back from the dead after two hundred years, and I wondered if anyone else in Glen had had the same experience? We would all agree that folk museums have their uses in preserving the objects and artefacts indicative of a particular culture. Alas, they can't preserve the elusive flame that illumines folk memory and tradition and helps create and inform a unique and living community.

As I look back now, I realise that the 1950s and early 1960s were a golden age in Glen, a time when the old culture was still vibrant and a time to which many people of my generation return in their thoughts with affection. It was as if Glen had become a large open-air monastery with McDyer as abbot. There were friars, the chosen few who hung on his every word, and also lay brothers who laboured in the fields and brought in the harvest. There were sisters as well, the Children of Mary, who wore blue veils at Mass on Sunday, tended to the abbot's every need, and did the cooking in the monastery's many kitchens. There were even one or two anchorites, holy men who lived lives of hardship and prayer in lonely places in the hills, unique among their brethren in having renounced all worldly gain. Everyone was expected to take vows of obedience and chastity, a vow of poverty being optional. To this requirement, the dissenters were too few to obstruct the general sense of purpose and unity. Glen had become a community of living saints. There were no scholars, but frankly we didn't miss them.

PART II

Home and Family

8

House and Farm

Our house, which my father in his reductive way referred to as the shack, was a snug little thatch-roofed cottage consisting of a kitchen and two bedrooms. The kitchen wasn't just a kitchen; it served as living room and dining room as well, and it was the centre of all life in the home. It was there that my mother cooked our meals, and it was there that we gathered round the hearth fire on winter nights to talk and make fun.

To the right of the fireplace was a curtain, and behind the curtain was an outshot bed, set in a kind of alcove. Because of its proximity to the kitchen fire, it was the warmest bed in the house. I remember it well, as my brother Peter Joseph and I slept in it during our school years, while my sisters Tina, Mary and Bernadette, slept in our parents' bedroom. Sometimes I would pretend to be asleep, and with both ears cocked lie listening to things I wasn't meant to hear, as my father and mother sat talking by the fire, going over the events of the day.

When I think of our house now, I think of the kitchen first of all. People who came to visit sat round the kitchen fire and more often than not they said that it was 'a cosy wee house'. My father, who was not a man to ignore a compliment, assured them that all you needed for a cosy house was good turf to make a good fire. He was an expert on turf, and naturally he took pride in the quality of the turf he cut and 'saved' on our bog at the top of the hill. He would explain that he kept the black turf for the winter, and that black turf, as opposed to brown, was every bit as good as coal. During the winter he made it his business to keep the hearth fire roaring. He would bring in basket after basket of black turf from the stack at the back of the house, and if he went to the village for tobacco, he would complain on his return that we had allowed the fire to die down.

As I look back now, I wonder how the kitchen could have been so cosy, because there were two doors, the front door facing south and the back door facing north, and neither had a porch for shelter. We rarely opened the front door except in summer. All entrances and exits were made through the back. On winter nights the north wind came in under the back door, crossed the kitchen, and went out under the front door with a song that went 'furroo-fur-roo'. Then my father would put more turf on the fire or roll up an old sack and lay it at the bottom of the back door to keep out the draught.

There was one window in the kitchen and it looked across the road on the end-wall of McGlinchey's, our nearest neighbour's house. As I stared out of the window, I often thought that the end-wall would make a bigger and better screen than the one they had for showing pictures in the Spink Hall. Behind McGlinchey's was a rock-strewn hill on which a few tattered sheep grazed in the company of a cow or donkey. It was not an inspiring scene. I envied boys who lived in Doonalt and could see the sea from their window as soon as they got up in the morning.

The road that ran past our house was almost level with our windowsill. As a child looking out, I saw first of all the boots of people passing up and down. To discover to whom the boots belonged, I had to raise my eyes to the sky or so it seemed to me at the time. When I mentioned this strange phenomenon to my father, he blamed what he called 'the old people' for building the house below the level of the road. 'Forever digging down for shelter,' he would say. 'Now everyone wants a house on a height because everyone wants a view.'

Our kitchen had a lovely flagstone floor, which my mother swept several times a day with a besom made from heather from the hill. Some of the flagstones were square and some oblong, and they were cut beautifully to fit together like a jigsaw and make the smoothest but not necessarily the warmest of floors for little feet. We had an open fireplace with a cobbled hearth and a wide chimney-brace tapering towards the roof. My father claimed that the cobbles had been set in till or boulder clay rather than concrete. All I can say with certainty is that none of them ever became dislodged. For some odd reason I attached importance to the hearth cobbles. They were smaller than those in any of the neighbours' houses. Worn smooth by the feet of many generations, they were lovely and warm on the soles. Behind the fire was a large flat backstone that protected the wall from excessive heat. Whenever it split, we didn't have to go to the shop to buy a new one, as there was no shortage of suitable stones on the hill.

By modern standards our kitchen was sparsely furnished. There was a dining table, and a chair for every member of the family. By the back door stood a form or bench for buckets and basins, and next to it was an ancient dresser with rows of delph bowls and willow-pattern chargers that were never used. Some of the bowls belonged to my father's uncles, who had gone to work in Scotland. One belonged to his Uncle Charlie who was drowned off the Doonalt coast when my father was a boy. Throughout my childhood my father drank his tea from a bowl, not because he was a great respecter of family tradition but because tea cooled more quickly in a bowl than in a mug or cup. Whenever we tried to poke fun at him for his faddishness, he would explain rather tersely that there was nothing worse for a man's gut than scalding hot tea.

Above the kitchen was what we called a garret consisting of eight thick planks and a wooden tester supported on three cross-beams. It was used to store old fishing nets and other equipment no longer in everyday use. My father said that the tester was once part of the kitchen bed, and that the planks and beams had been washed ashore after a shipwreck. To me, the thought of a shipwreck made our little kitchen a place of wonder and mystery. I used to look up at the planks and imagine the sailors who were made to walk them with their hands tied behind their backs.

The most mysterious place in the house was the loft above my parents' bedroom, which could be reached only from the kitchen by means of a step ladder leading up to a dark door that was rarely opened, and then never by anyone except my father. When I asked him once what the loft was for, his reply was not very enlightening. 'Old trunks, old suitcases and old lumber' was all he said, but it was enough to make me long for the day when I would climb up the ladder for an afternoon of undisturbed exploration. It was the word 'trunk' that set my imagination racing. A trunk was like a sea chest. It suggested travel to faraway places. God knows what it might contain. In my innocence it seemed to me that the loft was full of secrets, that everything I wished to know, everything that my father didn't want me to know, was to be found in those trunks among the cobwebs.

When finally I was old enough to climb the ladder unaided, I spent a wet afternoon going through the old trunks and suitcases by the light of the small, single-pane window. I discovered one or two things belonging to my Uncle Paddy who was a civic guard and died of tuberculosis two years before I was born. There was a policeman's whistle, a pair of handcuffs, some useful-looking knuckledusters, and some old copies of *The Strand Magazine* with illustrated short stories by P G Wodehouse and Arthur Conan Doyle. Of family history and family secrets there was not a hint. Nothing more personal than some old copies of *The Derry Journal*, yellow and crumbling with age. Just as I was about to give up the search, I came across a heavy box in a corner, containing six hefty volumes entitled *Six Centuries of English Literature*, published by Blackie and Son in 1933. The volumes contained passages in prose and poetry from the works of English writers from Chaucer to Browning as well as short biographies complete with pictures and photographs. Quite excited by my discovery, I took the six volumes down to the kitchen and showed them to my father, who said that Uncle Paddy had bought them shortly before he died. 'You'll be the first to read them. He was barely given time to open them.' I opened the first of the heavy, musty-smelling volumes and began thumbing through it, looking at pictures and reading the odd paragraph and caption. The poets and prose writers I was studying at secondary school were all there, but it was a revelation to learn that they had faces as well as names, that they were real people with wives and mistresses, enemies and friends. It brought home to me the relationship between literature and history, and with a sense of discovery I realised that writers are rooted in their times as a tree is rooted in the earth.

Indeed it was the beginning of my love affair with literature, and with English literature in particular.

My aunt's bedroom lay behind the kitchen fireplace. Unlike my parents' bedroom, it didn't have its own fireplace because the heat from the kitchen fire came through the party wall. My aunt had a bureau with brass handles, in which she kept her personal belongings. What interested me was the packet of digestive biscuits that she kept hidden in the top drawer. Though I raided the drawer from time to time while she was away teaching at her primary school in the mountains, I knew better than to be greedy. While it was possible to pinch one or two biscuits without arousing suspicion, to eat the whole packet might prompt her to find a new hiding place. In another corner of the room was an old harmonium with two pedals for working the broken bellows. From time to time I would try to play the first few bars of 'O'Donnell Abu', the Donegal anthem, with one finger, but the sounds that emerged from the reeds bore no relation to what I was expecting to hear.

Behind our house stood the outhouses: a byre for the animals and a barn where my father kept potatoes, corn and straw as well as tools and farming implements. The garden was surrounded by a dry-stone wall and sheltered on all sides by bourtrees, sycamore, ash and cherry. Under the cherry trees wild garlic grew in clusters. My father said that the seeds had originally come from a sailing vessel that had been wrecked off the coast in the previous century. Every autumn he collected the cloves as they ripened and hung them up by the fireplace to dry. The cloves, which were smaller than those of cultivated garlic, were much in demand by old women as a cure for colds and coughs during the winter.

We children prized the bourtree or elder above all other trees because the soft pith could be removed from a straight piece of branch to make a very serviceable pop-gun. The cherry trees were old and neglected and did not produce much in the way of fruit, but the sycamores and ash trees were good for climbing and hiding in. But the best place of all for hiding was Andy's garden, next to ours. Andy and his family had moved to a new house, leaving the old garden to revert to its natural state. It was full of tall trees, tall grasses and nettles, and so sheltered that on a calm day not a breath of air came to lift the lightest leaf.

On a warm summer day it was like entering a luminous tent of green in which light slumbered among the limp foliage. I would make my way to my favourite tree to watch white butterflies rising and falling in the sun, going here and there and round about, anywhere but as the crow flies. It was a boy's Garden of Eden, pathless, wild and overgrown, a place in which to hide from seekers, a place with its own mysterious history, a place of peace.

Our farm extended from the house down to the rabbit warren on the far side of the shore road. Each field had its own name, and the names lent the places an air of romance, speaking as they did of the work of generations long since gone. Below the house was the Brae, from which you could see the sea and the north side of the valley extending eastwards like a newly opened scroll. *Garraí na hEorna* (the Barley Garden) hearkened back to a time when barley was grown for poteen making. The field by the shore road, called *Carraig na Sían* (The Rock of the Young Glassan), got its name from a large, flat, table-like rock, on which young saithe were once spread to dry in the sun.

What we called the Sand below the shore road was the best place for potatoes and carrots, provided you could protect them from the rabbits. The soil was dry and friable, unlike the claggy soil of the garden, and contained not a single stone or pebble. Potatoes grown in the Sand had lovely smooth skin, and carrots grew straight and long, never forked or crooked. My father, who had a practical explanation for everything, told me that the sandy soil had been enriched over many generations with peat moss carried down in creels from the bog. 'Before the Famine there were three or four men in every house,' he explained. 'They had to do something to pass the time, I suppose.' He had a way of explaining the past in the light of his personal experience. Though not based on scholarship, his views made excellent sense to me at the time, and he was the first to make me think about the difference between the past and the present.

9

My Father

My father was a serious man — serious about his work and serious about the business of bringing up a family, two things that had an immediate effect on my early life. By the time I was ten I had already come to the conclusion that he was different from other fathers. For a start, none of them was as strict as he was. Other fathers were more relaxed, more ready to share a joke with their children and more inclined to take them into their confidence, or so it seemed to me. They would tell their children about their own childhood experiences and all the devilment they had got up to on the sly, and how they'd pulled the wool over their teachers' and parents' eyes and got away with it.

My father never told us anything about his childhood. For all I knew he might never have had one, and at times it seemed to me that he was bent on making sure that I didn't have one either. He saw that I was intelligent and good at school, and he was determined that I should 'get on in life' and not repeat the mistakes that had kept him bound to a few acres of stony ground. Not content with giving a word of fatherly advice, he loved to preach a sermon, and to my great discomfort most of his sermons were directed at me.

As a boy, it was not in my nature to challenge him, but still I had my own way of looking at things. I found it difficult to believe him whenever he said to me, 'No one would stay here', and I wondered if he himself really believed it. I loved Glen and I couldn't imagine a better place. Perhaps he wanted everyone to emigrate so that he could have the whole parish to himself. The thought kept coming back to me: an empty glen with one man free to roam the hills and dales as he pleased, not caring where the sun went down on him. One night he would sleep in Straboy, high up in the mountains, and the next by the sea in low-lying Malinbeg. It seemed an ideal life, very much like the life of the legendary heroes of ancient Ireland, and I wondered if my father in his heart thought the same.

I asked him once why he himself hadn't emigrated. 'There was no one else to look after the place,' was his reply. So in spite of all his sermonising, looking after the place must have mattered to him. He was not the kind of man who would have left his father and mother to fend for themselves in their old age. In spite of what he said, he was attached to the farm and the work that went with it. He thought of nothing else, and most of the time he talked of nothing else. There was nothing he liked better than good weather and the joy of being further ahead with the work than any of the neighbours.

I can understand his attitude now, as I am old enough to know that there is no surer way to happiness in life than to love your work and take pleasure in doing it well. He meant well too in preaching the importance of a good education, and I can only thank him for it, but what he called 'getting on in life' was the last thing I wished to think about when I was six. As a boy I never felt entirely at ease in our house, where at an early age I learned to mind my language, especially in recounting what I'd heard and seen outside the family. I learned the value of discretion, when to speak and when to keep my mouth shut. And now when I think of childish fun, I don't think of home. Instead I recall the hours I spent in neighbours' houses, playing with other children and listening to their parents telling stories.

I enjoyed going to school for that reason, as it too was a way of escaping from the house and my parents' supervision. I was friendly with another schoolboy, James Gillespie of Beefan, who caught a baby rabbit one spring and told me that he would give it to me for helping him with his sums. One morning he brought the rabbit to Cashel in his schoolbag and tethered it behind a ditch by the Scáthlán. At lunchtime he and I went to have a look at it, just to make sure that a cat or dog hadn't taken it. It was the loveliest baby rabbit I had ever seen. No bigger than a week-old kitten, its fur was soft and silky, and you could feel its fine shoulder blades moving beneath the supple skin. After school I ran home with the rabbit and put it under an orange box in the garden, since I didn't have a proper rabbit hutch. Then, in my innocence, I told my mother about my new pet and plucked some grass for its dinner. When my father came back from fishing, my mother told him about the lovely baby rabbit. To my surprise he showed no interest and just asked me where I was going to get young carrots to feed it. I got up early the following morning to give the rabbit its breakfast, but to my horror the orange box had been overturned and the baby rabbit had gone. When I told my father, he said that the dog or the cat must have taken it. 'Maybe, it's just as well,' he added. 'It would only attract other rabbits to the garden.'

I didn't believe him. I knew in my heart that the cat or the dog could not have overturned the orange box because I had put a heavy stone on top of it before going to bed. It was my first experience of bereavement, as if all the joy had gone out of my life. When I told James Gillespie about what had happened, he said that he would bring me another rabbit the following day. I didn't tell him about my suspicions: I just asked him to wait until I was a bit older and could find a safe place for a pet. It took me a while to get over my loss. The incident of the rabbit had taught me a lesson and I had come to see my father in a new light.

Now I realise that I may have judged him too harshly. He was intelligent, level-headed and knowledgeable within the limits of the life he knew. He had a practical mind, more concerned with 'How?' than 'Why?' He was good with his hands and at working out how to do things in the quickest and simplest way. In the business of improvisation he was highly creative. If he lacked the right tool or material for a job, he'd soon find a serviceable substitute. At the same time he had a good vocabulary and he was quick at mental arithmetic. When I went to boarding school, I was surprised to discover what a good letter-writer he was. He had the kind of mind that would have benefited from a good education. In a different world he might have studied engineering and found a means of expression for his creative side.

Given his concern however with practical things, he had little time for anything that didn't advance the work of the farm. He rarely read a book and he had a reductive cast of mind that killed all possibility of indulging in verbal embroidery and other tricks of the shanachie's trade. We children loved listening to ghost stories, but my father's gift lay not in telling them but in explaining how they'd come about. One of his favourite stories concerned two poachers who took their catch to the local graveyard in order to divide the spoils in peace. As neither of them could count, they had to find an alternative method of division. A neighbour returning from the pub after closing time heard a ghostly voice coming from behind the grave-yard wall, saying '*ceann damhsa, ceann duitse*' (one for you, one for me) over and over again. Understandably, he took fright and, running home to his wife, told her that he'd just heard God and the Devil in the graveyard counting souls.

'That's how ghost stories come about,' my father would tell us triumphantly. 'A man has too much to drink and then puts the wrong construction on something he's seen or heard.'

It was not what any boy who loved ghost stories would wish to hear. In fact there was nothing I liked better than being scared out of my wits on a winter night while knowing all the time that I wasn't in any physical danger.

My father firmly believed that certain things must not be spoken of in front of the children. Anything to do with animal copulation was one of them. He used to dis-appear with one of the cows from time to time and come back two hours later, the cow looking weary and a bit unsteady on her pins.

'Where are you taking her?' I asked on one of these occasions.

'Out to Glenmalin for a walk,' he replied.

'Can I come?'

'No, you'll find plenty to do about the house.'

I knew perfectly well why he was taking the cow 'for a walk'. I knew to look at her that she'd come round. 'Tak-ing her out to Glemmalin' was only a euphemism for taking her to the bull.

When the other cow showed signs of being on heat, I told him that she was 'bulling'. At first he pretended not to hear. After a while I said, 'Will you be taking her out to Glenmalin, then?'

'No, why should I?'

For the next twenty-four hours I kept a watchful eye on both the cow and my father but he never took her anywhere. That confused me utterly. Was he deliberately trying to fox me or had I misread the signs? I couldn't very well ask my mother or my aunt, and I was too shy to ask Jamie Boyle or one of the other neighbours. My thirst for knowledge about animal copulation knew no bounds, and my father's determination to keep this vital information from me only further inflamed my curiosity.

At school the following day I made what I thought were subtle enquiries among the older boys, some of whom seemed to know more than any yet. One or two of them boasted that they had been out to Glenmalin with their fathers several times, and they gave me a graphic account of the whole effortful procedure. On one occasion the undernourished bull couldn't find the right place to put it and the owner had to give the desperate beast a helping hand. This was the cause of so much mirth in the playground that I didn't quite know what to make of it. Were they telling the truth or were they making fun of me? Clearly, the pursuit of knowledge was not a straightforward matter. Rather it required resources of deviousness and cunning, of which I was not yet capable. I resolved to be less direct in my enquiries, if ever the need should arise again.

My father was equally secretive about cows calving and went to great lengths to keep us all in the dark. Obviously, he could not conceal the fact of a cow being in calf, and invariably I waited anxiously for the new arrival. I don't know how my father managed it but our cows always gave birth while I was fast asleep in the middle of the night. I'd get up one morning and my mother would tell me that the cow had calved. The whole thing seemed quite miraculous. There would be the cow calmly chewing the cud with hollow flanks, and a lovely calf on long legs with long dribbles of frothy milk hanging from its chin. There was never any sign of the afterbirth. My father, in his obsession with concealment, had probably buried it in the garden, as if it were the most damning of incriminating evidence.

During the winter months, when the weather was bad and there was little work that could be done outside, he would sit in his chair between the kitchen bed and the fire, smoking his bent Peterson in silence. Suddenly, out of the blue he would say, 'Inmudeelis, infirtaris, inoaknoneis'. No matter how many times he repeated it, I couldn't work out what it meant. One day I asked him if it was something the priest said at Mass on Sunday.

'It could be bog Latin or maybe bog English,' he replied.

'But what does it mean?' I persisted in the hope that he would give in.

'It's a kind of riddle,' he said, repeating the rhyme so that I could hear each word distinctly:

In mud eel is
In fir tar is
In oak none is.

It still didn't make much sense to me but I learned it off by heart anyway in the hope that I might impress and confuse my friends at school. The following day in the playground I stood on a rock and said the rhyme with as much authority as I could muster.

'I know a better one than that,' an older boy said cockily. '*Ad Deum qui laetificat juventutem meam.*' I'd picked the wrong victim, an altar boy from Ballard who'd learnt the Mass responses in Latin. I jumped down off the rock, resolving to keep my new-found learning to myself in future.

It wasn't the only rhyme or riddle my father taught me. Another of his favourites was:

'Sisters and brothers, I have none.
That man's father was my father's son.'

I was supposed to work out the relationship between the speaker and 'that man'. I repeated the couplet to myself many times but still the relationship eluded me.

'What is the answer?' I asked my father.

'It will come to you one day. When it does, you'll know as much as I do.'

I thought he might tell me if I kept pestering him but he would always fob me off, more often than not with a totally different rhyme. One day I came to him and told him the answer.

'What did I tell you?' he said. 'You've worked it out for yourself. Now you'll never forget it.'

But just in case I might think that I now knew as much as he did, he began a long sentence with the high-sounding 'Extricate the quadruped from the vehicle…' which he translated for my benefit as 'Unharness the horse from the cart…'. In time I became accustomed to his old rhymes and sayings, which I could see gave him pleasure because he would laugh and repeat them without warning and at the oddest times. Nor did it seem to matter to him that they were completely unconnected with what he'd been talking about only a moment before.

He was particularly proud of his capacity to eat what-ever was set before him. 'Like my father and grandfather, I have a good gut,' he'd say. 'It's the greatest blessing any man can have.' That, of course, did not mean that he was not a discriminating food critic. He liked going to houses where the housewife could cook, and he claimed to eat as little as possible in houses where the housewife lacked basic culinary skills. His tastes were simple, needless to say. Most of the time he'd be happy with a boiled egg, but few were the housewives who could boil an egg to match his expectations.

'Cooks!' he'd say. 'What cooks? Most of them can't even boil an egg for a working man.' At home he insisted on timing the eggs, and I had to admit that they were always done to his, if no one else's, satisfaction, neither too hard nor too soft. As he never consulted a watch or clock, I couldn't help being impressed by his unerring instinct. He would continue with his conversation and to all intents and purposes forget about the eggs in the saucepan. Then suddenly he'd break off in mid-sentence and say, 'Those eggs are done.' If I asked him how he knew, he'd explain that what some housewives didn't understand was that all depended on the size of the eggs and the state of the hearth fire rather than clock time. 'Sometimes an egg will take three minutes and sometimes four. The tricky ones take three minutes and three-quarters.' I was still none the wiser, but his comment made a lasting impression on me. Now, fifty-five years later, I still think of him on those rare occasions when I have to fend for myself and boil an egg for breakfast.

As soon as I went to boarding school, his attitude towards me changed. Having put me on what he saw as the highroad to success, he no longer preached at me. He had done his bit; he could now leave me to my own devices. And so when I began working alongside him on the farm during the holidays, I got to know him for the first time. I enjoyed working with him for the sudden shafts of humour that would light up his conversation, and I could now see him as another human being with his own strengths and failings. We used to talk at length about whatever was on his mind. His conversation was mainly about the work of the farm, and he never gossiped about the neighbours. He tended to judge other men by how good they were with their hands. The most damning thing I've ever heard him say about anyone was, 'He never did a hard day's work in his life.' I came to admire him for his seriousness and sincerity, qualities which I had already found in short supply in the world of men. He has left his mark on me, I suppose. The question I still ask myself about someone I've just met is a simple one: 'Is he or she capable of sincerity?'

He had a good memory and a mind that was well-stocked with all sorts of unlikely information. He often surprised me with his knowledge of Scottish words that had fallen out of regular use in the local dialect but which I knew from my reading of Scott, Burns and Dunbar. Once, when we were cutting turf together, I made some comment he didn't agree with. He didn't contradict me, he just told me that as I grew older my mind would 'shire'. When I asked him what he meant by 'shire', he said that my mind would become clearer, like a muddy liquid left to settle until the dregs fall to the bottom of the jar. I didn't quite know what to make of that and thought it best to say no more.

I still find it difficult to understand his fastidiousness, if only because it was not what I'd expect of a countryman. In later years I often thought of reminding him of how secretive he had been about simple and natural things when we were children, but somehow I felt that he might not appreciate my sense of absurdity. Now I prefer to remember him as he was in his sixties and seventies, always ready to see the amusing side of an incident: as if in middle age he had finally shed his inhibitions and found a more philosophical way of looking at the world.

10

My Mother

My mother's name was Mary Ann. She was born in Garveross, a townland less than half an hour's walk from where we lived. Her maiden name was Heekin and she came from a family of five. After emigrating to America in her early twenties, she came back on holiday six years later and took up with my father whom she had known before she went away. They were married in 1935.

My mother talked a lot about Garveross. She used to refer to it jokingly as 'the land beyond the Jordan', the Jordan in this case being a channel of the sea called the Deán. During spring tides the sea came up over the low-lying land, and for a time Garveross would almost become an island. When I was a boy, there was only a narrow concrete footbridge over the Deán. A horse and cart couldn't get across, and all provisions had to be carried. My mother used to tell us that when she was a girl there was only a rather primitive swing-bridge, which provided an occasion for many amusing incidents. I took great interest in my mother's stories, which for me gave Garveross a quality that made it quite different from any other place in Glen.

She was fond of telling us about her girlhood and the fun she and her brothers and sisters had growing up. She told us about her father who died in middle age, and her grandfather Jamie Heekin, who rode a mare in his late eighties and lived to be ninety-nine. She used to tell us that the first of the Garveross Heekins, a man called Matha Mór (Big Matthew), 'came from the sea'. I had visions of him rising from the waves, like a giant in a storybook, but I imagine that what really happened was that he had been shipwrecked off the coast and swam ashore, where he married a girl from Garveross who had given him food and shelter. It all sounded highly romantic, like something from the heroic legends of ancient Ireland. When I asked my father where the McGinleys came from, all he could say was 'Scotland,' which sounded prosaic by comparison and more than likely wasn't true.

She would also tell us a story about a man from Garveross who disturbed a weasel's nest one day while mowing a meadow. He could tell that the mother weasel was angry with him, and as he mowed he kept an eye on her and she an eye on him. After a while, when she thought he wasn't looking, she approached a noggin of milk he had left in the shade of a rock to slake his thirst. He was not at all surprised when she spat in the milk, knowing as he did that a weasel's spittle is poisonous. Just to see what she'd do next he went back to the nest and rearranged it so that it looked exactly as it was before. He continued mowing, still keeping an eye on the weasel. Eventually, she returned to the nest and examined it. She then approached the noggin again and began going round it in circles, coming closer and closer to it each time. Finally, she overturned it with her rump and spilt the poisoned milk.

'Wasn't that a good one,' my mother would say. 'And some people think that animals don't know the difference between right and wrong!'

Now and again she would tell us about her time in America, about the different types of people from all nationalities and the big department stores that sold everything you could ever imagine. She told us about what she called the American twang and the strange words they had, words you'd never hear spoken in Glen. She would also tell us about going to the theatre and the movies, but strangely she never went to the pictures in Glen. When I asked her why, she laughed and said that the seats in the Spink were too hard.

She could tell a story to beat the band, and some of them filled my young mind with terror. One of her stories told how her grandfather was on the mountain one dark night making a run of poteen, when a big black hound entered the still-house and stood eyeing him with weird expectancy from the doorway. Knowing there was no black hound in the parish, he sensed immediately that he was in the presence of something otherworldly, an animal that had come 'from nowhere good'. Making a hollow in the earthen floor with his heel, he poured out a generous measure of the newly distilled poteen. The hound came forward and drank the liquor, licked its lips in gratitude, and vanished into the night. I can still recall the creepy feeling I had as I listened to that story. How I could see the black hound in the doorway by the weak light of the lantern and my great-grandfather regretfully pouring out the poteen, which he'd rather have drunk himself. My father, who never believed any story, said that he'd probably drunk enough of it already. I kept badgering my father for stories about his grandfather, but if he knew any he wasn't telling.

Light-hearted and carefree, my mother enjoyed talking, and she had a joke for every occasion. Whenever she went to Cashel to do the shopping, she would come back full of news and stories. Everyone she met seemed to have something unusual to relate, and if they hadn't, she'd find a way of making whatever they'd said amusing. She was an accomplished mimic, particularly good at imitating accents and facial expressions and gestures. She would remember exactly how something had been said and how the speaker looked as she'd said it. I couldn't help feeling that people must have had a special way of talking to my mother because I could never detect any of these amusing quirks myself.

In many respects my mother was the antithesis of Auntie Kate, my father's sister, who also lived with us and could spend a whole day in Cashel without ever meeting anyone amusing or having anything strange to relate. In spite of their different personalities they both got on well together. My aunt always asked my mother if she'd met anyone on the way and she seemed to enjoy my mother's stories and her way of recounting the events of the day. It was as if she knew that my mother had the knack of making people say things that they'd never have said to anyone else.

My mother also had an old wind-up gramophone, which she had brought back from America. Whenever she was in a jolly mood, she would put on a record and we'd all gather round and listen. She had only about ten or twelve records, mostly Scottish songs by Harry Lauder. Some of the records were so worn that I would have to put my ear to the soundbox to try to make out the words. I particularly remember 'Roamin' in the Gloamin', 'I Love a Lassie', 'Just a Wee Deoch-an-Doruis', and 'Ticklie Geordie', which I thought was best of all. Sometimes the McGlinchey girls would come in from next door and dance to the music, which added to the fun.

However, we didn't get a chance to listen to the gramophone very often. Usually, my mother was busy doing housework, and when she wasn't doing housework, she was carding wool, spinning, knitting or sprigging, which was working floral designs on handkerchiefs as piecework. She didn't like close work because her eyesight wasn't good, and preferred, I think, working with my father in the fields. During the spring she would help him plant the potatoes and in the summer she would help gather in the hay while he made hand-cocks, but that was only in the early years when we children were too young to be of much help.

My mother was particular about dress and appearance. She liked to look her best going to Mass on Sunday and on the rare occasions when she and my father went to old-time dances in the Spink hall. After coming home from Mass she would comment on what other women were wearing, especially those who were a cut above everyone else and saw themselves as arbiters of 'fashion' in the glen. My mother didn't have an extensive wardrobe, but the clothes she had she wore well. Most of them came from her sister Cassie in America, who used to send her dresses and coats. The arrival of a parcel from America was always an occasion of great excitement in our house. The postman usually came around noon, and the big cardboard box would be opened and the afternoon devoted to trying on dresses and coats, deciding what could be worn with what, and what needed to be altered to make it fit. I suppose it was the nearest my mother got to the fun of a shopping expedition, which she remembered from her time in America and would talk about whenever she was in a mood for reminiscence.

When I went to boarding school at thirteen, the person I missed most was my mother. During the holidays I spent my time working with my father in the fields or on the bog, and my relationship with my mother remained unfulfilled, as she died when I was twenty, and before I had a chance to get to know her as a mature man. There

were many things I wished to find out about the McGinley side of the family that only she would have told me.
If I asked my aunt, she would have said something in one
sentence to discourage me from asking a second question.
My father would have said, 'Let the dead rest. It's all
ancient history now.' Looking back, I think that my
mother was the most natural person in the family. Open
and companionable, she could talk to anyone. She felt at
home in her skin and utterly at ease with the world. Her
untimely death was the hardest blow I've had to endure.

11

Auntie Kate

Auntie Kate's real name was Mary Kate but Auntie Mary Kate would have been a mouthful, so we called her Auntie Kate. She was a primary teacher who spent weekdays at her school in Lougheraherk and came back to stay with us at weekends. Quiet and serious, she rarely laughed and sometimes she seemed to catch her breath as she talked.

I was fond of Auntie Kate. She helped me with my sums at weekends, and when I got them right she would give me a sweet or a biscuit from the seemingly endless store she kept in her room. On Saturdays she went to morning Mass in the village, and she would do her washing when she came back. She would cook dinner on Sunday, and in the afternoon she would take her bicycle and set off once again for the mountains, and I would feel sad because the house seemed empty without her. Sometimes I would go down the field and look at the purply blue hills in the east and wonder if she was still on the road. Her journey was uphill. She would have to push her bicycle most of the way but coming back on

Friday evening she could freewheel. She wouldn't let rip, though. She would go slowly because she wasn't one for speeding.

Eventually, she must have got tired pushing her bicycle because she started hiring a hackney car to take her back and forth to Lougheraherk, where she taught. I was delighted by this change in her routine because sometimes she would ask me to come with her in Tom Maxwell's Ford Prefect, which was an opportunity to see what lay behind the purply blue hills. On my first visit what struck me above all else was the bare landscape around the school. From Cashel school you could see other houses, whereas Lougheraherk school stood alone in a bleak expanse of sedge and heather. In the marshy hollow below the school lay a little lough with reeds round the margin and a single white swan sitting all alone. I remember wondering if any other swan would come to visit her in such a desolate place.

My aunt opened the schoolhouse door with a big key. It was cold inside. The wind sang in the chimney, tugged at the door, and rattled the window sashes. There was only one large room, which surprised me because there were three rooms in Cashel school. There was an easel with a blackboard, on which I recognised my aunt's perfect handwriting, and there were desks with inkwells and a big empty fireplace. It was in every respect a smaller version of Cashel school.

I stood on a chair and looked out of the window at a bleached brown wasteland. 'Do you ever get lonely here?' I asked her.

'Why should I get lonely with all the children round me?'

'It's a lonely place,' I said.

'You only think that. You should hear the noise at playtime when they're all out in the yard.'

Tom Maxwell brought her bicycle into the yard. She would use it to travel back and forth to Gara's in Kilty-fanned, where she would stay for the rest of the week. It was strange leaving her all alone with her books in the empty schoolhouse. I was reluctant to go back but if I stayed for an hour or two it would have been a long way to walk before nightfall. Tom gave me a lift back to Kilgoly Bridge and I walked the rest of the way. I was pleased that she had taken me to see her school because now I could imagine it and I could also imagine the journey there. I had made a discovery. It was like seeing a new country or at least a new glen. If, as my father said, a glen was a hollow between two hills, the glen where I lived was not the only glen. There were glens within Glen, which was something I had not thought of before.

Now and again my aunt took me on shopping expeditions to Donegal Town, thirty-five miles away. On these occasions we took the bus to Killybegs and then the rail bus to Donegal. The rail bus was more interesting than the bus. Almost like a train, it ran on rails and went clickety-click as it rattled along. It ran through wild countryside, away from roads and houses, snaking through cuttings between rocks. The only time we saw the road was at level crossings where the traffic stopped to let us through. The thing that interested me most was how they turned the rail bus round at the station for the journey back. The driver drove the coach onto a big turntable and strong men pushed with their backs until it faced the other way. When I got home, I told my father about it. He pretended not to be surprised but I knew that at last I had seen something that he hadn't. I also told the other boys at school but they didn't seem to understand and said that I had imagined it all.

Another time my aunt took me to Derry. This time we went on a proper train with a locomotive that burned coal and belched smoke. We stayed the night at a hotel and were served dinner in the restaurant by a waiter instead of a waitress. When my aunt had done all her own shopping, we went in search of a bow for my father's fiddle. The search took well over an hour, because my aunt had to make enquiries in several shops, until at last a kindly old man came to the door and pointed us in the right direction.

The music shop was full of instruments I had not seen before. A tall, elderly man with a pronounced stoop and long fingers stood up as we entered. He had been sitting behind the counter reading *The Derry People*, a newspaper I recognised from home. When my aunt said that she was looking for a fiddle bow, he seemed to have no idea what she meant. Then she pointed to the wall where some fiddles and bows were hanging.

'Ah, you mean a *vi-ol-in bough*,' he exclaimed in an accent that was new to me.

After much discussion and comparative pricing, my aunt bought one of the four violin *boughs* on display, which he wrapped first in tissue paper and then in stiff brown paper secured with string. Finally, she bought some rosin, which she put in her handbag. As he bent down to do the wrapping, I realised that he must be very old. His hands shook and his cheeks were the colour of altar candles. He seemed to be speaking to himself as he wrapped, but I could not understand a word he said.

'All Derry people don't talk like that,' I said to my aunt on the way back to our hotel.

'He isn't from Derry, he's English. He thinks that a fiddle bow should be pronounced like the bough of a tree.' It was my first encounter with an English accent and for years afterwards I harboured the illusion that all English people talked like that.

Looking back now, I realise that my aunt's life could not have been easy. It was a life of work with little time for recreation. In the early years in particular, before she bought a car, she used to cycle everywhere in wind and rain. In winter she wore an oilskin cape, souwester, and pull-ups to protect her legs but more often than not she would arrive back from school soaking wet. She rarely went on holiday, and when she did it was only for a few days.

She was a quiet, contemplative person, a fact I came to appreciate more and more as I grew older. At weekends and during holidays she would spend a lot of time in her room. Sometimes I would find her kneeling by the bed saying the rosary or reading a prayer book, of which she had several, including Thomas á Kempis's *Imitation of Christ*, which she encouraged me to read without much success. Unlike my mother, she was not a great talker. She never wandered down the tortuous lanes and byways of conversation, making new pathways and unexpected discoveries. Instead, she spoke in well-constructed sentences, as if words were precious coins that must on no account be squandered, and when she uttered one sentence she would allow several seconds to elapse before uttering another. She was at her best summing up succinctly after someone else had spoken at length, using more words than was strictly necessary. After I went to boarding school, she used to write to me in beautiful nineteenth-century copperplate that I could not even begin to emulate. Her letters were short and factual with here and there an unobtrusive piece of good advice. She avoided flowery language and anything that might smack of exaggeration. If she had been a feature writer paid by the column inch, she'd have found it hard to earn a living.

Her sense of humour was also strictly her own. Now and again in the middle of a conversation, she'd make a joke that not everyone would see. Conversely, if someone else made a joke, she would not necessarily oblige by laughing. For that reason I used to think up things to see if she'd find them funny. The surest way to make her laugh was to say something absurd but not downright silly, or something outlandish that might just conceivably be true. In this my father was more successful than the rest of us, probably because she and he had been brought up together and he knew her better than anyone else. She would laugh at my jokes, but not always, and even when she laughed at them, I'd be inclined to ask myself, 'Is she laughing with me or at me?' When I mentioned this to my father once, he said, 'Don't feel bad about it. Getting her to laugh at all is a job well done.'

I learnt a great deal from listening to my aunt and paying attention to what she had to say. While my mother merely wanted me to be happy and enjoy a life less limited than her own, my aunt was more ambitious. She could see that I was interested in books, and for her all serious study must lead ultimately to the priesthood, which, she said, was the greatest goal any young man could set himself in life. She told me to pray for what she called a vocation, and as a first step she encouraged me to become a Mass server. My father probably had his own view of the matter, but wisely he kept it to himself. All he wanted for me was to do something useful with my life and not waste it in back-breaking toil.

Now I realise that all three of them left their own individual mark on me. From my mother I inherited a capacity to enjoy what pleasures come my way. From my father I inherited a restless and fault-finding mind as well as a certain detachment from the world, while from my aunt I learned the value of personal ambition as a spur to achievement. For a time, as a boy, I thought that my future might lie in the Church, but my experience of the priests who ran my boarding school soon put paid to that fond idea.

PART III

Growing Up in the Glen

12

Openings

On a windy night in November during the war years, I was playing with my brother and eldest sister before the fire while my mother sat carding wool, preparing it for spinning. My father had gone out to Loughunsha to collect a pup from Daniel McGinley, a remote relation of ours. My aunt was at her school in the mountains. We were alone with our mother, enjoying the warmth of the fire while we played our games on the hearth. As we didn't have any toys, the games we played were simple: 'Put your finger in the crow's nest, the crow is not at home' or making cats' cradles with a piece of knotted string. The only sound in the kitchen was the clacking of my mother's two cards, the drone of the wind in the chimney, and now and again the low sigh the fire made when the coals fell into place as the turf burnt down and shrank to ash.

From time to time we'd ask her if Daddy would be back before bedtime, but she was careful not to give us much encouragement. She merely repeated that it was a long way to Loughunsha, that he was bound to be late. None of us had ever been to Loughunsha. We didn't even know where it was. She told us that it was on the road that ran out over the hill to Carrick, and that it was at least two miles away. The three of us talked among ourselves about the pup, wondering if he'd be black and white like the old dog and if Daniel had already given him a name. We were excited by the prospect of having a pup to play with. He would tug at our clothes and run after us up and down the field.

My mother made porridge for supper and gave us milk from an enamel jug to put on it. Shortly after we'd eaten, she said that it was past our bedtime. When we told her that we wanted to stay up till Daddy came home, she wouldn't hear of it. We were already preparing for bed when we heard the sound of his hobnailed boots on the street. He lifted the latch and opened the door, his peaked cap pulled well down over his eyes.

'Where's the pup?' we asked in unison.

'You'll have to wait another while,' he said. 'Daniel gave it to a man from Clogher this morning. Everyone seems to want a pup these days.'

'I thought he had more than one,' my mother said.

'The dog had a litter of three. He gave two away, he's keeping one for himself.'

We could hardly contain our disappointment. Coming back from Loughunsha without the promised pup was like coming back from the fair without any sweets.

'You had a long walk for nothing,' my mother said.

'I got back dry, and that's something. There were openings in the southwest as I was coming in the Line.'

'Openings? What's that?' I asked.

He told us that 'openings' were bright patches in the clouds caused by distant lightning. You couldn't see the path of the lightning, only a vague brightness, and you couldn't hear any thunder either, because it was happening so far away. It all sounded quite magical. We wanted to go out to see the 'openings' but he said that it was too cold for us, that we'd see them another time.

My father took a great interest in the weather. When he got up in the morning, the first thing he'd do was to go out and look at the sky. He took particular interest in the way the wind was blowing and he could read the sky like a book. It came from being a fisherman and having to know the effect the direction of the wind would have on the sea. The way the wind blew would also give him a fair idea of whether he should expect rain. He was not the only one who was obsessed with the weather. His closest friend and neighbour Andy Gillespie was also a fisherman and liked to give his own forecast. The first thing he and my father always talked about when they met was the weather. My mother used to laugh at them and say they talked of nothing else. Belonging to a generation of men who had grown up before the coming of radio, they had learnt to rely on their own skill in interpreting the signs rather than on the predictions of the Meteorological Office, and more often than not the weather proved them right. Perhaps it wasn't all that difficult in Donegal. If you forecast rain or at least showers, you couldn't go too far wrong.

I must have been at least ten when he showed me the famous 'openings' which I later discovered to be the same as sheet lightning. Another time he took me out on a clear night to the end-wall of the house and showed me the northern lights above Glen Head. These were luminous rays like those coming from the headlamps of an approaching car, except that they were much more spectacular because they flashed green or even red. He told me that another name for them was 'aurora borealis', which made me laugh because it sounded funny and unreal like 'abracadabra'. Sometimes he would come in on a winter night and say, 'Aurora borealis. He who cannot spell it is a dunce'. We never did learn to spell the word because the answer he always gave with a smile was '*I-T*'.

My first sight of 'openings' has remained with me, and over sixty years later I can still see that diffused brightness in the clouds. As a boy, it seemed to me that that was how my life would unfold: as I entered the magical world of manhood, everything would open up before me. I would see things clearly and steadily, I would know everything I wished to know, and all would turn out as planned. Life, I discovered in time, was not so simple. The more you know, the more you desire to know and the more there is to know. For me the magic that lasts longest is to be found in books and music. Yet there is no satisfying the human mind and imagination. Life's magic is fitful and evanescent, never where we hope to find it, and life itself is best lived with a sense of wonder, not as a problem with a definable solution.

13

Forbidden Knowledge

D r Johnson said that knowledge is of two kinds. 'We know a subject ourselves, or we know where we can find information upon it.' When I was eight or nine, how-ever, I came to a radically different conclusion. First, there was the knowledge I had gleaned at school, which was legitimate but dull, and, secondly, there was the type of knowledge that made people look away and change the subject whenever I made enquiries. They obviously knew things I wasn't meant to know, and before too long I came to the conclusion that they were ashamed of this knowl-edge and that it must therefore be sinful. The priest spoke of the Tree of Knowledge of Good and Evil in the Gar-den of Eden. Eve plucked an apple from the tree and gave it to Adam to eat. You didn't have to be a genius to work out that this was no ordinary apple. There were no apple trees in our garden at home, but I had eaten the odd apple from a neighbour's tree without being caught by God or anyone else. Quite obviously, the apple in the story of Adam and Eve was neither apple nor pear. It was something else entirely.

My aunt had a book in her room called *Hell Opened* with pictures of naked men and women struggling with huge serpents that coiled themselves round their bodies and bit them all over without ever consuming them entirely. One woman who was up to her waist in a lake of fire had a blindfold over her eyes and two big apples on her chest. When I asked my father if she had gone to Hell for stealing apples, he thought it funny. He said that people don't go to Hell just for stealing apples. I didn't want to tell him that these were no ordinary apples. The woman in the picture was naked, and so were Adam and Eve in the garden. I realised that I myself had wandered into the Garden of Forbidden Knowledge, and I thought it best to say no more on the subject for the time being.

I used to lie awake in the kitchen bed facing the wall while my brother slept at my back. I often stayed awake deliberately, waiting for my father to come home from Doonalt whenever he went to 'rake' in Dominic Andy's. Pretending to be asleep, I would close my eyes and imagine the moon shining on the sea and the lonely shore road that he must walk all the way back. It was a struggle to remain awake, because the regular clicking and clacking of my mother's knitting needles on the other side of the bed curtain had the effect of a strong soporific.

I wanted to remain awake because I enjoyed listening to him as he told my mother the news. It was interesting to hear what they talked about when no children were present to spoil their conversation. He'd tell her what Dominic's wife had said to Hughie Cunnea and after that what Hughie Cunnea said to Dominic. I had seen these men at Mass on Sunday, but in this way I got to know many things I wasn't meant to hear.

My mother had her own ideas about what she wished to hear. Sometimes, if she wasn't altogether happy with my father's version of events, she would question him further in case he'd left out something important or, worse still, forgotten it. Unlike my mother, my father was not a mimic, and very often all he would give were the bare bones of what had passed. My mother wanted meat on the bone. She expected him to remember the very words of each speaker, so that she could hear them being uttered and repeat them to herself in the very accents in which they had been spoken. She had an innate sense of drama and in this case an intimate knowledge of the dramatis personae.

Now, as I look back, I can understand her passion for accuracy and her impatience with my father's unvarnished narrative. He was concerned purely with the facts and it wasn't in his nature to embroider them. In fact, if anything, he would be inclined to reduce the import of what he'd heard, and he certainly would never go so far as to speculate on what a speaker really meant as opposed to what he'd actually said. My mother, on the other hand, had a fertile imagination and a gift for psychological analysis. There was nothing she liked better than probing someone's cast of mind as revealed in his turn of phrase, and pouncing on a hidden motive with all the joy of a water diviner discovering a spring many feet below ground level.

One night I was slipping along the selvage of sleep when I heard my father's footsteps on the street outside. I pulled the bedclothes up over the back of my head and waited for the click of the door latch.

'It's a clear night,' he told my mother. 'You'd pick needles off the road, if there were any.'

'Anyone in Dominic's tonight?' she asked, going straight to the point.

The conversation meandered along until my mother was satisfied that he'd delivered up the last gobbet of news. Then she pulled back the bed-curtain ever so slightly to make sure that my brother and I were asleep. I could tell that the curtain had moved because I could sense the lamplight on the wall through my closed eyelids.

'I saw a funny thing today,' she said in a hushed voice. She'd stopped knitting, for I could no longer hear the clicking of the needles. 'I looked over the ditch into Andy's garden and guess who I saw.'

'Who?'

She said one word I didn't catch. Then she added in a voice almost as low as a whisper, 'He was standing there under the sycamore with his trousers down, staring at it.'

'Did he see you?' my father asked seriously.

'No, I only looked for a second. He must have been waiting for one of the girls.'

'Maybe he was just admiring it,' my father said.

My mother laughed out loud. 'At first I thought it was you having a joke on me,' she said.

'Shhh, you'll wake the boys,' my father said.

I put my hand over my mouth in case I should laugh, too. I had never heard my father say anything like that before. It made me realise that when he was alone with my mother he was an entirely different man.

The mystery man who was looking down at 'it' would not let go of me. The following day I kept thinking about him at school. In the afternoon I climbed through a gap in the wall into Andy's garden and waited. The garden was full of bushes and briars, ideal for hiding in. I waited for an hour or more, listening to people up and down the road, but no 'admirer of it', to use my father's phrase, came next or near me. For a week or so I kept an eye on the garden, but at the end of the week I was none the wiser.

For want of an alternative strategy, I began observing birds and animals in the hope that I might solve for myself one of life's greatest mysteries. Blackbirds chased each other in the garden, and my mother had a high and mighty rooster that trod the hens so often and so mercilessly that they used to run away whenever they saw him coming. That in itself was a mystery because it didn't quite accord with my theory that the hens must enjoy being trodden by His Lordship. Young heifers were another puzzle. Though lacking what I considered to be the necessary equipment, they often mounted each other for no reason that I could discern. That didn't accord with the information I had gleaned from older boys that it was the bull that did the mounting. The whole business was highly confusing, and to make matters worse, there was no dependable source of enlightenment to which I might turn.

I still listened to my father and mother's conversation whenever I managed to stay awake at night, but they never again alluded to what was uppermost in my mind. Their conversations had made me realise how little I knew about life, how little I knew even about my parents. I wanted to grow up quickly, to understand everything people said, and to make grown-up talk like my father and the other men around. One day I asked him when I'd be a man. He looked surprised. 'Why do you want to be a man?' he asked.

'I want to understand things,' I said.

'What things?'

'What you and Andy talk about when you're not talking about the weather.'

He must have thought that funny because he laughed. 'You'll be old in time enough, and when you are you'll regret it.'

If he had told me that he himself didn't know everything, I wouldn't have believed him. I knew in my heart that he knew all the things I wanted to know and that he was determined to keep them from me. Sexual knowledge

was a contraband commodity in the Ireland of my boyhood, and I was at university before I found satisfactory
answers to my simple biological questions.

Now at the end of my active life I realise that I am
back where I began in Glen as a boy, still in a state of
wonderment and uncertainty. The things I now wish to
know are not to be found in any book, least of all in scientific manuals. We are walking mysteries: we see only the
surface, and from the surface draw tentative conclusions.
The human heart is a source of endless puzzlement. We
are aliens to each other and to ourselves, and those who
think they know themselves and everyone else miss the
best of life's tantalising music.

14

Passing the Time Pleasantly

On wet days when I couldn't play outside, I used to go to the neighbours' houses to escape unwelcome supervision at home. In neighbours' houses no one took any notice of me; the conversation flowed on as if I wasn't there. I liked going down the field to a house in which there were four growing men, all of them keen footballers whose conversation ran on sport and the kind of rough-and-tumble fun that was frowned on at home. I envied them their freedom because it seemed to me that they were up to every enjoyable devilment, including smoking improvised cigarettes made from butts rolled in strips of newspaper.

One of them had made a 'corncob' pipe by hollowing out a cotton spool to serve as the bowl, and by removing the pith from a bourtree twig to make a serviceable stem. I thought it all highly ingenious, the very epitome of the freedoms denied me as a boy, freedoms that all young men enjoyed or would like to enjoy. Visiting neighbours' houses made me realise that every house was different, and it made me long for the day when I would be able to go here and there and act on whatever whim came to mind.

Though I enjoyed playing with other children on the hill we called the Corr Mhalaigh, there were certain things I preferred to do alone, and looking for eels in the stream was one of these. The stream was shallow for the most part with here and there an occasional deeper pool, and its bed full of stones that had been coloured brown by the water. My father told me that the water contained iron, which gave the stones their rusty colour, and sometimes the water itself looked rusty too.

The stream began somewhere on the hillside, running down through rough mountain pasture until it reached the Corr Mhalaigh where it vanished between high banks, forming a private world from which you could see nothing except the steep banks and the sky above. After that it flowed along the park we called the Upper Pound into a concrete tank or reservoir, which supplied piped water to the parochial house. At that time the priest was the only person in the whole townland of Killaned who washed in water from a tap. Then the stream ran under the road through a culvert, which was full of cobwebs and big spiders, and finally down along the Lower Pound, flanked on each side by bushes and briars.

I would make my way down the stream lifting stones to see if there were any eels beneath them. Whenever I lifted a stone, the water would become muddy and I would have to wait for a minute or two until it cleared. Catching eels in this way wasn't easy, and I often wondered if perhaps there was a touch of madness in my method. Not that it mattered — as in my heart I knew it wasn't the prospect of catching an eel that attracted me but the sound of flowing water, the shapes of the stones in the stream, and the feeling that there was nothing else in the world that could intrude on me. The sound the water made varied from pool to pool. The best sound of all was in the reservoir, because there the water flowed over the concrete wall like a never-ending transparent curtain. The stream was a world in itself — the most satisfying place I knew. There was nothing I liked better than sitting silently by a pool in the shade of overhanging bushes, listening to birdsong as I waited for an eel to poke its head out from under a stone.

After heavy rain, while the stream was in spate, little brown trout sometimes came up from the Murleen River and became stranded in the pools. I remember spending a month or more trying to catch one that had made its home under a rock on which I used to sit. I got a sally rod from the garden and a few yards of fishing line from my father. Fashioning a hook from one of my mother's safety pins, I baited it with a wriggling earthworm that I thought should look attractive to a trout. I soon discovered, however, that fish were not so easily deceived.

After approaching the pool as quietly as I could, I would take up my position without a sound. At first there was never any sign of the trout but after a while it would appear out of the shadows, as if by magic. I would sit on the rock, watching it facing upstream as it moved its fins and tail ever so slightly to maintain its position in the current. Sometimes it would move its jaws as well but whenever I lowered a baited hook into the pool, it never showed the slightest interest. I tried earthworms large and small and beetles both black and brown; I even tried breadcrumbs to no avail. It was as if the little brown trout had a sixth sense that told it of the deadly hook in the bait. I didn't tell any of the other boys about the trout but I mentioned it several times to my mother. She laughed and said that I mustn't become obsessed with one trout, that there were more than one fish in the river. Disappointed by her lack of seriousness, I turned to my father who said that the day was too bright for fishing. He said that I should try again after a heavy rainfall when the stream would be fast flowing and the water less clear.

After the next night of rain I acted on his advice. The water was tumbling and gushing between the rocks and my head did not cast a shadow, but I did not consider it satisfactory because the water was so brown that I could not see the trout. Still, I knew that it must be there. I dropped the baited hook into the pool and held it against the current without letting it sink to the bottom. After a while I felt a nibble and then a tug as the line went taut. The trout came wriggling out of the water and I held it up, watching its gills opening and closing as it gasped in the destructive air. It was a lovely little trout, only five inches long, with little red speckles on its sides. I ran home with the fish still attached to the hook and showed it to my mother.

'I've caught him at last,' I said proudly

'What will you do now?' she smiled. 'You've caught the only fish in the stream.'

'I'll eat it for dinner,' I said.

'It's too small to eat at dinnertime. I'll cook it now and you can eat it before the others come in.'

She cleaned the trout and cooked it and gave it to me on a plate with a glass of milk and a slice of buttered bread. It was the first time I tasted river trout and it was delicious. I asked my mother to taste it as well. At first she was reluctant. Then to please me she took a piece on a fork.

'It's the freshest fish you'll ever eat,' she said. 'Even the fish Daddy brings straight from the sea take longer to get to the pot.' She was right. I was never to come across precisely the same flavour again.

The following afternoon I went back to the stream, hoping that another trout would have taken the place of the one I had caught. I sat for an hour looking down into the shadows in the pool but there was not a sign of life stirring. It seemed as if my mother was right. I had caught the only trout in the stream, and I could not help being saddened by the knowledge that I could not catch it a second time. The pain of never-again was a truth I'd experience many times throughout my life. Some things you can enjoy only once, after which the memory of enjoyment becomes ashes in the mouth. Having caught and eaten my trout, I felt that there was an empty space in my life, and I gave up going to the pool. In time I forgot about the trout, though some years later I was reminded of it at boarding school when I came across a poem by W B Yeats called 'The Song of Wandering Aengus':

> *I went out to the hazel wood,*
> *Because a fire was in my head,*
> *And cut and peeled a hazel wand,*
> *And hooked a berry to a thread;*
> *And when white moths were on the wing,*
> *And moth-like stars were flickering out,*
> *I dropped the berry in a stream*
> *And caught a little silver trout.*

I read the whole poem several times, thinking it the most magical piece of verse I'd come across. It inspired me to read poetry at a time when I might otherwise have found it a tiresome chore.

When I was about nine something happened that made me see myself in a new light. I invented a drink I called Dabra after 'abracadabra', a word I'd heard used by the juggler in Fossett's Circus on one of their rare visits to the Green Field. To tell the truth, I do not quite know whether I invented or discovered the precious liquor. All I remember is that I first made it by chopping up a fistful of dock leaves, stuffing them into a whiskey bottle, pouring cold spring water over them, and burying the corked bottle in the garden for a fortnight. When I dug it up again, I found that the water had turned green. I sipped some of it from a spoon by way of experiment, only to discover that it tasted foul. I was not easily discouraged, however, and I made some more Dabra, first using sycamore leaves, and later nettles, but I still could not drink the concoction.

When I shared my secret with another boy at school, to my surprise he didn't make fun of me. Instead, he told me that what I was trying to make was wine and that his elder brother had made excellent wine from ripe sloes. 'First, you slice up nine sloes,' he said. 'Then you cover them with water, put the mixture in a bottle, and bury it for nine days and nine nights until it ferments.'

I could tell from his use of the technical word 'ferment' that he knew what he was talking about, and I went home in a state of excitement. We didn't have a blackthorn in our garden but a neighbour had a sloe bush, which was the same thing. I waited anxiously throughout the summer, keeping a weather eye on my neighbour's sloes. When autumn came and the sloes had ripened, I picked a pocketful and took them home, where I followed my friend's instructions to the letter. I even crossed off the days on a calendar I had specially made for the purpose. But when I dug up the bottle again, the water inside was still quite clear, which didn't seem right. The only wine I'd ever seen was altar wine in the sacristy and that was dark red. Obviously, I must have done something wrong.

'What makes wine red?' I asked my friend at school.

'What makes the sky blue?' He was never one to be stumped for an answer but it was not the answer I needed.

Next day I consulted his elder brother who told me that I had done everything right, except that I hadn't buried the bottle deep enough. 'The cork of the bottle must be nine inches below ground level,' he said.

There was nothing for it but to begin from scratch again. I was determined not to be discouraged, as I had visions of myself making wine on a commercial scale for consumption by my pals at school. This time, with the aid of a tape measure, I buried the bottle to the correct depth and waited patiently for the ninth day. At first I couldn't find the exact spot where I'd buried it, but at last I came upon it by prodding the ground with an old poker. To my disgust, the water still hadn't turned red and my tongue shrivelled in my mouth when I tasted it. My father, who'd watched my efforts in silence, said, 'I expect there's more to wine-making than you think.'

'What do you need to make proper wine?' I asked.

'Grapes,' he said. 'They don't grow in Ireland. The climate isn't right.'

It was a deflating piece of information. Suddenly, I felt older and sadder. Dabra was for younger boys. I never tried to make it again.

Soon afterwards, Big John McNelis, a relation of my father who'd spent the best part of his life in America, dropped in on us for a chat. He was a cheerful, slow-moving man, full of fascinating stories about a place he called 'New Yark'. Before he left, he asked me what I'd like to do when I grew up.

'I'd like to go to New Yark,' I said, thinking he might give me sixpence.

'That's a journey for the feet.' He pointed down. 'The best journeys are in the head.' He tapped his forehead with his forefinger.

He left without giving me the longed-for sixpence. Disappointed, I asked my mother what he'd meant by journeys in the head.

'Big John is a bit soft in the head,' she said.

'He was telling you to read more books,' my father explained.

I didn't believe him. Surely Big John must have meant something else, something my father didn't want me to know. He was like that, my father, full of advice I didn't want to hear. Wherever I turned, I faced a blank wall. My Dabra had come to nothing, and now the journey in the head. It seemed to me that Big John knew all the things I wanted to know, and he was the kind of easygoing man who would tell me, given half a chance. The following summer he was drowned off the Doonalt coast. Another avenue of information had closed.

15

Talk about Death

I had spent a lot of time trying to find out about sex with no success, but the same could not be said about death. It seemed to me that people talked of little else. We lived in a parish where everyone knew everyone else within a radius of seven miles. As most of the young people had emigrated, there was a preponderance of the middle-aged and elderly, one or two of whom were nearly always either dying or close to death. Whenever two adults met on the road, one was bound to say to the other, 'I hear so-and-so has been anointed' or 'I hear so-and-so is for death'. References to death were always direct and to the point; no attempt was made to sidestep its finality. No one said, 'John has passed away' or 'Mary has gone to her reward'. It was always: 'John died this morning, may God be good to him' or 'Mary didn't last very long, poor creature'.

Everyone took an interest not only in death but in the process of dying. When someone was seriously ill, there would be regular reports on progress, whether they were eating, and whether they were 'raving' or in pain. There would be daily reports on what a sick man had said, whether he'd asked after an absent friend, and whether he had come to favour a particular food in his last precious hours. As there was no professional undertaker in the community, one or two neighbours would prepare the body by washing it and laying it out for waking and burial. In this way everyone had direct experience of the death of several acquaintances or neighbours. People had a personal knowledge of death rarely found in modern urban communities, and they talked openly and freely about the experience. Death, unlike sex, was an accepted fact of life. To take more than a passing interest in the subject was not seen as morbid or voyeuristic. By the time I was six, I knew more about death than life, merely from listening to the adults around me. People talked in a matter of fact way about the death rattle, a gurgling in the throat of a dying person, and the *marbhfháisc*, a strip of cloth tied round a dead person's jaw to keep the mouth closed, as if these things were as common as sunrise and sunset. One man was so blasé about death that when asked how he felt he would say, 'Just waiting for the minute.' We all knew he wasn't being serious, rather that it was his way of whistling in the dark.

Unlike the elderly, the young saw death as a remote, theoretical event that always happened to someone else. The untimely death of a young person would evoke the sympathy of young and old, of course, but the death of someone who had lived long beyond his expected span was often seen by the young as an occasion for irreverent fun at the wake. After the rosary had been said over the deceased at midnight, the people of the house would go to bed to snatch a few hours' sleep, leaving neighbours to keep vigil over the body till morning. Sometimes one or two youths would go out and raid a neighbour's henhouse and prepare a nocturnal feast of chicken and potatoes for all present. There would be fun and laughter, and stories would be told of past wakes at which 'tricks' had been played on the corpse. The dead man would suddenly sit up in the bed with the aid of a concealed rope, for example, causing any young girls present to flee in terror. I find it difficult to believe that such unseemly events were other than rare. It is possible that they happened in the distant past, and that the stories they inspired survived merely as a source of ribald entertainment.

Among the adults, sudden or accidental death was feared above any other. Death was seen as a rite of passage that required careful preparation — a visit from the doctor to be followed by a visit from the priest who would administer the Sacrament of the Sick and speak words of consolation and encouragement. Most people believed that if you'd lived a good life, you had nothing to fear. Only the wicked died a bad death. In the way of things some people who didn't deserve it suffered horribly before dying. Such suffering was seen as 'putting in your quarantine' before arrival in the world beyond. Great suffering here meant less suffering there. Most people, given a choice, would rather postpone the suffering till later. After all, today was real and tomorrow a long way off.

No one wanted to die in hospital: it was best to die at home in one's own bed surrounded by the family with a wife or daughter to hold your hand. Some went gently downriver while others struggled heroically against the inevitable. Sometimes it was difficult to know when someone was on the point of death. There was a story of an old man who took so long over dying that he severely tried his wife's patience. Again and again she held his hand, convinced that the hour had finally come.

'Don't fight it, John,' she kept saying. 'Just let go and the tide will carry you.'

John opened his eyes and looked at her. 'You're still there, are you? You'll never give me a minute's peace, now will you?' he said and breathed his last.

Much was made of what a dying man said on his deathbed and whether he was still in full command of his faculties. As far as I know there were no famous last words. The most distinctive exit I've heard of was that of a neighbour who suddenly sat up in bed and shouted, 'Nebraska!' Then, satisfied as to his whereabouts, he sank back against the pillows and expired. His wife, who was not in the least put out, said that he must have had a vision of the next world, which was so wonderful that he thought he was in America.

One summer afternoon, as we returned from the Big Strand, my aunt took me into a house I had not been in before. We were shown into a bedroom where an old man was lying on his back with his head propped up on three pillows. He was wearing a dark beret and his lips were black. His face was drawn and pale and his chest rose and fell as he breathed. A woman came into the room with a cup and wet his lips with water from a spoon.

'He's been like that since yesterday,' she said. 'Nothing but water. Not even a spoonful of soup.'

My aunt sat quietly by the bedside. I had a suspicion that she was praying but I wasn't sure. I couldn't take my eyes off the sick man's hands, which were lying on the bedspread like the two rusty grapples my father kept in the barn for hooking and holding timber cast in by the tide. After a while we went into the kitchen and my aunt talked to the woman of the house and one or two neighbours.

'Why is he wearing a beret in bed?' I asked my aunt when we were alone on the road again.

'He's suffering death,' she said.

I wondered if each townland had a beret that was put on the head of anyone who was dying, so that everyone else would know.

'Do all dying men wear a beret?'

'No, of course not. He's wearing a beret in case his head gets cold.'

'But there was sweat on his forehead and the woman mopped it.'

'It's what's called cold sweat. People break into a cold sweat when they're sick.'

'Where will he go when he dies?'

'To heaven in the sky above the clouds.'

A week later I watched a coffin being carried down the road by four neighbours. Men and women were walking behind the coffin, my father among them.

'Is it warm in the coffin?' I asked him when he came back from the funeral.

'It depends on the weather. It's cold in the winter and warm in summer, I suppose.'

'Is it dark in the coffin?'

'Yes, but it doesn't matter. You can't see with your eyes closed.'

'What did they do with him?'

'They put him in a grave in the ground.'

'Auntie Kate said he went to heaven.'

'His soul is in heaven, his body's in the graveyard. And that's all I know about it.'

I wanted to ask him how you could be in two places at once, but I could tell that he was getting impatient. He could talk about work until the cows came home but other things didn't interest him in the way they interested my mother. Further information would have to wait for another day.

When I became an altar boy, I accompanied the priest at funerals and I got to know more about how they were conducted. The coffin would rest on the front benches in the church, and I would imagine the dead person lying inside in a brown shroud with his hands folded over his chest. I would hold the aspersorium for the priest as he sprinkled the coffin with holy water and later the grave itself. The grave was frighteningly deep, and four men would lower the coffin down into it on ropes. The priest would then say the graveside prayers in Latin, ending with the *Pater Noster*. Finally, he would drop three shovelfuls of earth on the lid of the coffin, and each time he would say *Memento homo quia pulvis es, et in pulverem reverteris*, which my aunt told me meant 'Remember you are dust and into dust you will return'. The earth falling on the coffin lid always made a hollow sound, as if the coffin were empty, a thought which I found quite scary and always tried to dismiss from my mind.

The priests ensured that we were all experts in eschatology. They had briefed us so thoroughly on the Four Last Things that no one was in any doubt about the importance of a happy death. As the end approached, many became anxious that they might be weighed in the balance and found wanting. Even hard-nosed shopkeepers nearing their end became worried about overcharging and short measure. At such moments the comfort of Extreme Unction, the Sacrament of the Sick, and the reassurance offered by a priest was a godsend. No one who was dying was likely to complain that it was the priest's thundering sermons that had caused the disquiet in the first place.

The priests told us that dying was like going on a long journey and that viaticum, the Eucharist given to the dying, meant food for the journey. Not everyone was willing to face up to the approach of death. I heard a story about an old man who never had much time for churchgoing. In his final illness his wife told him that she had sent for the priest and asked him to be ready to make his Confession. 'You must think I'm in a bad way,' he said. 'It's you who's dying. Dying to see me go. Well, I won't kick the bucket yet.'

She told the priest to take him gently, that on no account must he mention death. The priest sat by the bedside and talked about the weather and this and that, trying to put his mind at rest. Finally, he asked him how he was feeling.

'I never felt better,' the sick man replied. 'Seeing you again has done wonders for me. I'll be getting up as soon as you go.'

The priest finally lost all patience. 'Do you ever think about death, Paddy?'

The sick man sat up in the bed. 'It isn't my job to think about death; I don't depend on it for a living. Like any well man, I'd rather be dead than think about death.'

The priest left in a huff and the man died unhouseled that night. Some people blamed the priest for being hasty. Others said that Paddy had lived a good life and that maybe he'd had no need of a priest. His wife wasn't worried: she said that she'd whispered the act of contrition in his ear as he expired, which was as much as any priest could have done.

The general fascination with death had its practical advantages. Even people who had lived lonely lives on their own were seen as part of the community, and the community would feel diminished by their death. Neighbours would shake their heads and say, 'We'll all miss him, may he rest in peace' or 'Back Street won't be the same without her', as they offered support and sympathy to those in bereavement. After a funeral they would visit them in their homes to drink tea, to bring words of comfort, and to share memories of the dead. Stories would be told and amusing incidents recalled, and the mourners would feel that they were not alone in their grief. In giving comfort people received comfort. At times it seemed that death had been created solely for the well-being of the living, while sex had been created for their discomfiture and embarrassment.

16

Going to the Pictures

Life in Glen in the 1940s meant work and little else, apart from the occasional football match or game of pitch-and-toss at the village crossroads on Sunday evenings. Now and again we were blessed with a visit from a travelling swingboat company or a circus that consisted largely of clowns, monkeys and horses rather than lions, elephants and tigers. Otherwise we would have been totally innocent of the frivolities of the great world but for 'the pictures'. Once a week Frank Quinn from Dunkineely came to Glen to show a film in the Spink Hall, three hundred yards east of Cashel village, which was more famous locally as a ballroom of romance than an occasional cinema. People came to the dances from as far away as Carrick, Kilcar and Ardara, but for us children it was the once-a-week cinema that mattered.

The Spink was owned by a right-wing benevolent group with the high-sounding title of the Ancient Order of Hibernians. I have no idea what the Hibs, as they were commonly known, did in Glen apart from owning the Spink Hall, but in retrospect we should all have been grateful to them for providing such a necessary social facility.

Quinn came to the Spink on Wednesday evenings, which for many people made Wednesday the most important day of the week. 'Going to the pictures' was something they looked forward to from one week to the next, in spite of the fact that the seating accommodation in the Spink was nothing short of spartan. Going to the pictures also involved an hour or so of tense expectation beforehand, during which certain questions arose in the minds of all film enthusiasts. Would Quinn arrive on time? Would he remember to bring in the advertised picture? Would his temperamental projector work until the end of the film or would there be 'a technical hitch' in the middle of the second reel? However, no one took any of these questions too seriously because everyone was intent on enjoying the evening and no one was in a desperate hurry to go home.

On one or two occasions Quinn found out halfway through the programme that he had forgotten the third reel, so we all waited patiently in our seats while he drove the six miles to Carrick to fetch the missing ending. Serious film buffs seized the opportunity to debate among themselves what was likely to happen next, and the business of predicting the ending gave rise to heated discussion. Though no one actually came to blows, there was a general feeling that the ending mattered as much as the outcome of any real-life situation. For a precious hour or so we could all enjoy the the illusion that we were well-paid Hollywood scriptwriters with powers of life and death over the characters.

The evening usually began with a B-movie to whet our appetites for the main feature. As we never knew in advance what to expect, we were more than grateful for small mercies. Very often the B-movie was a Western, which sometimes was more enjoyable than the film that followed. To keep us on tenterhooks, Quinn was also in the habit of showing serials over a period of ten weeks or so. Each instalment lasted for about twenty minutes and ended with the heroine at the mercy of the villain or the hero's life hanging by the thinnest of threads. It was as if Quinn's whole vocation was to provide us with fodder for discussion until the next instalment was due.

Watching the film was only half the pleasure. Discussing it afterwards and comparing it with other films was as good as seeing it all over again. Admittedly, film criticism fell short of high sophistication. Films were praised for telling a good story or having a strong love interest, and criticised for having no story, for being dull or downright silly. Heroes were praised for being manly and resourceful in a tight spot, but not necessarily for their looks. Victor McLaglen, whom no one would have called handsome, was greatly admired for teaching John Wayne a trick or two in *The Quiet Man* during a fight that seemed to last for all of half an hour. Indeed there were freethinkers who said that he would have licked John Wayne if it had been a real boxing match rather than a film.

I greatly enjoyed listening to adults discussing films, particularly films I hadn't seen, because imagining the action was the next best thing. Now sixty years later there are certain films I think I may have seen as a boy, though I can't be altogether sure. *The Blue Dahlia* is one of these: do I really remember seeing Alan Ladd kissing Veronica Lake or had I merely listened with eager interest as two of my neighbours went over the film in detail the following day? Did I really see *Gilda* with Rita Hayworth peeling off those long black gloves as she danced?

From what I remember of adult discussions, no one fell desperately in love with the out-of-reach goddesses of the screen. No one marvelled at their long, long legs, perfect hair, rising breasts, and sophisticated way with a cigarette holder. No one argued over the relative endowments of Barbara Stanwyck, Lauren Bacall and Deborah Kerr, but I remember listening to many conversations comparing the manly attributes of Gary Cooper, Humphrey Bogart, James Stewart and John Wayne. These men were seen not as actors but rather as living heroes, embodying virtues that every man in his right mind would be pleased to possess. It was a matter of simple fact that the leading actor determined the outcome of the action. I once heard a man argue passionately that if Gary Cooper rather than Clark Gable had been the hero of *Gone with the Wind*, the film would have had a more satisfying ending.

Many of these discussions took place on the pavement outside Jamie Byrne's shop in the evening. Some I recall now with a certain amount of nostalgia, if only because the participants are long since dead. Once I heard an old man complain that Quinn had cut a certain film because he was in a hurry to get home to his wife.

'He didn't show the half of it,' he insisted. 'One minute we saw a man leaving his house and within seconds he was going into another house miles away. What happened to him in between? That's what I'd like to know.'

This piece of film criticism gave rise to a lot of mirthful joshing on the part of more sophisticated *cinéastes*. One told him that it wasn't Quinn who cut the films and that if we were shown every piddling detail, we'd all be in the Spink till doomsday. To which the old man pulled two inches of film from his waistcoat pocket and held it up against the light of the shop window.

'Look at this, will you,' he said triumphantly. 'Now tell me who is it.'

'It's only a man on a horse,' someone said.

'It's Tom Mix on Tony, that's who it is! In the picture you saw last week. And where did I get it? On the bank behind the Spink. It's a piece of film Quinn cut and then threw out the window so that no one would be any the wiser.'

All this led to a highly technical discussion that was miles above my head. There was talk of the film breaking in the projector and of Quinn having to splice it together on the spot, but nothing would convince the old man that he hadn't won the argument. He drew out his pipe and put the 'proof of the pudding' back in his pocket.

'There's no talking to any of you,' he said, heading down the street. 'Quinn is pulling the wool over your eyes and you don't know it. I'll never go to one of his pictures again.'

My interest in the pictures was not without its attendant heartache. My parents wouldn't let me go every Wednesday, which meant that I had to make do with a summary of the story the following day from more fortunate boys. My parents were not as broad-minded as I would have liked. They thought that some films were less suitable than others, whereas I was convinced that I was missing the most interesting pictures. Their censorship meant that I saw more Westerns and slapstick comedies than films of any other genre. At first I liked Laurel and Hardy films best, but when I was about twelve I saw a Western called *The Ox-Bow Incident* that lived with me for days. It was my first serious film; I simply couldn't get it out of my mind.

The Ox-Bow Incident told a story of frontier justice going badly wrong. A cattleman is murdered and a posse hastily formed to hunt down the killers. The posse surrounds three homesteaders by their campfire in the middle of the night and finds the murdered man's rustled cattle grazing nearby. The leader of the posse is an ignorant bully who has no time for the law's delays; he is absolute for justice on the spot. To complicate matters, the three homesteaders are a mixed bunch. One is an upright, civilised man played by Dana Andrews, another a shifty, unprepossessing Mexican played by Anthony Quinn, and the third a confused old man who accuses the Mexican of the murder. The to-and-fro argument between members of the posse and the three homesteaders goes on all night while in the background three ropes dangle from a leafless tree. Not all the members of the posse want to hang the men. A cowboy played by Henry Fonda argues for giving them a fair trial but the majority is for instant revenge. At dawn the three men are hanged. When the posse gets back to town they find that the cattleman is still alive and the men who attacked him and rustled his cattle have been caught.

It was a grim story that was meant to move and instruct rather than entertain. Young and impressionable at the time, I don't think I've ever again found a film as disturbing as *The Ox-Bow Incident*. Looking back, I think that I gained more from the films I saw in the Spink than from any other source of information. There was no television at the time, and in the absence of a library of interesting books, films were the only imaginative entrée I had into the great world outside the glen. Quinn showed many good films over the years, and anyone who went every week would have seen most of the seminal films of the 1930s and 1940s.

Sadly, the golden age of cinema in the Spink was not to last. In 1953 a new parish hall was built by Father McDyer, who began showing pictures soon afterwards. As we might have expected, the quality of the films deteriorated. Gone were the glory days of *film noir*, on which we had been educated by Frank Quinn. Now we had sentimental musicals and other innocuous offerings that the good priest thought might provide healthy entertainment without endangering our immortal souls. With the opening of the parish hall, the Spink soon fell into disuse both as cinema and dancehall, and Quinn's films became a fond memory among the older generation. It was a regrettable development but no one, except the more discerning film addicts, seemed to mind. As one of them pointedly put it, 'The pictures aren't what they used to be. Bugger Ann Blyth and *Rose Marie*. What we need is Bogey and a new *Casablanca*, or even a new *Key Largo*.'

17

Childhood Journeys

The first journey I made on my own was to the village of Cashel, about three hundred yards from our house in Killaned. My father used to call Cashel 'the metropolis', which was the first big word I learned. When he told me that a metropolis was a capital city, and that Cashel was the capital of Glen, I thought it high praise indeed. Then he ruined it all by telling me that a travelling rhymester called Micheál 'ac Coradáin had described the metropolis as *Caiseal na nDearnad* or Cashel of the Fleas. I didn't quite know what to make of that, especially since my father explained that travelling rhymesters, like all travellers, were probably great carriers of fleas themselves.

Cashel is built on a slope. Consisting of one street running between two crossroads, it is not what you might call a pretty village. It is bare and windswept but its great merit is that it gives the visitor a sense of openness as opposed to enclosure. Whereas in villages like Carrick and Kilcar you are aware mainly of shops and houses, from Cashel you can see the wider reach of the glen on each side. As you walk down the street, the north mountain, Glen Head and Glen Bay unfold before you.

When I was growing up, there were fifteen inhabited houses in the village. These included three grocery shops and two pubs, McShane's and McNelis's. Fortunately for the shopkeepers and publicans, they weren't solely dependent on the other villagers for a living. Instead they had a large hinterland as Cashel was the hub of all commercial life in the valley. The shops sold everything from groceries to ironmongery, including scythes, spades, shovels, crowbars, six-inch nails, and nuts and bolts. At the time, however, I was interested mainly in biscuits and sweets, especially liquorice sticks and bull's-eyes or brandy balls.

I passed the shops and pubs every day on the way to and from school. Passing the pubs, I would peer through the gloom inside to see what was going on. Pubs were mysterious places and for us children forbidden territory. The only pub I went into was Annie McNelis's, because she ran a grocery counter as well as a bar. Going into McNelis's was more exciting than going into Jamie Byrne's grocery shop. For one thing the bar seemed to be in a state of permanent twilight. There would be one or two drinkers sitting on stools at the high counter, and the air would smell strongly of stout, beer and whiskey. At first I wouldn't recognise the drinkers, but gradually my eyes would become accustomed to the gloom.

Then Annie would struggle out from behind the high counter and stand by the low grocery counter. If I bought a pound of tea or sugar for my mother, Big Annie, as she was called, would put her hand in a big glass jar and give me a brandy ball as I was leaving. I was related to her on my father's side of the family. And I had heard that my grandfather was friendly with her father, Paddy John, and that he went to McNelis's to 'rake' every evening. McNelis's was the largest house in Cashel. In the old days it was an inn as well as a pub. It was there that the English composer Arnold Bax stayed on his frequent visits to Glen before the First World War.

On the way home from school I used to go into the forge in Back Street to watch Condy, the blacksmith, work the bellows. The interior of the forge was dark and mysterious, with piles of what looked like 'junk' along the walls. Apart from the ever-open door, the only source of light was one small grimy window. There was an anvil with a horn on which Condy beat glowing red metal into whatever shape he required, a crowded bench with two vices, a drill with a big wheel and handle, and a green oil-drum in a corner surrounded by an entanglement of metal, which Condy would go through now and again as he searched for a suitable piece of iron. The forge looked the very picture of chaos, but I could see that Condy knew where to lay his hand on any object he might need.

At school we had learnt a poem about a village blacksmith who was a mighty man with 'large and sinewy hands' and brawny arms 'as strong as iron bands'. Condy, who never spoke to us children, wasn't in the least like the blacksmith in the poem. He was a lightly built man, more wiry than brawny, and among the grey hairs on his chest was a faded tattoo of a crucifix which my father said he had acquired in Scotland while serving in the merchant navy as a young man. When I said that he wasn't as strong as the blacksmith in the poem, my father told me that Condy was greater than any blacksmith, that he was a wheelwright as well and that there was nothing he could not turn his hand to. I had to agree. I had seen him shaping felloes for a cartwheel and then putting the hub, spokes and felloes together to form a perfect wheel with an iron rim, which was the nearest thing to a miracle my young eyes had seen, especially since it was all done haphazardly over several days in a forge that looked dark, cluttered and chaotic. As he hammered a piece of metal into shape, he smoked nonstop, and as the ash of his cigarette grew longer and longer, I could not help wondering when precisely it would fall to the floor. He would stand with one arm raised to work the bellows and the other hand resting on his hip, while the coal fire glowed and the metal reddened and whitened before our eyes.

My father was friendly with Condy. They had fished together from the same boat and our bogs were next to each other on the hill. Whenever we were working on the bog, my mother would be sure to pack some lunch for Condy, who lived on his own and had no one to prepare his meals. My father said that Condy was as hardy as a snipe; that he had experienced life in the navy; and that provided he had enough cigarettes to keep him going, he could go without food for a day and never feel hunger.

As a boy I was fond of bridges. I loved crossing them and I loved standing on them to look down at swirling water. When our cows ran dry, my mother would sometimes send me down to Hughie the Bridge's for milk. It was an opportunity to stand on Gannew Bridge and look upriver and down. Gannew Bridge was relatively new, the old bridge having been swept away on the night of the big flood in June 1935, which I'd heard grown-ups talk about. Another bridge I liked crossing was the bridge on the way to Curreen to see my mother's Auntie Mary, who was married to Ned Lyons. Like my mother, Auntie Mary was born in Garveross. Though she was an old lady when I knew her, she was still good-looking, and she made the best country butter I've ever tasted. I enjoyed going to see her because she was such a pleasant woman, and because her granddaughter Maureen used to give me copies of the *Beano* and *Dandy* comics, which we didn't get at home.

Best of all was going to see my grandmother and Uncle Patrick in Garveross because I had to cross two bridges to get there. The first of these was the Minister's Bridge across the Murleen River, which divided the Glen into north and south. It was built of mortared stone and it had a small arch and a larger arch with a breakwater. You could lean over the parapet and look down at water swirling between brown rocks and the irises that grew on both banks. For me it was the most interesting bridge in Glen — the kind of bridge I thought I might like to build when I grew up.

After the bend beyond the Minister's Bridge came a short slope called Ard Bochtóige. A *bochtóg* was a kind of guardian, a female fairy that lived in the sea and came to land from time to time to warn certain families and individuals of death or impending danger. Some people said that *bochtógs* were really the souls of people who had been drowned at sea and liked to keep up their association with the families of which they had been fond as living human beings. My father's Uncle Charlie was drowned off the Doonalt coast as a young man. Naturally, I wondered if his spirit still lived as a *bochtóg* in the sea.

'They say that some families have a *bochtóg* and others don't,' my father told me.

'Do the McGinleys have a *bochtóg*?' I asked hopefully.

'If we do, I haven't seen her.'

'Will I see her?'

'Look out for her at Ard Bochtóige next time you go to Garveross.'

I realise now that he was making fun of me, but at the time I thought he was being serious. On the way to Garveross I always walked slowly up Ard Bochtóige, hoping that a girl fairy might come out of the ditch. I knew what a girl fairy should look like: she'd be wearing a red pixie hood, a short green skirt, and brown cloth shoes that turned up at the toes. Needless to say, I was always disappointed. Whenever I go to Garveross now, I go by the Minister's Bridge and Ard Bochtóige. I still haven't seen the McGinley *bochtóg* but I can't help paying my respects to the folk imagination that conjured up the lovely idea of the guardian fairy.

The next landmark on my journey was Garveross Bridge, which was then just a footbridge across the Deán, a tidal channel of the sea. It was made of concrete, and because it was so narrow, it looked very long, longer than any other bridge in Glen, or so it seemed to me. The central piers, which were built on sand and silt, were surrounded with wooden piles. When someone with hobnailed boots walked across, it rang with a hollow sound, not unlike the sound of a great army marching. Whenever I reached the other side, I looked back because it seemed to me that I was leaving the rest of the glen behind. It was a good reason for going to Garveross, which was a glen within a glen. It was different from Killaned, different from any other place I knew.

When I was about eight, I began going to the bog with the donkey to bring home turf for the fire. During the summer holidays, when my father was busy with the harvest, I sometimes made three trips a day to lay in a supply for the winter. We brought home the turf in two creels or panniers, which hung on pegs on either side of the donkey's graith or harness. The graith was made of pleated straw covered with sacking, and attached to it was a wooden straddle from which hung the creels. It was kept in place by a belly band and a crupper, which we called an *éiseach*.

For some odd reason we boys found the word *éiseach* highly amusing, and we used it as often as possible. The *éiseach* was made of rope swaddled in cloth to protect the donkey from crupper burn coming back downhill under a load. Our donkey had a sensitive behind, and to protect it further my father made a cloth wheel for its tail to keep the crupper from skinning the poor beast. This wheel caused a great deal of merriment among us boys, and we referred to it constantly as the steering wheel. I suppose there wasn't a great deal to amuse us at the time, and it was just as well that we found enjoyment in simple things.

Our bog was at the top of the hill above Killaned, but the road went the long way round to avoid the steeper slopes. That accounted, I suppose, for the two S-bends, the Wee S and the Big S. We used to rest at the Big S and look down at the glen below. You could see nearly every house in the valley, not to mention the Big Strand and the sea in the west. On a fine day it was a lovely scene. If you had a pair of binoculars, you could see who was doing what around the houses and in the fields. It occurred to me that Glen was no place for a secretive person who didn't like being seen by his neighbours.

On the way to the bog I used to pass a field where an old man with a grey stubble lay in the lee of a rock 'herding' one hungry-looking cow. He would lie on his side under the rock in fair weather and foul, and now and again he would strike the side of his leg with the switch he always carried. I have no idea why he considered it necessary to supervise a cow grazing because the field was surrounded by a wall that no cow could jump over, and there was nothing growing in the field such as corn or potatoes that needed to be protected from her attentions. Once he was standing by the road as I passed, and I got my first close-up view of him. His skin was as grey as his hair and stubble, his sunken eyes were large and wild, and he was wearing clogs with wooden soles, and short-legged trousers with knee-straps. He wasn't wearing a shirt; rather his chest was bare beneath his brown mackintosh. As I looked into his eyes, I experienced an unaccountable surge of fear, though he had not uttered a word. When I reached home, I told my father that I had seen a ghost on the way to the bog. Surprisingly, he did not make fun of me. He merely said that what I had seen was an old hermit who had come back from the desert after a long fast. My father was like that. He never seemed to agree with me. When I was a bit older, I came to realise that he had his own individual way of putting things.

The bog was bare and windswept, and even on the warmest day of summer there was a lovely cooling breeze. On rougher days the wind, blowing close to the ground, made a high-pitched whine in the sedge grass and heather. The turf stacks looked like long black huts, and between them were mounds of turf mould and fragments of clod marking the sites where stacks had been built in the past. When I told my father that the mounds looked like the graves of giants warriors, he told me that the only warriors he'd heard of were the men who'd cut the turf and stacked it over the centuries. He laughed at that and looked at me as if he expected me to laugh too. My father kept our bog neat and tidy. He made a kesh or improvised crossing over a little stream with bog oak, heather and sedge. It looked like a small arched bridge when he had finished, a miniature version of the Minister's Bridge. I had to admit to myself that he was very good with his hands.

Alone on the bog I felt that I was in strange territory because I could no longer see the rest of the glen. For that reason going to the bog was like going on holiday, an excuse to get away from the house. I liked walking through heather and between the tufts of sedge that grew here and there and that even the mountain sheep would not eat. When I was older, I began going out beyond our bog to the loughs to look at wild duck and the odd skart or cormorant. I was already looking forward to the day when I could set off up the hill on the other side of the loughs and continue in a straight line until I came to the foot of Slieve League, a mountain that then seemed impossibly far away.

Whenever I return to Glen, I always go up to the bog, just to look at familiar landmarks. No one cuts turf there any more, but the little footbridge my father built and the old turf stack mounds are still there. Though the glen has changed out of all recognition, the old bog remains the same.

18

Places and Stories

From an early age I liked to hear about places and how they got their names. As a boy I didn't know that the lore attached to place names was a much studied branch of Old Irish literature, and neither did I know that it would form part of my university education. My father told me that Killaned, where we lived, was named after Fanad, a local saint who once had his cell on land belonging to one of our neighbours. Killaned is a transliteration of the Irish *Cill Fhánaid*, meaning Fanad's cell or church. The cell, which we called the *Úig*, or 'cave', was built of rough, unmortared stone. It was full of holes, through which the wind blew, and it had a low, flat roof of heavy slabs. As you might expect, it was the most basic of habitations. There was no window, no fireplace or chimney, not even a stone bed for the holy man to lie on.

My neighbour, who was not a noted devotee of saints, used the cell as a pen for his lambs. In this way he was keeping up a sanctified Irish tradition of finding a new use for something that no longer served its original purpose. Thus, an old iron bedstead often found new life as a gate, a fallen branch filled a gap in a ditch, and a broken shovel shaft served as a makeshift post in a fence.

My father was knowledgeable about local place names and their meanings. From the stories he told me, I got the impression that the social history of Glen was embedded in the place names, most of which made little sense in English but made excellent sense in their original Irish versions. Meenamohog is a meaningless name but its original Irish form *Mín na mBothóg* (Plain of the Bothies) refers to a time when transhumance or 'booleying' was practised in Glen. During the summer months the young girls of each family went to live in huts on the mountain to herd cattle that had been transferred from the low-lying farms for seasonal grazing. The girls milked the cows and made butter. From time to time they would bring home the butter and equip themselves with a fresh supply of food before returning to the mountain. They were not lacking in entertainment in their lonely outposts. Young men would visit them in the evenings, providing an occasion for singing and dancing and other even more traditional pastimes.

Most of the place names in Glen are in Irish or derived from the Irish. In the townland of Malinmore, however, there is a fair sprinkling of original English place names that show the influence of the Scottish and English planters who acquired some of the best land in the area from the seventeenth century onwards. Thus we have the Sandy Hole, John's Hole and Rocky Point side by side with Poll na Péiste (the Serpent's Hole), An Charraig Uasal (the High Rock) and An Choiscéim (the Step). It is possible, of course, that the places with English names once had Irish names that gradually fell into disuse and in time slipped entirely from folk memory.

In the Glen valley original English place names are rare. One of the few places on the Killaned hill with an

English name is the Black Flags, but that is a direct translation of the Irish Leaca Dubha, which refers to a steep cliff face of black rock that was notoriously dangerous for cattle. While grazing, cattle would often go right to the brink, trying to reach down to the long sweet grass on the ledges below. Once or twice cows fell down the cliff and had to be destroyed. My father often sent me up the hill to drive our cows out of danger. It was a task I didn't much care for, because it seemed to me that the cows were quite capable of looking after themselves and that my well-meaning intervention might only confuse them.

During my boyhood, the landscape was dotted with ruins and roofless houses, bearing testimony to a time before the Famine when the parish was more heavily populated than it is today. Some of these 'ballogs', as we called them, were to be found on hillsides far from the nearest road, places where no one would dream of living today. There is one on the Killaned hill called Ballóg Dhonn-chaidh (Denis's ruined cottage), of which nothing is left but a few broken walls standing near a level piece of rough pasture that still bears the marks of lazy beds or ridges to show that it had once been tilled. Local tradition had it that many of these cabins had been built and roofed in a single day. Places like these fascinated me: they spoke of a sad history of hardship and deprivation, giving the stories I had heard about the Famine the keen edge of implacable reality. It was difficult to believe how anyone could have lived in such places or managed to wrest a living from a few roods of shallow ground among heights and rocks and encroaching sedge and rushes.

The Martello Tower on Glen Head speaks of a different facet of Irish history. It was built by the English around 1810, when there was genuine concern among the ruling class that a French invasion was imminent. According to local lore, the work was done by local craftsmen using stone quarried from the nearby cliff face. A fine example of cut stonework, it stands like a solitary sentinel in a wild, uninhabited expanse of cliff and moor with the Atlantic pummelling the rocks beneath. As you approach it up the slope from the Beefan side, it rises unexpectedly out of the landscape ahead of you, an alien structure that makes you wonder what on earth it is doing there. What struck me the first time I saw it was the stark contrast between its precisely cut stone and the crude stonework of Ballóg Dhonnchaidh, which probably dates from the same period and indicates the primitive nature of the cabins in which the Glen people then lived. Of course, the Martello towers were not built as homes. Rather they were fortifications designed to signal the approach of an enemy and to withstand an enemy attack. Even today, after two hundred years, they look as if no expense had been spared on their making. The Glen Head tower would still be in nigh perfect condition if one of its parapets had not been struck by lightning some years ago.

There were other places whose names had a resonance for me, not for any historical reason but because of the stories associated with them. One of these was Mullaigh na gCros (the Hill of the Crosses) on the old road over the hill from Killaned to Glenmalin. According to the story my father told me, a man was once going out to Glenmalin on his way home from the wheelwright's. He was carrying two spinning wheel legs on his shoulder, and just as he came within sight of Rathlin O'Birne Island, he noticed another island between Rathlin and the horizon, which he had never seen before. He stood looking at it, convinced that it was one of those enchanted islands that, according to legend, rise from the waves once every seven years and are visible to mortals from only one particular spot. He knew that if he left the spot where he was standing, he might never find it again, so he tied the two spinning wheel legs together in the form of a cross and stuck them in the ground as a marker. Then he went to the nearest house to get a crew together to go out to the island in a boat.

The skipper, however, told him that the only way they could keep the island from sinking under the sea again was to throw a live coal ashore, because coals are blessed, so they got a bucket of burning coals from the hearth fire. He then took the skipper and his crew back to the spot where he had seen the enchanted island, so that they could establish its location for themselves. But when they reached the hill, there wasn't just one cross but several hundred, all of them exactly alike. They spent an hour going from cross to cross looking for the island until at last one of them found the real cross and the spot from which the island was visible. When they had taken its bearings in relation to Rathlin O'Birne, they set off for the boat slip. They rowed out and sure enough, once they'd cleared Rathlin, the enchanted island rose up in front of them.

In all their lives they'd never seen such lush landscape. There were tall straight trees, lovely green lawns and orchards with apples and pears, not to mention oranges and bananas. They kept an eye on the island as they rowed in, just in case it might vanish, and when they were within a stone's throw of the shore, they spotted a beautiful young woman under a tree knitting a white sock on three needles. As soon as she spotted them, she took a ball of wool from her lap and flung it in their direction. The ball fell short but instead of sinking, it bounced off the waves and landed on the floor of the boat. The boat began to rock so violently that they thought they'd all end up in the water. Meanwhile, the beautiful young woman continued knitting her sock, as if totally unaware of their predicament. They knew at once that she was not of this world. Frightened out of their wits, they tried to cut the thread with a knife but it was as strong as any cable. Finally, one of them picked up the ball of wool and flung it into the bucket of live coals. The thread immediately shrivelled up and broke and the boat stopped rocking. The men were so relieved that they forgot all about the island, and getting out their oars, they made for the slip at Log na dTruán as fast as they could pull. No one ever saw the enchanted island again, but the hill where the man from Glenmalin placed his cross in the ground is called Mullaigh na gCros to this day.

The story of how Mullaigh na gCros got its name had all the components I could have wished for: an enchanted island that was rarely visible, a familiar hill covered with crosses, a beautiful young woman with a magic ball of wool, and orchards with trees bending under the weight of oranges and bananas. I felt shattered when my father in his reductive way said that the story was probably invented to explain the place name.

'You mean to say it isn't a true story?'

'It's another fairy tale. The old people loved nothing better.'

Though my father had a way of puncturing my expectations, I am now grateful to him for all he told me about local place names and their origins. The stories embodied in what is called the *dinnseanchas* gave the landscape a living presence, and myself a sense of personal possession, as if my knowledge of these stories endowed me with a place in the unwritten history of the Glen, a sense of being the inheritor of a family legacy handed down from father to son through countless generations. These stories still remain with me, and on my last visit to Glen, as I went over Mullaigh na gCros, I stood and looked out in the direction of Rathlin O'Birne, feeling blest for that enchanted island beyond with its luxuriant orchards lending the lonely road and the bleak hillside a contradictory, romantic glow.

19

Seasons

Whenever I thought of the seasons as a child, I imagined an enormous clock with Christmas at twelve, Easter at three, bonfire night on June 23rd at six, and Hallowe'en at nine. As the months passed, a single hand would travel round the clock face and point to the particular season or festival. Like most children, I thought of Christmas as the best time of the year. If nothing else, it came when it was most needed: had it come in the middle of summer, it wouldn't have been half as magical. It was a time of warmth inside and freezing cold out — at least that was the Christmas in everyone's mind, which was the only Christmas that mattered.

The best part of Christmas was the week or two before it, wondering about presents and reading the Christmas cards that Davy the postman brought for my aunt and parents. The Christmas on the cards was a festival of the imagination that none of us would ever experience: a Christmas of horse-drawn carriages and jolly men in red jackets drinking from tankards by glowing log fires. The real Christmas in Glen was another thing altogether. I would go to bed early on Christmas Eve in order to wake up early on Christmas morning. Once I woke in the middle of the night and looked out of the window, hoping to see Santa Claus. The sky was clear and full of stars, and with the tail of my eye I spied a shapeless bundle vanishing down McGlinchey's chimney. In the morning when I told my father about what I'd seen, he said it must have been Father Christmas making a delivery. 'It didn't look like a man,' I said in genuine puzzlement. 'It must have been his bag you saw,' he explained. 'Father Christmas climbs down the chimney first and pulls his bag down after him.' I couldn't but believe him. And such is the force of suggestion that for years I was convinced that that was indeed what I had seen, and I still believed in Santa Claus when most of my friends had progressed beyond the stage of mere uncertainty.

Some parents told their children the truth about Father Christmas as soon as they were out of nappies, so that they wouldn't expect presents that no one could afford. In our house Christmas was a time of great expectation and undeclared disappointment on the day. In the war years toys were hard to come by and those that we got were simple and mostly homemade. One year my father made me a cart from a wooden box with wheels adapted from cotton spools, and another year my Aunt Sarah, who worked in Dublin, sent me a toy flute. Sadly, it got broken in the post and I had to hold both pieces together with a sheet of newspaper wrapped round them. In spite of my best efforts, I never managed to play more than one note. What's more, the sound I made was uncomfortably shrill, which caused my mother to put her hands to her ears and say that I should play my flute only while Daddy was playing his fiddle. Another time Aunt Sarah sent me a picture book of witches and giants with long hair and warty faces, and animals that walked on their hind legs and wore baggy trousers with a big check patch on the seat. That was the best present I ever had. I read the stories over and over again and I can visualise some of the pictures to this day.

After Christmas came a dreary stretch of short dark days when nothing much happened. Thankfully, our kitchen was small and cosy. While we played games on the hearth in the long nights, my mother knitted socks or pullovers and my father smoked his pipe. Sometimes he read *The Derry Journal*, a weekly that brought us news from every parish in Derry and Donegal. I couldn't understand why he found it so interesting, as it seemed to me to be devoted entirely to reports on deaths, the weather, the poisoning of foxes, and court cases concerning poteen-making and disputes between neighbours over land and marauding dogs that killed sheep. It was full of words and phrases that made no sense to me, including 'remanded in custody' and 'bound over to the peace for a year'.

Now and again my father would put aside his pipe and take down his fiddle from where it hung by the kitchen bed. He would tune it with his ear close to the strings and rosin the bow with great care. It was an old fiddle with a cracked soundbox and a semicircular mark where the varnish had been worn away by his stubbled chin. After he had played with the pegs for a minute or two, he would draw the bow across each of the four strings until the emerging sound pleased his exacting ear. Then, with his eyes closed, he would begin playing unrecognisable tunes that were vaguely reminiscent of other tunes. After a while my mother might say that it was time he got a new fiddle, that a cracked fiddle was worse than a tin fiddle, that she had no idea what he was trying to play. Whatever it was, it must have given him solace and pleasure. Sometimes, when he was in a mood for music making, he would go to the bedroom and play to himself in the dark. These moods were rare, however. It was probably a source of regret to him that he couldn't play well enough to please my mother.

On winter days he foddered the animals and did odd jobs about the house. Sometimes he made creels for carrying turf, knitted net covers for lobster pots, or opened drains on the land. Then gradually the days grew longer. Around St Patrick's Day the first lambs would appear on the hillsides, looking impossibly white beside their bedraggled mothers, and on good days lark song poured down out of the great nowhere in the sky above our heads. The lambs and the lark were a signal that a new working year had begun. My father would take down his slane from its place in the barn and go to the bog to cut the turf.

Easter was the next milestone. It was different from Christmas, more serious and subdued, and a time of church-going. Good Friday in particular was a day when even people who weren't particularly religious experienced something resembling a sense of loss. Everyone kept the fast and drank black tea. By tradition it was a day when early potatoes were planted but little other manual work was done. After the rigours of Lent and Good Friday, Easter Sunday brought with it a sense of release and celebration. We children made fires in the open and boiled as many eggs as we could eat. I have no idea how this custom arose. Perhaps an egg was once seen as a symbol of fertility and new life, or perhaps the eating of eggs was an inexpensive and convenient way to celebrate the end of Lent and six weeks of short rations.

On May Day we discarded our shoes and went to school barefoot. I don't recall any child in good health wearing shoes during the summer. Going about barefoot gave us a sense of freedom, especially while running on grass. After all, the ancient Fianna who hunted the deer barefoot were so agile that they could pluck a thorn from their heels without slackening their pace, which understandably was something none of us ever managed to do. From time to time we used to suffer from stone bruises and grass cuts between the toes. Grass cuts could be quite painful, and a serious stone bruise meant walking with a limp for a week. As far as I can tell, there is no record in the literature of any member of the Fianna suffering from either infirmity.

Bonfire Night on St John's Eve, the 23rd of June, ushered in the summer. I loved the holidays from school, the long days and evenings, the taste of new potatoes, and the scent of new-mown hay. When my father took the scythe from the barn and began sharpening the winter-dulled blade, it was a sure sign that summer had finally arrived. The sharpening stone made a ringing sound on the blade, which became more songlike and musically complex whenever two or three men sharpened their scythes simultaneously in adjacent fields. The blade went through the meadow grass with a rhythmic swish and the grass fell in neat, straight swathes, giving off a sweetish aroma. We then shook out the swathes and left the grass to dry for a day or two. After that we turned it with a rake to make windrows, by which time it had already lost its fresh green colour. Whenever the weather was wet and the hay was not dry enough for hand-cocks, my father would make grass-cocks or lap-cocks. Then we would have to shake them out again on the next good day, which was why he used to say that bad weather meant double labour.

When the hay was sufficiently seasoned, it would be made into large haycocks which we called tramp-cocks. There was a sloping field below our house called the Brae, which was exposed to sea breezes and sudden gusts of wind. According to my father, building a tramp-cock on a steep slope was something every Tom, Dick and Harry couldn't do. He was so particular that he would never allow anyone to build a tramp-cock on the Brae except himself, and his proudest boast was that he never had to put a prop to one. He once told me that he would rather pull down a listing tramp-cock and start afresh than use a prop to keep it upright.

We used to make the haystack in October, by which time the corn would be cut and the corn stack already made. The days would be shorter and the cows on after-grass in the fields. Lifting the potatoes and putting them in pits until they were needed was all that remained to be done, before the coming of Hallowe'en and the mysterious mummers with their rhymes and macabre masks announced the approach of another year end.

The mummers were local boys who went from house to house in grotesque dress, singing and demanding money for their performances. They entered each house one by one, and as they entered they recited a rhyme declaring the name of the character they represented. Jack Straw, dressed from head to foot as a straw-boy, declared:

'Here comes I, Jack Straw,
Such a man you never saw...'

Then Wee Devil Doubt, who could have been descended from a character in a morality play, entered saying:

Here comes I, Wee Devil Doubt
With my shirt turned inside out...'

Once all of them had entered, they would sing a traditional song or two and rattle the coins in their tin can to remind us of the reason for their visit.

The success of a mummers' act was judged on the effectiveness of their dress as disguise, their acting ability, and the quality of their singing. When a neighbouring boy told me the following day that he had played Jack Straw, I found it hard to credit. It was a revelation to think that a straw coat and hat could so successfully conceal someone's identity.

Now and again the weight of the dark winter months was lightened by a visit from a troupe of travelling actors who would stay for a week and put on four or five plays in the Spink Hall. My father and mother weren't playgoers, and they didn't see me as one either, so I was delighted when one year my aunt said that she'd take me to the Saturday matinée. I had already seen the posters in the village, and earlier in the week I had seen one of the actors on the Lower Line on the way to Doonalt. A tall man of striking appearance, he kept spouting his lines aloud and gesturing extravagantly, as if the road were a stage and the hills on each side an enraptured audience. As we met, he looked at me with wide, horrifying eyes and flung up his arms in a gesture of utter despair. It was something I had never seen my father or any of the neighbouring men do.

At the matinée I sat in the front row in case I should miss anything. The curtain rose on a scene outside a country inn. The characters on stage were at sixes and sevens, arguing among themselves about a stranger called the Gambler, questioning if he would arrive as promised. I was getting impatient with all the talk when a man of commanding stature, dressed in tan jackboots, green trousers, green shirt, brown cape and wide-brimmed hat, entered and looked magisterially about him. As he stood in the centre of the stage with a crockery jar slung over his shoulder, from which he refreshed himself every so often, I recognised him immediately as the actor I'd met on the road. He was the most dandified gambler I'd ever seen, and he looked all-powerful, a magician who could bend anyone to his will. There was total silence in the hall; all eyes were upon him; no one dared cough or move in his seat. It was hard to credit that anyone could have such power over an audience, or achieve such a transformation in his appearance in so short a time. I couldn't wait to see what he'd do next. It was my first introduction to the magic of theatre, and though I may have forgotten the name of the play, I haven't forgotten the stylish wayfarer who made such an indelible impression on my uninformed mind. Years later, when I saw Tischbein's *Goethe in the Campagna* during a visit to Frankfurt, the first thing that came to mind was that the 'gambler' I'd seen in the Spink as a boy had been wearing Goethe's hat. I have seen many plays over the years but none that left me with such a sense of the magical and with so many questions that no adult of my acquaintance cared to answer.

20

Church-Going

In the Glen of my boyhood, religion in its outward expression was there to be witnessed at every hour of the day. There were May devotions, October devotions, the family rosary, Lenten fasting, the Stations of the Cross, and first Fridays to name but a few. The pervasive sense of religion was even embedded in the imagery and idioms of the spoken language. 'God bless us and save us' and 'God between us and all harm' were among the many references to the Almighty that passed every lip at least once every day of the year. But in spite of all that, religion could not be said to govern the transactions and small change of everyday living. What bound people together as a community and gave their lives meaning and purpose was the cycle of the seasons with its attendant work on land and sea. When all was said and done, people depended on each other and on themselves. Religion in its purest form did not exist among either clergy or laity. What endured was a sense of human life being at the mercy of unpredictable forces that must be placated or appeased by frequent supplication and regular ritualistic observance.

In many ways we lived in the shadow of an older pagan society, by which I mean that the practical expressions of religion were never far removed from something resembling superstitious belief in the power of charms. People were known to go to the priest complaining of the toothache, and if a cow fell sick they would get the priest to say an 'office' for her rather than pay for an expensive visit from the vet. If the priest's office did not work, no one complained. It was put down to *toil Dé* or God's will, which most of the time was inexplicable and always to be accepted without question. The governing philosophy by which people lived was a form of pessimistic fatalism tempered by an unshakeable belief in the power of prayer. It was a way of life that created the possibility of contentment and now and again even happiness.

On Sunday all work ceased and everyone, except the very young, the very old and the sick, went to eleven o'clock Mass in Cashel. As there were only four cars in Glen in the 1940s, most people walked or cycled to church, some coming from places over five miles away. Anyone receiving Communion was obliged to fast from the previous midnight, a rule that was particularly hard on people who came long distances on foot. It was not unknown for old women to pass out during Mass from sheer exhaustion. There would be shuffling sounds as two strong men carried them outside to revive them in the sharp sea air.

The Catholic church, or chapel as we called it, was a T-shaped building with transepts to the east and west. It was simple and austere in structure with little in the way of decoration to distract the eye. If the aim of the architects was to concentrate the mind on one central experience, they succeeded. The interior was airy, giving an impression of lofty space, and the high-arched windows ensured that daylight and at times sunlight kept flooding in. When I grew up and began visiting other churches, I found them gloomy and dark by comparison.

There were two stained glass windows, one on each side of the altar, with two life-size statues in front of them. The walls were hung with colourful pictures representing the Stations of the Cross, which frightened the life out of me as a child. The altar was of carved wood and the tabernacle at the centre had a gilt door that shone like a torch, reflecting the sun at certain times of the day. Women sat on the right and men on the left, though there were one or two independent spirits who sat wherever the whim took them.

Sunday was the only day on which people from outlying areas came to the village. After Mass women took the opportunity to do a bit of shopping or enjoy a restorative cup of tea with a friend, while some of their menfolk had a drink in one of the two pubs before facing the long trudge home. For that reason Sunday was a busy day for shopkeepers and publicans, at least for the first hour after Mass. Shopkeepers took the precaution of sitting at the back of the church so that they could make a quick exit with a view to being ready for the first customer.

As an altar boy, I usually got up early on Sunday. When I was eight I learnt the Latin responses for the Mass, and my aunt made me a surplice and soutane on her Singer sewing machine. She trimmed the surplice with lace, which she crocheted herself, using an odd-looking needle that she called a hook. It was strange learning the Latin responses because the words meant nothing to me, and some of the responses, particularly those in the *De Profundis*, were real tongue-twisters. When I asked my aunt why we had to gabble in a language we didn't understand, she told me not to be silly; that God and the priest understood Latin and that that was what mattered. She must have thought about what I had said because some time later she gave me her missal and told me to learn the English translation as well so that I would know what was going on.

The priest told us that the sanctuary was reserved for God and that we must be careful to act with reverence once we entered this holy place. We had been chosen to assist the priest in the celebration of Mass and Benediction, and we should always remember that. In the sanctuary there was to be no talking or whispering, and no dashing about. We had to move quietly and keep a straight face at all times. It was a tall order for an eight-year-old, and for the first month or so I felt that I might not be able to cope. Gradually, however, I came to realise that God was not going to come down on me like a ton of bricks if I forgot myself for a moment and mispronounced a Latin word. He was not a schoolteacher. That is, he didn't shout and he didn't wield a cane, but, in spite of that, he was every bit as real as Master Boyle. For the first time in my life I knew that I was doing something my father hadn't done, and something my aunt, as a woman, wasn't allowed to do. Quite by accident, I had found a role I could be proud of, though I had to be careful because pride was one of the Seven Deadly Sins.

The first priest I served for was Father Peter McGuire, a quiet, contemplative man in his middle years who enjoyed fishing and who used to talk to himself in the sacristy and while out walking. As you might expect, he was an unworldly man, and he found punctuality difficult. Eleven o'clock Mass on Sunday could be held at any time between eleven and eleven-thirty. Most people didn't mind his imperfect sense of time. They turned up at eleven and stood outside the chapel talking until he chose to make an appearance. One or two parishioners who were out of step with the local culture wrote to the bishop about how difficult it was to plan their Sunday since they could never be sure when Mass would begin or end. The bishop wrote to Father McGuire who preached a sermon about busy-bodies who were so busy minding everyone else's business that they had forgotten how to mind their own. He then continued to celebrate Sunday Mass at whatever time suited him best.

There was much speculation as to the identity of the busybodies. Most people had their suspicions but no one was willing to name names, apart from observing that those who were good with the pen were few and far between. Every sensible person said that the priest was a saintly man who had better things to think about than the clock. We altar boys were particularly fond of him. He never said a cross word to any of us, and we liked to think that he wouldn't take any notice if we ourselves were late. We were sorry when he was eventually moved to another parish about thirty miles away.

Our next priest was Father Arthur O'Friel, a young man from the northern end of the county. My mother liked him from the start. She came home from Mass on his first Sunday in Glen and said that he was the most handsome priest she had ever clapped eyes on. Sadly, his health wasn't good, and I could tell that he was in pain from the way he used to sigh while saying the prayers of the Mass. His time in Glen was short for he left within three years and died shortly afterwards.

Altar boys used to take turns serving Mass on week-days. Sometimes we would have to serve at a funeral, which none of us liked. All the funerals I remember seem to have taken place in the middle of winter when the wind nearly blew the surplice off the priest at the graveside. At that time offerings were collected over the dead. Someone from the village would call out the name of each individual and the amount he had paid. The most common payment was a shilling, but neighbours and close relatives would pay half-a-crown. As you might expect, the amount of offerings collected at a funeral would depend on the financial standing of the deceased. A man who had paid generously at funerals during his lifetime would be likely to attract heavy offerings when he died, and his family would be pleased by this mark of respect. Funeral offerings, which were divided among the priests of the parish, gave rise to much irreverent comment. One village freethinker used to describe the custom as a case of 'auctioning the corpse', thus leaving the family of the deceased deep in debt to those who'd paid. No one liked the custom, and no one complained when it was discontinued in the 1960s.

Whenever there was a high requiem Mass, which was not very often, Canon Ward and one other priest would come in from Carrick, making three concelebrants in all. I liked High Mass because of the plain chant and I particularly liked the *Dies Irae* because it went with a galloping rhythm and it rhymed. Gradually, I got to know bits of it by heart, and I used to repeat them to myself in imitation of Canon Ward:

> *Dies irae, dies illa*
> *Solvet saeclum in favilla*
> *Teste David cum Sibylla*

A low requiem Mass without plain chant cost ten shillings, and a high requiem Mass cost five pounds. Only those who didn't have to struggle to make ends meet could afford to leave this world on a cloud of incense and soaring Gregorian chant. My father always said that he'd have ten low Masses instead of one High Mass because ten would be said over several weeks and would have a better chance of attracting the attention of the Almighty. To me as a boy, sung Mass was a moving experience, and my youthful imagination found three priests in white albs and black chasubles more impressively powerful than one. At an early age I decided that if I lived long enough I'd make provision for a High Mass to be said over me when I died. The Pope and bishops, however, had other ideas. They abolished the old Latin Mass, and the *Dies Irae* vanished from the liturgy. When I wish to hear it now, I listen to it on my CD player, and am invariably reminded of Canon Ward and the other priests who used to sing it on freezing winter mornings in Glen.

Canon Ward was a distinguished-looking man, tall and thin with white hair and long, sensitive fingers. It was said that he had been a great athlete in his youth and that he'd got his long fingers from playing the piano. My mother, who was inclined to notice these things, used to say that he was ladylike in his movements, but that it would be a mistake to think that butter wouldn't melt in his mouth. Though he never as much as looked at me, I was scared stiff of him, perhaps because he was older than the other priests. Many years later a neighbour told me that he was a 'holy terror' in the confessional box, and that he was particularly hard on married men who practised premature withdrawal as the only practical form of contraception then available to them. As my neighbour said, those were the bad old days when the most dreaded question in confession was, '*Ar chaill tú síol?*' or 'Did you spill your seed?' The answer determined whether the penitent got a severe ticking-off as well as three Rosaries for penance.

The five years I spent as an altar boy in Glen changed my way of looking at things. Growing up, I was surrounded by farmers and fishermen like my father, practical men who were concerned mainly with the quickest way to get something done before the next shower. It was a world of harsh exigency, where unwanted things happened in spite of all human effort to the contrary. A farmer could toil the longest day of summer in an attempt to get hay into a fit state for a tramp-cock, only to have his work undone by a sudden downpour.

The world of the sanctuary was a million miles distant from such everyday preoccupations, and priests were different from the other men I knew. They were quieter, gentler, and more serious, and the world they represented was hidden from human view. It was a world I could sense vaguely in the music of the requiem Mass. The prayer after Mass, which spoke of 'wicked spirits who wander through the world for the ruin of souls', stirred my imagination as vigorously as did the stories of Cuchulainn and Fionn Mac Cumhaill. It conjured up a world full of invisible spirits flying through the air, going here and there about their devilish business, which they did all the more effectively for being invisible. The thought of them made the world a more exciting place. It was no longer merely a place of things you could see and touch but a place of invisible powers and forces, where good battled against evil and did not always win.

I knew Father McGuire and Father O'Friel at a time when priests were seen as consecrated men with a God-given vocation. They were both studious men who bore their learning lightly, and who had the knack of talking to country folk in their own language about their day-to-day concerns. They did not go about much, and spent most of their time in the solitude of the parochial house. Neither of them preached thundering sermons about hellfire, damnation or anything else, probably because it was not in their nature to do so. In this as in so many other ways they were untypical of their time. I consider myself blessed in having known them. Perhaps understandably, they inspired in me the hope that one day I might become a priest myself.

21

Looking for the Cure

Priests occupied a unique position in the folk imagination, a position that had its origin in a history of persecution and deprivation. During penal times priests were fugitives, living among the people outside the law and travelling long distances on foot to administer the sacraments or say Mass in the shelter of a hedge or in a crudely constructed *scáthlán* or Mass-house. They had little temporal power but their spiritual power in the eyes of their flock was absolute. In sharing the hardships of the community they became heroes, thus acquiring an unbreakable grip on the minds and hearts of the people. After the Catholic Relief Acts leading to Catholic emancipation, priests acquired a degree of temporal power and influence. They gained a foothold in the education system, and Catholic tenants depended increasingly on them as mediators in disputes with landlords and their agents. The image of the priest as protector of his community was greatly reinforced, giving rise to numerous folk tales exemplifying this priestly role. There are countless stories of the miracles performed by priests and stories of curses laid by priests on the enemies of their parishioners and their religion.

In the Ireland in which I grew up priests still occupied an unassailable position, especially in rural communities. They were accorded unswerving loyalty and respect, and they were feared for the illimitable powers they might unleash against anyone who disagreed with them. A common attitude was that a priest as the anointed of God must not be crossed, and priests themselves encouraged this belief. People expected great things from them. The priest was not seen as a man with a soul to save and subject to temptation like the rest of us. Instead he was revered as a Christ figure with Christ-like powers over nature and disease. Yet in the popular imagination not all priests were inclined to exercise the powers given them from above. The use of spiritual power to cure disease or forestall misfortune required prayer and personal sacrifice amounting to great suffering. A 'good priest' was a man who pitied the sufferer and was willing to take his suffering on himself. In times of illness and distress people would travel miles, frequently to another parish, to seek the help of a 'good priest' endowed with 'the cure'.

People went to the doctor with their ailments of course, but often, as a form of insurance perhaps, they went to the priest as well, especially if the illness seemed beyond the reach of medical science. The priest would say an office or special prayers, and bless salt, which would be put on the sick person's tongue. Most people went to the priest only with serious illnesses, but there were instances of priests being asked to say an office to cure trivial ailments.

When I was about ten, a wart appeared on my left forefinger. At first it was small, but within weeks it began to sprout lesser warts until it measured nearly half an inch in diameter. It was an ugly wart and I did not like the look of it. When it began to split into segments, I became worried that it might eventually cover the whole length of my finger. By then grown-ups had begun telling me that warts were lucky but I knew that they were only trying to console me.

My father, half-jokingly, said that the old people believed the only cure for warts was rainwater from a *ballán* or basin-stone, that is, a stone with a hollow or well ground into it. Some ballans dated from pre-Christian times and were used in pagan rites. I knew of one in the neighbourhood, and when I said that I would dip my finger in it, my father told me that that would not do. I would need to come across a basin-stone by accident, what he called a *tobar gan iarraidh* (an unsought well), because only then would the cure in the water do its work. I soon realised how difficult this was to achieve. Wherever I went, ballans were on my mind, so how on earth could I stumble on one by accident?

Meantime my aunt would have no truck with ballans. She told me to say a novena to Our Lady to make the wart go away. I duly said a prayer called the Memorare every day for nine days but for some reason best known to the Almighty my novena didn't work. That summer Canon Byrne, a priest from Malinbeg, came home on holiday. My mother said that a Canon had more power than an ordinary priest and that I should ask him to bless my wart. I served Mass for him the following Sunday, and after he had disrobed in the sacristy, I showed him the wart and asked him to make it go away. He took my finger and looked at it but he didn't touch the wart.

'If it's troubling you, you should go to the doctor,' he said.

When I told them at home what the Canon had said, my father laughed. He reminded me that somewhere in the gospels Christ commanded a leper he had cured to show himself to the priest. 'Now the priests are saying, "Go, show yourself to the doctor".' My mother didn't see the funny side and neither did I. She said that the least Canon Byrne could have done was bless it because a blessing never did anyone any harm. My aunt, who would not countenance any criticism of the clergy, said nothing.

A week later my wart got so itchy at school that I began poking at it with the nib of my pen. Ink from the nib eventually penetrated the wart, which changed colour and became less itchy, but I still kept poking at it until it was quite black. Then one day a piece of it fell off, revealing a patch of clear white skin underneath. Over the next few weeks little bits kept falling off every day until finally no trace of it remained.

My aunt said that a novena to Our Lady was never known to fail. My mother said that Canon Byrne must have had second thoughts and said a prayer for me after all. My father said, 'Warts come and go without any rhyme or reason.' As for myself, I was convinced that the cure was in the ink, and that it worked because the inkwell was a kind of basin-stone I had come across by accident, the unsought well my father had told me about. But I was sufficiently savvy to keep my discovery to myself. I knew the other boys would only laugh at me if I let them in on my secret.

22

The Mission

Like the other altar boys, I was sitting with my back to the mission preacher, facing the congregation, whose faces were a picture of rapt attention. The sermon was about sins of impurity, fornication and the like. It was a long and passionate sermon, and I had begun to wonder if it would ever end. The preacher paused and held up a wooden crucifix, pointing to the pale figure of Christ.

'Who crucified Our Lord?' he demanded. The people in the front seats, who bore the brunt of his stare, bent their heads. Like them, I knew the answer. It was the Jews, of course.

'The Romans?' he wondered aloud.

'No, it wasn't the Romans,' he said firmly.

'The Jews, then?'

'No, it wasn't the Jews either,' he answered himself. 'We did it. You and you and you and me. Everyone who was ever born. Everyone except Our Lady. She alone was born without original sin. It was our sins, yours and mine, that crucified Our Saviour.' He paused and looked round the church with challenging finality.

I watched as a tear trickled down the cheek of a woman who was noted for her devotion to Our Lady. It was my first mission as an altar boy, an event I would always remember. Parish missions, which took place every three or four years, were usually conducted by a Franciscan or Redemptorist missioner brought in for the occasion. The missioner would say Mass every morning, hear confessions during the day, and hold a service every evening at which he would preach with more eloquence and drama than any secular priest could muster. Mission week was one of total immersion in religion. People were urged to turn their back on the world and its wiles, and for these few precious days, give their whole attention to their eternal salvation.

Missioners didn't dress like ordinary priests. The Redemptorists wore a black soutane with a black belt into which was tucked a large crucifix. The mission I remember best was given by a Franciscan with a sandy-red beard. He wore a brown habit with a cowl, and a large rosary hung from his cincture, rattling and swinging as he walked. He went about in sandals, without any socks to protect his feet from the cold November wind. It was the first time I had seen a man in sandals, and when I mentioned it to my aunt, she told me that he was probably doing penance for our sins. Like Father McGuire, he was a quiet man. He didn't rant. Sometimes he spoke in a low voice to make you listen more attentively. Then suddenly he would raise his voice, perhaps for effect or to wake up anyone who was inclined to nod off.

People discussed his sermons afterwards with great seriousness, comparing him with other missioners they remembered. I got the impression that they would have preferred more fireworks with the odd clap of thunder thrown in for good measure. Looking back now after sixty years, it seems to me that sermons were judged by their emotional effect. Listening to a good sermon was supposed to be a moving experience. A good preacher could make his listeners hang on his every word and lose themselves in the drama of his performance, leaving them invigorated and renewed. Afterwards someone might say, 'Wasn't that a great sermon?' much as a theatregoer might say, 'That's the best *Hamlet* I've seen'.

Missions were usually held in late autumn or winter, when people weren't too busy with farm work. During mission week women went to church twice a day, to Mass in the morning and to a sermon and benediction in the evening. Men had a more pragmatic approach. They usually went in the evening when the day's work was done. They knew that the world could not be denied its due. Sin was unavoidable: after all Saint Augustine was a great sinner. And so was Saint Paul before he was blinded by lightning on the way to Damascus. That was taking things a bit far, though, as no one would want to be blinded by lightning on the way to Carrick or Ardara. What people wished and prayed for was a long, enjoyable life with time for repentance and forgiveness at the end — what was called 'a happy death'.

As an altar boy, I had to go to the mission both morning and evening. I listened to the sermons as best I could, but they were mostly about sins I was too young to commit. It occurred to me, however, that listening to missioners was a great way to discover new sins. At the end of the mission there was an evening for men only and another evening for women only. As I couldn't make out what the sermon was about on either evening, I thought one of the older boys might be able to enlighten me. He told me that it was all very simple. The missioner had been hearing confessions and had discovered that there were men's sins and women's sins, and that the women's sins were so bad that he couldn't mention them in mixed company. Then he said that maybe the missioner didn't want women to find out about men's sins in case they might start committing them themselves. I felt that the Franciscan must be a very interesting man, since he knew everyone's secrets, and I wondered if he and Father McGuire compared notes over dinner.

I wasn't in the least frightened of him. He wasn't old and grumpy and stiff like Canon Ward. There was a spring in his step, and he looked young and lively in spite of his beard. When he asked me in the sacristy one morning if I'd like to be a Franciscan, I felt flattered and said 'Yes' before I had time to think.

'Are you good at mathematics?' he asked.

'Mathematics, what's that, Father?'

'Sums. Are you good at sums?'

'I get them wrong now and again.'

'Study mathematics. That's where most boys fail,' he said.

He gave me what he called a miraculous medal and told me to pray for a vocation and not to forget my sums. On the way home I thought about what he'd said. I couldn't imagine myself going about in sandals with a beard and tonsure, having reached a stage of my life when I wanted to be a bus driver and nothing else. It was the last day of the mission. I never saw the Franciscan again.

Mission week changed the look of the village. With the missioner came five or six vendors of sacramentals, who erected their canvas-covered stalls on both sides of the street outside the chapel. The stalls were nondescript on the outside but inside they contained more riches than the Cave of the Forty Thieves. I stopped and looked wide-eyed at them every morning on the way to school. Inside were rosaries of all kinds, holy pictures, statues, crucifixes, medals, scapulars, wax candles, and a score of other religious objects. No wonder people crowded round as if they couldn't make up their minds what to buy. The morning after the mission ended the vendors dismantled their stalls and put them on a lorry to take them to the next parish. Cashel street looked empty and miserable — as if we'd only imagined it all.

23

My First Real Book

My parents were not in the habit of telling me bedtime stories. Now and again my father would teach me a nursery rhyme, and on rainy days, when he couldn't do any outside work, he might read me a story or two from one of my aunt's old school books. The story I liked best was called 'The Cruise of the Dolphin', which told of the adventures of four young boys who lived in a town near the mouth of a river. One summer they bought a rowing-boat between them, and on a day when there was no school, they went on a cruise to an island in the estuary. They had planned a picnic, and after pitching their tent they spent the morning fishing for their lunch.

While they were bathing in the afternoon, the wind got up and a change came over the sky and sea. They decided to shelter in the tent and make some lemonade to pass the time. One of them, Binny Wallace, whose name I shall never forget, volunteered to go back to the boat for the lemons. He had been gone only five or six minutes when they heard him calling out their names in distress. They ran down to the beach where they'd moored the boat. To their horror it was afloat with poor little Binny Wallace standing in the bows, facing the land with his arms outstretched as he drifted out to sea. There was a strong gale blowing and the sea was covered in white caps. The water was so angry that he couldn't swim ashore and, unfortunately, they had taken the oars in order to use them as tent poles. The sky grew darker as the boat drifted farther into the distance. Soon the figure of Binny Wallace was no longer visible, and the boat itself had dwindled into a white speck on the black water. Finally, it went out like a spark and the three boys on the beach saw it no more. They spent a harrowing night on the island while the storm blew itself out. The following morning their parents came to rescue them. The Dolphin was found floating keel up and a little later the body of poor Binny Wallace was washed ashore.

It was a heart-rending story. At night in bed I kept hearing the phrase 'poor little Binny Wallace', and kept seeing his forlorn figure standing in the boat, reaching out with both arms to his three friends on the shore. I imagined the boat growing smaller and smaller until it vanished under the darkening sky. Again and again I asked my father to read me the story, and sometimes I would take the book myself and pretend to read, fully convinced that I was, as I knew many of the sentences off by heart. Many years later I discovered that 'The Cruise of the Dolphin' came from *The Story of a Bad Boy*, a semi-autobiographical novel by the American writer Thomas Bailey Aldrich, first published in 1870, and the story that first awakened in me the desire to read stories for myself.

Some time later my aunt taught me to read and write a few simple words and she also gave me an old primer and a jotter to practise on while she was away at her school. She came back every Friday evening, and on Saturday she would have a look at what I'd been doing. The primer she'd given me wasn't very interesting. It had writing and pictures but no story like the one about Binny Wallace. What I wasn't to know was that even if it had stories I wouldn't have been able to make much sense of them. In my innocence I asked her for a storybook and she said she'd bring me one next weekend.

While she was away, I found an old book with a battered cover in her room. It didn't look like a child's book; the pages were covered in small print and there were only fourteen pictures in all. I went from one picture to another, trying to read the writing underneath. They were pictures of desperate men wearing strange clothes and shoes with buckles, and some of them had pistols and others knives or what looked like short swords.

The first picture in the book, and the most frightening, showed a fierce man in a cloak standing on a cliff edge with a scar on his cheek and a long metal tube in his hand. He was gazing into the distance, and I could not help staring long and hard at his face, wondering what he could have been looking at or if he'd seen a ghost. Underneath the picture was a caption that said, 'The Old Sea-Dog Bill'. I knew the word 'old' and the words 'sea' and 'dog' but the word 'bill' meant nothing to me. In the picture there was no sign of a dog and no sign of the sea either. The man was broad and burly and all alone. I kept repeating 'The Old Sea-Dog Bill' to myself until finally I asked my father the meaning of the word 'bill'.

'Bill?' he repeated. 'It's the beak of a bird.'

'But there's no bird in the book,' I said, showing him the picture. 'And there's no dog either.'

He threw back his head and laughed.

'A sea-dog isn't a dog like Fido but an old sailor,' he said. 'And Bill is the same as Billy. It's a picture of the pirate Billy Bones.' He laughed again without telling me what was so funny. Then he picked up the book and read a paragraph or two aloud before putting it down.

'It's a bit too advanced for you.' he said. 'But if you learn enough words, you'll soon be able to read it for yourself.'

Still, I had discovered something new. The same word could stand for different things. A sea-dog was not a dog that barked in the sea. It fact it wasn't a dog at all. I began looking at the other pictures and trying to read a word here and there, but though I could read one or two in each line, I couldn't put them all together to make any sort of sense. Disappointed, I went back to my aunt's reading book. It didn't have any sea-dogs, only stories about animals and birds. It was not as interesting as the Old Sea-Dog Bill but my aunt told me that if I wanted to read about him I would have to master the reading book first.

A year or two later I was old enough to read *Treasure Island*, or at least make enough sense of it to enjoy the story. And what a wonderful story it turned out to be. It had a boy called Jim Hawkins who was both brave and resourceful and well-able to hold his own, even in the company of pirates. It had a blind man with a stick, a sea-faring man with one leg, a faraway island, and buried treasure for which the pirates were prepared to kill. I was so taken with the story and the characters that I read it not once but several times, reliving the danger with Jim Hawkins as he found himself alone on the *Hispaniola* with Israel Hands. And where I found myself alone too, pointing both pistols at the pirate and telling him calmly, 'One more step, Mr Hands, and I'll blow your brains out.'

It was not Israel Hands who troubled my dreams as I lay in bed at night, however, but blind Old Pew. I could hear the tap-tapping of his stick on the frosty road while Jim Hawkins and his mother waited in terrified silence inside the darkened house. I could hear the handle of the door being turned and the rattling of the bolt as Old Pew tried to enter, and I shared their sense of relief as the tapping recommenced and gradually died away.

For a long time I began every new book that came my way in the hope of finding another *Treasure Island*. As I grew older, I came to realise that I was expecting the impossible. Every good book is unique and no other book can ever recreate the same world or provide the same experience. Even today *Treasure Island* occupies a special place in my thoughts. It was my first real book, the book that turned me into an avid reader. I've enjoyed many books over the past sixty years, but none of them quite filled my waking and dreaming hours with the all-absorbing immediacy of Long John Silver and Old Pew when I was nine or ten.

24

Reading Irish History

I do not recall my first encounter with Irish history. But I think it must have been through poems and ballads that told a story of unwavering courage and heroism in the face of the enemy. As I look back, it seems to me that I've always known 'The Rising of the Moon', 'The Convict of Clonmel', 'Dark Rosaleen', and 'The Memory of the Dead'. Everyone knew these poems and ballads. My father, who was not much given to reading poetry, would recite snatches of them from time to time. I didn't have to go to school to learn them.

As a boy I believed every word I read. My aunt's old schoolbooks were full of poems and stories that greatly excited my interest in Irish history and mythology, for I was not aware of any distinction between the two. Cuchulainn, Fionn Mac Cumhaill, Conn of the Hundred Battles, Niall of the Nine Hostages and Brian Boru all inhabited the same heroic past, and that was all that mattered. It was a golden age that promised to last forever and my only regret was that I hadn't been born into it. At that time I thought that Irish history was one good story after another, and there was nothing I liked better than a good story. The first indication that things were about to go wrong came with the arrival of the Vikings towards the end of the eighth century, but to my inexpressible relief Brian Boru stopped them in their tracks at the Battle of Clontarf in 1014.

Naturally, I expected a second golden age to follow, but after the death of Brian Boru nothing seemed to go right any more. There were too many kings, none of them willing to yield sovereignty to any other. Even to read about it was nothing short of heartbreaking. But worse was to come. My history book told me that the arrival of the Normans in 1169 was 'the beginning of Erin's evil,' an evil that had still to be fully and finally eradicated. From then on things went from bad to worse with every battle. It was like supporting a football team that never won a match.

While reading about the Nine Years' War waged by Hugh O'Neill and Red Hugh O'Donnell against the armies of Queen Elizabeth I, my hopes briefly rose again. O'Neill and O'Donnell were Ulstermen in the grand tradition of the ancient Red Branch Knights. More importantly, O'Donnell was a Donegal man, whose ruined castle I had seen near Donegal Town only 35 miles away. At last I had found heroes who were worthy successors of Brian Boru. I was overjoyed when both of them routed the English at the Battle of the Yellow Ford in 1598. It seemed to me that at last the tide was on the turn but my sense of relief was short-lived. Three years later the Battle of Kinsale 'sealed the fate of Ireland' as my school history told me. From then on there was no consolation. Just reading about it gave me a cheerless pain in my gut and I had to steel myself to keep turning the pages. Now even the names of the players on the Irish side weren't Irish: Wolfe Tone, Robert Emmet, Thomas Davis,

Charles Stewart Parnell. My teacher Frank Boyle did his best to make it all sound interesting, but for me Irish history had become just another dull subject, like arithmetic, which I had to learn in order to pass exams. I was fully convinced that I would never take any pleasure in it again.

Then, unexpectedly, two things happened that changed my mind. My aunt had a copy of Eleanor Hull's *A History of Ireland*, which I found myself leafing through one wet Sunday. There was a heart-rending picture of Hugh O'Neill, old and blind as an exile in Spain, and there were portraits of Donal O'Sullivan Beare, Sir George Carew, and Lord Mountjoy, all of them characters in the Elizabethan Wars. Reading the odd paragraph here and there between the pictures, I chanced on a quotation from Edmund Spenser's *View of the Present State of Ireland*, describing Munster after Carew had laid it waste:

> *The trees are bare and naked…the ground is cold and wet…the kine are barren and without milk…besides being all with calf for the most part, they will only through much driving and chasing, cast all their calves and lose their milk…*

The quotation stood out because it was written in the present tense, unlike the other sentences round it. Slowly, it dawned on me that the man who wrote it had been there and had seen the aftermath of war in Munster with his own eyes. It was written in simple English and it was about cows losing their calves and their milk, which was something I'd heard about and could understand. This wasn't the history we were learning at school. It was as real as the present. I could see it. I could feel it in my bones. It was like hearing about something that happened that morning. Later I was to discover that scholars don't think much of Eleanor Hull as an historian, but that did not matter to me at the time. I shall always be grateful for that quotation from Spenser in her book.

A few months later Eamonn Gillespie, who lived over the lane in Killaned and was a few years older than I, lent me a book called *On Another Man's Wound*, a memoir by Ernie O'Malley describing his experiences in the struggle for Irish independence from 1916 to 1921. Eamonn and I used to go to the bog for turf together and on the way we'd talk about the comics and books we lent each other. I don't know how he managed to get his hands on Ernie O'Malley's book, which was not typical of the books we'd been reading. I had never read anything about twentieth-century Irish history before. I didn't know much about the Black and Tans, except what I had heard about the day they came to Glen and shot Michael Heaney in Malinbeg. To my surprise I greatly enjoyed reading *On Another Man's Wound*. Ernie O'Malley had a natural gift for descriptive writing, and I accompanied him on his travels all over Ireland, slept with him on wet hillsides, and heard the heavy tread of the sentries as he lay in his prison cell. This was living history, written by an eyewitness, and reading it was probably as near as I would ever get to having been there.

As my interest in the past reawakened, I came to realise that history was not confined to books. Glen itself was a history museum, dotted with Stone Age dolmens, Celtic slab-crosses and the remains of saints' cells, but these held little interest for me then. The only archaeological feature that stirred my imagination was a 'tunnel' under the Protestant graveyard, which we called *Poll Foulds* (Foulds' Hole). As children, we were told that if we didn't behave ourselves we would have to spend the night in *Poll Foulds* among the dead. It was a frightening prospect, which led me to imagine a damp, dark passage beneath the graveyard littered with human bones. Local storytellers said that the tunnel extended for three miles from the sea to a place called the Leachtaí, and that monks used it to escape from the Vikings, and priests to escape from the English during penal times. All that was fanciful speculation, and it is now thought that the so-called tunnel is really a souterrain dating from the ninth century, which was rediscovered in 1832 by workmen digging a grave for a man called Foulds. A crowbar slipped from the hand of one of the grave diggers and vanished through a hole in the ground. According to local lore, the men were so startled as they heard the echoing noise it made on its journey downwards that some of them fled, thinking that the crowbar had vanished into the nether regions beneath their feet. The rector, however, took a less alarmist view. He had the site excavated, and a souterrain measuring 19 feet by 7 feet was found underneath the graveyard. The souterrain may have been a chamber originally built as part of an earlier church on the site. Today it may be entered through a trapdoor in the graveyard directly in front of the present Protestant church.

Something else that aroused my interest were the previously mentioned ruins of stone-built cottages and broken walls marking the boundaries of old farms. These were the footprints of dead and forgotten farmers, the vestiges of lives departed, of a time before the Famine when the glen was more heavily populated and when farms were to be found on hillsides now recolonised by heather and rushes.

There is something mysterious about the ruins of a Famine cottage that moves us to reflect on a past we can never truly know. We seek it in the naked stonework, the layout of the rooms, the empty fireplace, the floor flags, and the gaping windows like empty eye sockets through which the forgotten inhabitants once gazed. It is an experience that quickens the imagination and touches us in the very core of our being. With a pang we read the stones like the annals of lost lives, the only annals they've bequeathed us. The ruins of old cottages were my first indication that the landscape could be read like a book. All you needed to know was what to look for. This realisation made me more observant. An old wall was no longer so many rows of grey stones: it was a symbol of something else, a different kind of alphabet. As my father once said to me, 'The old people who went before us could neither read nor write but they're not forgotten. They left their signature on the land.'

Another thing my father told me was that the Killaned houses were once grouped together in a clachan or hamlet, and he pointed out the site where you could still see what remained of the foundations of the old houses. He told me that in the early nineteenth century the landlords abolished the rundale system, under which each tenant farmed several detached fields. In 'striping' the land, the landlords sought to ensure that each tenant had his own separate holding and that each holding formed a single unit. They also helped with the building of new houses, each on the farm that went with it. That explained why Killaned was no longer a village and why the houses were dotted here and there along the roadside, from twenty to a hundred yards apart. It made me wonder what it would have been like to live under the old system with the houses in a cluster, facing this way and that and with very little space between them. It made me realise that the past was different from the present and that the life my great-grandfather led was not the life I knew.

Over the years I've enjoyed many happy hours reading history. The Irish history we learned at school was a history of easy certitudes that told of a classic confrontation of good and evil in which the Irish, as underdogs, represented the morally unassailable and the superior English, the forces of darkness and oppression. As I grew older, I learned to question the old certainties, comforting though they were, and I came to appreciate the difficulty of knowing the past in a real sense. At best we see only the tip of the iceberg. The rest is submerged in a turbid sea that is proof against scientific exploration. We may know the sequence of events, and something of the actors in the unfolding drama. What is more difficult to establish is the nature and strength of the actors' beliefs, feelings and motivation, and the obscure interactions that give rise to great events. The past is a house of many mirrors, in which too many historians see only their own reflection and that of the age in which they live. For me what gives the past its fascination is its essential mystery. In a sense we all invent a past for ourselves, and in another sense historians invent a past for all of us. Perhaps it is just as well that definitive history is impossible. If our knowledge of the past were cut and dried, there would be less grist for the omnivorous intelligence and imagination to grind. While the universities spew out more and more historians, the past will never be allowed to grow stale.

PART IV

Learning About Living

25

Boarding School

My father was in the habit of reminding me that I wasn't as strong as other boys of my age and that, unlike him, I would not be fit to hack it on land and sea. There was only one thing for it in his view: stick to the books. It was a piece of advice that I did not welcome, if only because of the far more pleasurable things I could be doing out of doors. Now I know that he meant well, but at the age of twelve it seemed to me that I would never have any peace while I remained at home.

Fortunately, a convenient escape route beckoned. A scholarship exam was held every Easter for boys and girls applying for entry to one of the preparatory colleges for students wishing to become primary teachers. When my aunt told me that I could sit the exam at the age of thirteen, I wasn't in the least reluctant. I had a year to prepare for it, which seemed to me then to be far too long. My teacher Frank Boyle helped me in every way he could, especially with arithmetic, history and geography. At weekends my aunt gave me lessons in Irish and English grammar. When Easter came, I went out to Teelin to do the exam and came home two days later knowing in my heart that I hadn't done as well as I had hoped. As I was only thirteen, I was still young enough to have another crack at the exam the following Easter, but somehow I had made up my mind that it was do or die the first time round.

When the results came out, two boys from the parish were offered a place but there was no brown envelope in the post for me. To give my father his due, he said nothing and neither did my aunt. I went to the village for a pound of tea for my mother and met Pat Boyle, an irascible old buffer noted for his sharp tongue.

'Did you get the call?' he asked.

'No,' I replied.

He pulled a stumpy pipe from his mouth and looked down at me with watery eyes. '*Chac tú ar an bháinín,*' he croaked, which was a crude way of saying that I'd cocked it up. Then he put the pipe back in his mouth and went off up the street with the news. There was nothing he liked better than a well-turned Irish phrase, particularly a phrase that was both trenchant and unambiguous.

On the way home I kept repeating aloud what Pat Boyle had said. I could not help thinking that it must be true. After dinner I put the graith on the donkey and readied a pair of creels to go to the bog for turf. Going to the bog, I always found, was a good excuse whenever I wanted to get away from the house. It meant that I was seen to be doing something useful; that I wouldn't get up to any mischief for at least an hour. The bog road ran uphill, snaking round in a semicircle, and as I climbed the steep slope, the whole glen and the bay opened up behind me and all I had to do was look back and enjoy them. That day I stopped several times to take in the scene. Now our house seemed remote and insignificant, and nothing else seemed to matter. I met no one coming down, and no one overtook me on the road. It was one of those days when I was glad to be on my own.

There was a lovely cooling breeze on the hilltop, and when I reached the bog, I left Neddy grazing the rough mountain grass and went down to a little basin within sight of Loch an Airgid, thinking I might see some wild ducks or water hens feeding. I sat on the heathery slope and waited. Sometimes cormorants came in from the sea, and sometimes a pair of swans would fly in from the direction of Slieve League, but today there was no sign of wildlife of any kind. I was out of luck and it seemed to me that, though I might wait all afternoon, I was destined to be disappointed.

An audible silence had fallen on the day and I lay on my back with my eyes closed. I thought I could hear the grass growing by my ear, or was it the movement of beetles and other tiny insects? It did not matter: what held me was the heavy stillness in which I could hear the faintest sounds. I kept listening with my eyes closed, trying to imagine what was making the barely audible ticking. I forgot about the exam and Pat Boyle's crude dismissal. It seemed so unimportant compared with the workings of the natural world.

Then, as I got to my feet, a single crane came in from the west, its long legs trailing. I was expecting it to land on the shore below but it flew over the water and over the hillock to the east. Thinking it was making for the sister lough, I walked round Loch an Airgid and up the side of the hillock, where I stood looking down on Loch an Óir, scrutinising the edge of the water as I sought the hunched outline of the bird. I remained stock-still for a long time, half convinced that I had glimpsed something grey among the reeds on the far shore, before I began making my way down the slope. Though I had often heard the cries of swans and wild geese, I had yet to hear the screech of a crane, and I wondered how close I'd get, and whether she'd fly off wailing if I disturbed her. Suddenly my heart missed a beat as a crane broke cover on my left, rising from a place I had not spotted. There was no eerie wail, no screech, no sound apart from a dry rustle. I watched as she flew off towards Slieve League, her long wings flapping slowly and deliberately, as if she were daring me to catch her. While I was still distracted, her mate rose from the far side of the lough and followed her. It was as if they'd both been in cahoots to confound me. I felt a quickening surge of happiness and I returned to where the donkey was grazing and filled the creels with turf from a stack my father had already opened. It was something I had done many times before and felt I would do countless times again.

The following day a brown envelope arrived in the post. To my surprise and delight I was being offered a place at St Enda's College, Galway. It was to be the end of the life I knew. From then on I would come home only on holiday. My relationship with the place in which I had been brought up was about to change forever. One result of 'the call to Enda's' was that Loch an Airgid became a hallowed place for me, a place with all the resonance I later came to associate with a time of innocence and truth. There are more picturesque loughs in Glen but none that for me has the mysterious aura of Loch an Airgid. I have drawn comfort from the memory of its austere beauty in many uncongenial places and situations, and whenever I go back to Glen I make sure to pay it a visit.

In early September I got a lift to Galway with Enda Cunningham from Carrick, who was taking his brother Cathal to St Enda's for the first time. Enda was a past pupil of the college. He knew what was in store for us and on the way he told us stories about the teachers and the priests who ran the place. He told us to look out for

Peach, the president, and Gubby, the vice-president. The very names intrigued me; they were every bit as exotic as the names of the pirates in *Treasure Island*, Billy Bones and Ben Gunn. Enda made it all sound highly entertaining. I got the impression that we were in for the time of our lives.

We arrived in late afternoon and were welcomed at the main entrance by a short, dapper priest with an impressively large head. Everything about him was neat, particularly his feet and hands. He had an ash-grey face and large sunken eyes with tussocks of black hair sprouting where you'd expect to find eyebrows. He was wearing patent leather shoes and, as he shook hands with Enda, I couldn't help noticing the tufts of black hair on the back of his stubby fingers, which seemed odd to me because he had no hair whatever on his head. He chatted for a while to Enda in Irish, but I couldn't understand a word he said. It was my first encounter with the Connacht dialect, which sounded nothing like the Donegal dialect to which I was accustomed. It was not an auspicious start.

'That was Peach,' Enda told us when the priest had gone. 'But don't call him Peach to his face. He likes to be known as *An tUachtarán* or *An tAthair Ó hEidhin*.'

St Enda's was one of six preparatory colleges that had been founded by the government to educate young boys and girls with a view to their becoming primary teachers. There were two colleges for boys and four for girls. All subjects, apart from English, were taught through the medium of Irish, and Irish was the language in daily use by staff and pupils alike. Entry to the colleges was by examination only. As all pupils were of a high standard on entering, the Leaving Certificate exam was taken after four years rather than the usual five. The aim of these colleges was to ensure a steady supply of primary teachers who would be proficient in speaking and writing the Irish language.

Most of the boys in St Enda's came from the Gaeltacht areas of Galway, Mayo and Donegal. At first those of us who had come from Donegal had difficulty understanding the teachers and our fellow pupils from Connacht. It was a matter not only of pronunciation but vocabulary as well. Their pronunciation of such common words as *arán* (bread) and *scian* (knife) was totally different from ours and they had a word for potatoes – *fataí* – which we had never heard before, all of which provided occasions for amusing misunderstandings and good-natured ribbing.

After a fortnight, when I had just begun to get used to my new regime, I was summoned by Peach to his study. As I gingerly opened the door, I had an impression of twilight and late evening, though the day outside was bright. I found him seated behind a wide desk that made him look even smaller than he was. He was wearing his biretta, which I'd heard was a sign that something or someone had incurred his extreme displeasure. He pointed to a chair and I sat on it, wondering what on earth I could have done wrong. He fished out an envelope from his desk drawer and asked me to read the address. Recognising the handwriting of one of my old school chums from Glen, I read slowly and deliberately, wondering if Peach had found some ghastly spelling mistake.

'St Enda's College,' he repeated scornfully after me. 'This is *Coláiste Éinde*, boy. I thought I'd made that clear.'

'Yes, you did,' I agreed.

'Is this letter from your parents?'

'No, it's from one of my school friends, Father.'

'Write and tell him you are at *Coláiste Éinde*. Letters addressed to any other college are not accepted here. In future they will be returned to the sender.'

He picked up his fountain pen and began writing. He was still wearing his biretta as a judge passing the death sentence might wear his black cap. I hesitated, not knowing if he had finished. After a long minute he looked up and pointed to the door. I couldn't get to it quickly enough but before closing it, I looked back. He had taken off his biretta which now sat on the desk at his elbow, a tea cosy without its teapot. Outside in the corridor I breathed fresh air again. From the window I could see the gardener digging on the slope with a fork, a view that seemed familiar and strangely comforting. I'd had my first sight of Peach's study. It was an experience I had no wish to repeat.

Luckily, we didn't see Peach every day. He didn't take classes; instead he devoted his time to administration and perhaps more ethereal matters. He said Mass two or three times a week, and looked quite impressive in alb and chasuble. Now and again we'd see him in the distance, leaving the college or returning from town, wearing a black clerical suit and hat, which made him look like a caricature of himself. He was deadly serious about everything he did, and he was particularly serious about the grave responsibility of preparing a bunch of rough-and-ready country boys with a wicked sense of humour for what he saw as the unfunny business of life outside the walls. In the four years I lived under his rule I never once saw him smile. Sometimes I wondered if he had any human weaknesses, if he enjoyed his food or an occasional glass of whiskey at bedtime. Perhaps he listened to the news on the radio. I couldn't imagine him listening to any other programme, certainly not the latest pop tunes on Radio Luxembourg.

In our second year the bishop gave him the grand-sounding title of Venerable Arch-Deacon, which only reinforced our perception of him as a being who was remote from any world that we were ever likely to inhabit.

Perhaps it was this very remoteness that enabled him to exert such an inexplicable pull on our young minds. We were never entirely free of the thought of him. Even *in absentia* he was present as a restraining force, his influence always there in the background like a niggling sense of cheerlessness, an awareness that we must tread carefully, that such privileges as we enjoyed were not ours by right.

On the rare occasions when he supervised study, you could hear yourself breathe in the silence, and as he walked up and down reading his office, you could hear the creaking of his shoes and the swish of his cassock long before he approached your desk. Sometimes he would take off his reading glasses and stand in the centre of the study hall swinging them round and round in his right hand, as if he were silently counting the revolutions. Though we didn't realise it at the time, he probably felt ill at ease with us. His fastidious temperament rendered him incapable of bringing out the best in us, or encouraging us to find the best in ourselves. Quite possibly, he may have disliked us for the mess and disorder we would create if left to our own devices. He certainly never talked to us as growing men, not even in the last term of our fourth year when we were about to escape from his jurisdiction for ever. The only piece of advice he ever gave us was to go to the theatre whenever we could, because it was a more imaginative and creative medium than cinema. It was a piece of advice I found myself taking and for which I am grateful, though not for the reasons he gave us.

The vice-president, whom we called Gubby, was a priest from County Clare. He was younger than Peach, broad-backed and broad-shouldered, solid and strong. But for his clerical clothes, he could easily have passed for a well-heeled farmer who would know a good beast when he saw one and who'd be capable of dealing swiftly with anyone who tried to sell him a pup. He gave the impression of being Peach's equal in status and allowed us to infer that he was an independent thinker, which was not the same as encouraging independent thought in us. Quick-tempered and slow to show mercy, he was less predictable and therefore a more intimidating presence than Peach.

Though of average height, he looked short and stocky because of his broad shoulders. During the day he wore a cassock and never went anywhere without his leather strap, which he carried in his trousers pocket. He didn't use it every day, but when he did, it was not unbeknown to the unfortunate victim. Six strokes on each hand was the usual punishment but for hardened cases this tally could double. An appeal to extenuating circumstances was as futile as it was unwise. He expected boys to take their punishment like men, and any boy who didn't could have his punishment doubled without further explanation.

He exercised total control over us but in a different way from Peach. While Peach was the object of much ribald humour, Gubby was respected as well as feared. Unlike Peach, he had a human side: his passionate interest in hurling and Gaelic football and his unerring memory for who scored what and how. He taught us Latin and Christian doctrine, and supervised games and athletics. Now and again he would tog out and join the senior boys at football. He wouldn't do much running but he'd make enough noise to compensate for any lack of agility. I can still visualise him standing mid-field, shouting in his echoing voice, '*Buail í*,' which, roughly translated, means, 'Don't hug the ball, you fool. Kick it, for God's sake.' Now and again in class he would crack a joke at which he himself would laugh, but whether he expected us to join in the laughter was open to question. In spite of that, we felt that he wasn't beyond all understanding. You could have a short conversation with him, provided you chose the right subject and you had the good sense not to contradict him. Understandably perhaps, we had a sneaking affection for him.

In some ways life at St Enda's resembled that in a medieval monastery with its round of canonical hours. Every minute was measured out and accounted for. The loud ringing of a bell woke us in the morning, and the day began with Mass in the college chapel. After breakfast we had classes, and in mid-morning a bowl of soup and a chunk of bread. Then there were classes before dinner, and more after dinner, until it was time for games and recreation. Finally, after tea we had three hours' study until bedtime. It was a strict regime that presented few opportunities for self-indulgence. It made a virtue of rigid self-discipline and unwavering willingness to abide by a hundred written and unwritten rules. St Enda's was not a place for anyone who found it difficult to conform or do what everyone else was doing at every hour of the day.

I suppose the system we lived under could be described as totalitarian, leaving no room for even reasoned dissent. We were being prepared for a career as primary teachers, and in the Ireland of that time primary teachers had to work closely with the priests who managed the primary schools. It was seen as desirable that teachers should have unquestioning respect for their managers, so that priestly time was not wasted in unnecessary argument. If that was indeed the thinking behind our training, it wasn't very successful. We were an intelligent bunch of boys who had come mainly from country places where irreverent humour was part of the culture. What we were made to say was one thing; what we thought and talked about among ourselves was something else entirely.

The odd occasions when we were allowed to escape from strict routine assumed unparalleled importance in our minds. Going to town for a haircut was one of these.

Going out in a group to see a play or film was another. My idea of what constituted a good film was derived from the pictures I'd seen in the Spink in Glen. The films which Peach and Gubby chose for us — for the most part wholesome films like *Scott of the Antarctic*, starring John Mills, or harmless comedies starring Danny Kaye — were insipid by comparison. Now and again on Sunday afternoons in winter Gubby would take us for walks to Barna. On the way we would look at the bare countryside all round, and the austere drystone walls would remind us of home. Then we would turn round and walk back. At times these excursions seemed pointless but they provided a welcome break.

One of the things that made life at St Enda's tolerable was the sense of the ordinary, everyday world that the lay teachers communicated by their very presence. They reminded us of the life outside the walls, the world we'd left behind with our parents. Unlike the priests, the lay teachers didn't live in. They had families of their own, and went home to their wives every evening. Some of them even went home to lunch every day. It was extraordinarily reassuring to see them coming and going in their ancient cars and realise that the time they spent with us represented less than half their waking hours. It made us dream of the life we would one day lead, of the fabled world elsewhere.

There were six lay teachers in all. Unlike us, they were free to read the newspapers and they knew what was going on in the world. Apart from the subjects they were paid to teach, they had access to all sorts of 'forbidden' knowledge. Getting them to talk about it, however, required diplomatic skill and sheer persistence coupled with a gift for subtle flattery. Having discovered that the science and maths teachers would not be deflected from the curriculum, we concentrated our efforts on the more amenable teachers. Of these, Mike, who taught us music, drawing and woodwork, was the most forthcoming. He had the rare knack of imparting information almost without seeming to. He also told us stories based on the books he'd read, and if they were on the tall side he enjoyed telling them all the more. Above all, he knew how to tell a story in parts over the course of a week and leave us on tenterhooks for the next instalment. In his indirect way he taught us more about the workings of the great world than the rest of the teachers put together.

Among the lay teachers, Tom, who taught English, had the most commanding presence. A tall, well-built man in his fifties, he smelt strongly of pipe tobacco and peered down at us through rimless pince-nez, from which dangled a gold chain. In sports jacket and cavalry twills, he looked like a beneficent professor on holiday in the country. His catchwords and acerbic comments provided many occasions for mimicry and merriment when his back was turned. Boys who had not learnt their Shakespeare were promptly told to 'go back to the obscurity of Ballyhuppahane, whence you should never have emerged'. We all thought that Ballyhuppahane was a name he had invented, until some bright spark discovered that it was a real place in the foothills of the Slieve Blooms in Co Laois.

Tom was not one of those teachers who spoon-feed their pupils. Instead he told us that the finest thoughts in any language were enshrined in its poetry, and that the best poetry could not be paraphrased, not even by the poet who wrote it. Naturally, it was against his principles to explain every word and trope in a poem. He pointed out that there were almost two hundred pages of notes at the back of our poetry anthology, and that he expected us to read them. Among the poems we studied for the Leaving Certificate exam was Shelley's 'Hymn of Pan'. It wasn't

an easy poem, and we were pleased when he gave us only
one stanza to learn off by heart:

I sang of the dancing stars,
*   I sang of the dædal earth,*
And of heaven, and the giant wars,
*   And love, and death, and birth.*
*   And then I changed my pipings—*
Singing how down the vale of Mænalus
*   I pursued a maiden, and clasped a reed.*
Gods and men, we are all deluded thus!
*   It breaks in our bosom, and then we bleed.*
All wept, as I think both ye now would,
If envy or age had not frozen your blood,
*   At the sorrow of my sweet pipings.*

One smart Alec among us put his own construction
on the stanza. He was convinced that when Pan clasped a
reed, he was really clasping his penis, and that the line 'It
breaks in our bosom, and then we bleed' was a covert reference to ejaculation.

'No wonder Tom didn't explain it,' he laughed. 'I'll ask
him tomorrow, just to embarrass him.'

Things didn't work out as he had planned, however.
On hearing his question, Tom simply enquired if he'd
read the relevant note at the back of the book.

'No, sir.'

'Then read it aloud for the benefit of the whole class.'

The boy, rather sheepishly, read out a single sentence:
'Syrinx, an Arcadian nymph, was changed by her sisters
into a reed when fleeing from the enamoured Pan, who
afterwards cut this reed in seven (or nine) parts to make
the "Pan's-pipe" or shepherd's pipe.'

'Now, do you understand the meaning of the line?'

'No, sir.' The boy would not be put off.

'Write out the sentence fifty times for tomorrow. Then perhaps the meaning will dawn on you.'

We were all suitably amused, but after that we knew better than to try to embarrass Tom.

His method of teaching English was to make us learn by heart long passages from our poetry and prose anthologies. Anyone who couldn't recite them word perfect was given lines. He rarely told us anything about the social or political climate in which writers worked. He was also silent about their lives, perhaps because he considered them to be too scandalous. He had us learn passages from the essays of Joseph Addison as examples of the kind of prose style we should cultivate. In support of his opinion he would quote Dr Johnson: 'Whoever wishes to attain an English style, familiar but not coarse, and elegant but not ostentatious, must give his days and nights to the volumes of Addison.' Some boy with a sense of mischief once asked him for his favourite English sentence. He thought for a moment and said, 'We were now treading that illustrious island which was once the luminary of the Caledonian region...'. Perhaps it is not surprising that none of us ever succeeded in writing a sentence that met his expectations.

Nesfield's *Grammar* was his Bible. He gave us exercises in word parsing and clause analysis until we could do them in our sleep. He taught us to be on our guard against tautology, a cardinal sin in his book. One result of his teaching methods was that after four years we were all walking anthologies of English poetry. Though we would not have believed it at the time, it gave us a good ear for the rhythms and music of good English writing. I owe more to Tom than to any of my other teachers, for it was he who guided my early efforts at writing and directed my attention to what makes the study of great literature in any language such an enriching experience.

In spite of the restrictions of the regime, I enjoyed my time at St Enda's. All the teachers were hard working in their different ways. I did not fully appreciate the high quality of their tutelage until I went to university. We probably received the best education available in Ireland at that time. Undoubtedly, we were a privileged bunch of boys. Most of us would never have received a secondary education were it not for St Enda's and the preparatory college system.

By the time I reached my final year, I knew that I did not wish to become a teacher. I was dreading having to go to the teachers' training college the following year, and it seemed to me that the only way I could escape that fate was to win a university scholarship. I had not yet made up my mind about a career. All I knew was that it must be something different, something that would reflect my growing interest in literature.

26

Working with My Father

M y father was an exacting perfectionist, no matter what the work. At times I had the impression that no one, except himself, could do certain tasks entirely to his satisfaction. Turf-cutting was one of these. One Easter, while on holiday from boarding school, I offered to help him cut the turf. He handed me one of the two slanes he kept in the barn, and we both set off with the two ancestral implements on our shoulders. It was a mild April morning with a breeze from the south that bore a sense of spring and renewal. After a sedentary winter of study and little exercise I felt a surge of untapped energy stirring in my legs and arms. We climbed the winding bog road together while my father puffed happily at his pipe and told me about whatever work plans he had in mind while I was home.

Ours was an old bog that had been in use for several generations and was now almost cut out. At the top end the peat moss was shallow, only four spits deep, and the turf it produced were light brown in colour and burned quickly without giving off much heat. We used them mainly during the summer months when the weather was warm and a fire was hardly needed except for cooking. At the lower end, where the peat moss was seven spits deep, the turf was heavy and black and as good as coal for heat on a winter night. My father always began cutting at the lower end because it allowed any excess water to drain away as we went along, and because the black turf took longer to dry.

First, we pared away the top sod or scraw about a yard wide, which consisted mainly of heather and sedge with close, stubborn roots. We worked quickly and in silence, and when we'd pared about twenty yards, my father ran his spade down the face of the bog to remove any loose material killed or dislodged by winter frost. We were now ready to begin. My father insisted on taking the first spit, and when he had cut a length of about three yards, I started on the next floor below. After the heavy work of paring, the turf-cutting seemed easy. I began cutting and casting at speed, enjoying the ease with which the blade tore through the decayed roots and fibres and the smooth slither of the sods slipping off the blade as I cast them onto the bank. After ten minutes I felt that I could cut turf with my father any day. I was strong and eager and I was determined to make him realise that there was very little he could teach me. I increased my speed and he increased his, keeping the same distance behind me on the upper floor. For a while he said nothing. Then suddenly he stopped.

'Mind what you're doing,' he said. 'Look at the bog-face and the floor you're leaving behind you. You'll never make a turf-cutter at this rate. The floor should be even and the bog-face should slant a bit so that it won't cave in during the winter. And look at those sods, a big one and a small one and then another big one. The turf should all be the same size, as if they were cut by machine.'

'There's nothing like a bit of variety,' I joked.

'Everyone has his own natural cutting pace,' he said, pulling out his pipe from the depth of his trousers pocket. 'If you stick to what comes naturally, you won't go too far wrong.'

He didn't accuse me of trying to make the work into a contest, but I could see it was what he'd meant to say. When he'd got his pipe going, we started again. This time I worked with more deliberation. At first it wasn't such fun, but after a while I began to enjoy the rhythm of the work and to find satisfaction in leaving a floor and bog-face that was every bit as clean as my father's.

We worked steadily for the rest of the morning and, after we'd eaten, we worked again throughout the after-noon until evening. It seemed a long day and I didn't demur when he said that it was time to go home. He walked back down the length of bog we'd just cut, pulling at his pipe as he surveyed the workmanship.

'I'll make a turf-cutter of you yet,' he said. It was as near as he could get to an admission that I was catching on.

'There's nothing to it,' I said loftily.

'You wouldn't say that if you had to do it for the rest of your life. A short stint will only do you good, it will blow the cobwebs out of your mind.'

'Is there anyone in the townland who can cut turf to your satisfaction?' I thought I might tease him a little on the way home.

'John Una and Johnny Phaddy Johnny are both neat workers and they don't let the grass grow under their feet.' It was the ultimate in accolades, his *summa cum laude*, and I thought I could do worse than make an effort to deserve it. Every year, while I was at boarding school and univer-sity, I helped him with the turf-cutting during the Easter holidays.

'Have I passed the test?' I asked the year after I'd taken my degree.

'What test?'

'The turf-cutting test, what else?'

'You had a good tutor.' He gave a short laugh of self-congratulation, and then delivered one of the generalisations of which he was so fond.

'Some men work in mad spurts, and then spend half an hour smoking or chatting while they get their breath back. You're like me. You don't go at it in a fury; you keep up the same steady pace all day. A man gets more done that way, and what he does is neat and tidy.'

The other work to which he attached supreme importance was mowing hay with a scythe. When I was about sixteen, he bought me a scythe and a whetstone which, rightly or wrongly, I took to be a tacit admission that I had finally reached manhood. After that, mowing became one of my favourite jobs during the summer holidays. I enjoyed it because it required a certain degree of skill and because it was done at the loveliest time of the year. Besides, it provided me with a means of testing myself, of discovering the limits of my strength and of seeking to extend them. Listening to old men talking about mowing, I often felt that there must be something mystical about the skill. They would talk gravely about the importance of a good edge, giving the impression that not everyone was gifted in this way. A man with a good edge could sharpen a scythe with a few rubs of the whetstone and mow for the longest day of summer without undue expense of energy, whereas someone who lacked the gift would only dull the blade with each stroke and end up with backache. My father refrained from advising me about sharpening. Being a traditionalist, he took the view that it was a hereditary skill that could not be taught or learnt.

I soon realised that what mattered to him was the quality of the work rather than the amount of ground covered in a day. He showed me how to mow evenly by keeping the heel of the scythe close to the ground, and taught me not to take too wide a swathe and not to leave an unsightly field of 'ridges' or 'wings' behind me. In his view, it was a mark of slovenly mowing if you could count the swathes after the hay had been gathered into tramp-cocks. A newly mowed field should look as smooth as a newly planed piece of timber. 'It's like shaving,' he would say. 'You mustn't leave even one whisker standing.'

We worked together through the long days. I was young enough and eager enough to enjoy the rhythm of the work, the pleasant feeling of tiredness in my limbs in the evenings, and the satisfying sense of more days stretching ahead endlessly. What's more, I got used to my father's company and his selective sense of humour. I got to know which things must be talked about seriously, and which things were merely fit subjects for good-natured ridicule. He took his own word seriously. If he promised someone to do something, he wouldn't know peace until he had done it.

Curiously, he had little sense of family history, certainly no interest in going back over the past. I grew up knowing next to nothing about my immediate ancestors or my father's experiences as a young man. All I knew was that he used to play football in goal, that his father was obsessed with farm work, that his Uncle Charlie was drowned off the Doonalt coast, and that his brother Paddy was a civic guard who died of TB while still a young man. Whenever I questioned my father further, he would say that there was nothing further to tell. Yet I would not describe him as taciturn or humourless. On the contrary, he was an amusing conversationalist when in the mood.

It would be difficult, however, to give an adequate idea of the flavour of his conversation, if only because he had the gift of making conversation about next to nothing. He didn't need a subject; in fact he refused to have anything to do with subjects. His conversation was a kind of free association made up of quirky sayings, snatches of old songs, and old advertising slogans that struck him as funny, and if they weren't funny in themselves, he'd make them sound funny by the way he had of saying them. I don't think I've ever heard him say a simple thank-you. Rather he always said, '"Thank you Ma'am," said Dan,' which, he told me many years later, was the refrain from an old song about a man called Dan who came to court a young lady and was so eager to please her mother that he kept saying, 'Thank you Ma'am' throughout the evening.

Reasoned discussion was not his *métier*; he was content to give his opinion in one short sentence and leave it there for the rest of us to argue over. Often I had the impression that he was deliberately throwing us a bone of contention for his own private amusement. If he disagreed with your opinion, he would smile and say, 'You're welcome still your pipe to fill and smoke your own tobacco.' In spite of all appearances to the contrary, he knew his own mind. He had strong opinions about the things that got up his nose, including De Valera — 'the Devil in a black overcoat'; the Fianna Fáil government — 'a bunch of crooks'; and sheep farmers who turned a blind eye whenever their sheep strayed on to his land — 'the sheep are as hungry as their owners, they'll eat wherever they can get a free bite'.

The longer I worked with him, the better I got to know him. He was not an imaginative man, and had little or no time for idle speculation or homespun philosophising. What he had in abundance was unfailing common sense which he brought to bear on everything he saw and heard. As I grew into manhood, I couldn't help being impressed by his determination not to be deluded. Though I used to tell him some of the more outlandish things I'd gleaned from my reading, he never registered surprise at any of them. Instead he contrived to give the impression of having heard it all before. I don't think he was putting on an act either, as he had the kind of mind that did not marvel at things. One day as we were resting from our labours on the bog, I asked him half-jokingly where he'd got his wisdom. He gave me one of his quizzical smiles and said that he had no wisdom except the wisdom he was born with. That was how he saw life. Men of character and ability were born not made. As he would say himself, you can't make a silk purse out of a sow's ear.

For me the summer holidays were a time of self-discovery. In working with my father I tested the limits of my physical strength, and I gained an intimate knowledge of the 'mythology' surrounding work routines that gave me a sense of anchorage in my native parish. Every night I used to read into the small hours when the rest of the family were in bed, and in every book I opened I seemed to find sanction for my own thoughts and feelings at the time. Whereas I had been living under the illusion that my experience was in some way unique, in the novels and literary biographies I read I found an objective and at times critical reflection of my own, as yet largely unexamined, life. It was encouraging to discover that other people had been there before me, that my feelings and sensations were those of most young men, that I was not alone on the shore, that I was merely one speck of foam on the breaking wave of human life.

Whenever I recall those summers now, I think of a short poem by Ezra Pound:

And the days are not full enough
And the nights are not full enough
And life slips by like a field mouse
Not shaking the grass.

27

Reading Begets Writing

From an early age I was fond of stories. The first stories I remember hearing were told round the turf fire on the hearth, ghost stories that filled me with fear and wonder. A good storyteller could make you forget who and where you were. He could make you shiver with horror or laugh till tears came to your eyes. A good story took you out of yourself, providing an escape from the everyday world of school and household chores. It could change the way you felt; it could make you sad or happy; above all it made you want to tell the story yourself.

When I was about ten or eleven, my aunt gave me a book called *Old Celtic Romances*, which consisted of translations from medieval Irish by P W Joyce. There were six stories, including 'The Fate of the Children of Lir', 'The Fairy Palace of the Quicken Trees', and 'The Fate of the Children of Usna'. The story I liked best was 'The Pursuit of the Giolla Deacair and His Horse', a humorous tale concerning a trick played by an enchanter in the shape of a giant on the warriors of the ancient Fianna.

The giant, who gave his name as the Giolla Deacair, was ugly and fearsome. 'He had a large, thick body, bloated and swollen out to a great size; clumsy, crooked legs; and broad, flat feet, turned inwards. His hands and arms and shoulders were bony and thick and very strong-looking; his neck was long and thin... He had thick lips, and long, crooked teeth; and his face was covered all over with bushy hair.' In his right hand he carried an iron club 'which he dragged after him, with its end on the ground; and as it trailed along, it tore up a track as deep as the fur-row a farmer ploughs with a team of oxen.'

He held his horse by 'a thick halter, and seemed to be dragging him forward by main force, the animal was so lazy and so hard to move. Every now and then, when the beast tried to stand still, the giant would give him a blow on the ribs with his big iron club, which sounded as loud as the thundering of a great billow against the rough-headed rocks of the coast.'

The giant asks Fionn, the leader of the Fianna, to take him into his service for one year, mentioning that at the end of that time he would fix his wages, as was his cus-tom. Surprisingly, Fionn agrees, after which the giant tricks fourteen of Fionn's men into mounting his horse. The men find themselves stuck so firmly to the horse's back that they can move neither hand nor foot. The giant takes his leave and the horse gallops off with the men over the sea, swift as a swallow in flight. Most of the story concerns the pursuit of the giant and his horse by Fionn and fifteen of his bravest followers, and the marvellous adventures that befall them on the way. The story is full of fascinating details, such as Fianna warrior Diarmuid Ó Duibhne's custom of not eating any food left over from a previous meal. Accordingly, he would kill a deer for his dinner every evening and leave to the crows whatever he could not eat.

This carefree life among God's plenty under the open heavens was the very antithesis of the narrow life of economic astringency and tiresome Do's and Don'ts that I knew. I read the story again and again until I could quote whole passages from memory, recreating for myself a world I felt I had missed by being born into the wrong century. The enchantment described in the story was reflected in the enchantment I experienced in reading. My enjoyment was not just in reliving the excitement of the pursuit but in the language of exaggeration used to describe it. When I went to secondary school, I was disappointed to find that the books we were supposed to be studying included nothing as entertaining or imaginative as 'The Pursuit of the Giolla Deacair and His Horse'.

At St Enda's, as in all Irish secondary schools of that time, we had an anthology of English prose consisting of essays with such titles as 'Sir Roger at Church', 'On Going a Journey', 'The Deaths of Little Children', and 'Mrs Battle's Opinions on Whist'. Most of the essays were by English writers, including Joseph Addison, William Hazlitt, Leigh Hunt and Charles Lamb. As far as I can remember, there was not one Irish writer among them. As the subjects of their essays were remote from the preoccupations of my yearning imagination, I reluctantly came to the conclusion that what I sought from literature was not to be found in the prose essays on our English course.

Then, almost by accident, I came across a copy of *Sense and Sensibility* in the school library and began reading it one wintry afternoon. To my surprise I found myself enjoying it, not just for the story and the characters but for the writing itself. Jane Austen's world was remote from any world I'd experienced, but that did not seem to matter. I had gone through a door into a place and time that was new to me, yet one capable of being known and realised, a world of absorbing and inexhaustible interest. It was the first grown-up novel I read.

Soon I read another and then another and found myself asking questions about things I'd never thought of before. I felt transformed, if only while I was engaged in the act of reading. I would lose track of what was happening around me, would forget about my own preoccupations and the irksome school routines and live entirely in the minds of the characters the author had created.

During the Christmas holidays that followed, I came across three short stories: 'The Three-Day Blow' by Ernest Hemingway and 'The Tent' and 'The Fairy Goose' by Liam O'Flaherty. I hadn't heard of Hemingway before, so I read his short story first. It concerns two boys getting drunk in a cottage in the country on a blowy afternoon. The opening paragraphs paint a scene of uncluttered simplicity. The reader is made to feel that they can actually see the cottage, the wood, the lake, and the big trees swaying in the wind. It is autumn. 'The fruit had been picked and the fall wind blew through the bare trees.' The two boys, Nick and Bill, sit in front of a log fire drinking Bill's father's whiskey as they talk about baseball and their favourite books. They put a fresh log on the fire and do some really serious drinking and what they consider to be serious talking. They feel truly grown up as they discuss their respective fathers and what makes a man a drunkard. Their conversation is presented tongue in cheek: '"It all evens up," Nick said. They sat looking into the fire and thinking about this profound truth.'

Most of the story is in the form of dialogue, as if reported by someone listening outside the window. At first we do not enter into the mind of either boy. Then suddenly Bill begins talking about the recent breakup of Nick's relationship with Marjorie. Nick says very little. He feels uneasy, and for the first time we get a glimpse of what is going on inside his head. We begin to realise the ambiguity of his feelings for Marjorie. In what is a masterly piece of oblique narration, we sense the story behind the story that is being told. Nick is no longer drunk. The whiskey has died in him. He and Bill get down two shotguns and go out to join Bill's father by the swamp. For Nick nothing has been finally settled. The story doesn't 'end'. We are left feeling that it will go on: 'None of it was important now. The wind blew it out of his head. Still he could always go into town Saturday night. It was a good thing to have in reserve.'

As I read the last sentence, I could only marvel at how such a seemingly bare and simple style could convey so much in so few words. It was the antithesis of the florid and convoluted style of some of the essayists we were studying for our exams.

I had read some of Liam O'Flaherty's stories in Irish but I'd never read anything by him in English. Curiously, 'The Tent' was also set on a windy day. It was about a tinker, his two wives, and a stranger who comes to their tent seeking shelter for the night:

A tinker and his two wives were sitting on a heap of straw in the tent, looking out through the entrance at the wild moor that stretched in front of it, with a snowcapped mountain peak rising like the tip of a cone over the ridge of the moor about two miles away. The three of them were smoking cigarettes in silence. It was evening, and they had pitched their tent for the night in a gravel pit on the side of the mountain road, crossing from one glen to another. Their donkey was tethered to the cart beside the tent.

Unlike the world of Jane Austen, this was a world I felt I knew. The tinkers who came to Glen from time to time used to camp by the stream on the Line only fifty yards from our house. I remembered their tent and brightly painted caravan, and the tin clippings and heaps of broken straw they left behind by the roadside. The immediacy of O'Flaherty's prose transported me to a place at once familiar and strange. I found myself sitting on a box in the tent with the tinker, his wives and the sombre stranger. It was an unsettling and at the same time exciting experience.

The tinkers I had seen in Glen were dark-complexioned men who said very little as they went about their mysterious business of making tin cans. The women were swarthy and strong featured and they never seemed to smile. O'Flaherty's tinkers are also a tribe unto themselves, far superior to ordinary mortals like the stranger. The travelling man, whose name is Joe, is lithe and graceful. He looks almost feminine and there is something contemptuous and arrogant in his expression. His two wives are slovenly but strangely beautiful. They seem to get on well together and are sufficiently wicked to lead the stranger up the garden path. All three become tipsy on his whiskey, after which he makes an ineffectual pass at one of the women, and the story ends in a frightening burst of violence.

In some ways I felt that O'Flaherty's direct and forceful style was not unlike Hemingway's, though his rhythms were different. You got the impression that the words he used had only one meaning; you were never in any doubt about the author's intention. Objects and actions stood out starkly against the wild landscape that contained them. I could sense O'Flaherty's extraordinary powers of dramatisation, and reading 'The Tent' was like watching a play. I could see the action take place before my very eyes. What I liked best of all was that O'Flaherty, like Hemingway, was content to show me things as they happened and leave me to draw my own conclusions.

Avidly, I turned to 'The Fairy Goose', which was quite different from 'The Tent'. It was set in a time long past, a time of simple-minded superstition when credulous villagers stood in awe of an old woman who cast spells and feared the supposed supernatural powers of their priest:

> *Old Mrs Wiggins had by now realised that the goose was worth money to her. So she became firmly convinced that the goose was gifted with supernatural powers. She accepted, in return for casting spells, a yard of white frieze cloth for unravelling dreams, a pound of sugar for setting the spell of the Big Periwinkle and half a donkey's load of potatoes for tying the Knot of the Snakes on a sick cow's side. Hitherto a kindly, humorous woman, she took to wearing her shawl in triangular fashion, with the tip of it reaching to her heels. She talked to herself or to her goose as she went along the road. She took long steps like a goose and rolled her eyes occasionally. When she cast a spell she went into an ecstasy, during which she made inarticulate sounds, like 'boum, roum, toum, kroum.'*

This was a kind of story I'd never encountered before. I'd never met an old woman like Mary Wiggins, and I doubted if such a woman ever existed. Yet such was the author's skill with language that I did not need to believe in the characters or the events. It was a story that could be read and enjoyed as a fable. I could hardly believe that 'The Tent' and 'The Fairy Goose' had come from the same pen, and I read the two stories again to see if I could work out how O'Flaherty had achieved his effects. I knew from my reading that his Irish short stories were beautifully written, but his English was, if anything, more distinctive in its rhythms. I also knew that he had been brought up on the Aran Islands, and couldn't begin to imagine how a native Irish speaker could come to write English better than most of those who had been to the

212

language born. Truly, a writer was a superior being, a druid reborn with magical powers to transmute and transport. I was sitting at home by the kitchen window, looking out at the blank end-wall of McGlinchey's, when the thought occurred to me. I had discovered my life's ambition. I would and must become a writer.

After that my reading took on a deliberate purpose. I had outgrown adventure stories. I was reading for the pleasure of taking on cargo that might one day bring grist to my mill as a writer. I couldn't read a good novel or short story without wishing that I had written it. Surely, I told myself, writing must follow reading. I was too young to realise that there is a world of difference between the two. Again and again, I tried my hand at writing short stories without managing to produce anything that pleased me. My disappointment was such that I began to wonder if reading, like drinking, provokes the desire but takes away the performance. I was too inexperienced to know that I wasn't really writing. I was only trying to imitate the style of the authors I happened to be reading at the time.

28

Fishing with My Uncle

From listening to my mother I knew the Garveross place names long before I got to know the places themselves: Páirc a' Mhíodúin, Cúl a' Gharraí, Píosa Neddy, Oileán na gCapall, Tóin a' Foinse, Áit Dhomhnaill Bhuí. Through long repetition, and because I had never seen them, the places acquired in my young mind an aura of legend and romance.

Granny Heekin lived in Garveross. On Fridays she went to the post office to collect her pension, and sometimes she came up to Killaned to pay us a visit. Like other elderly ladies of that time, she dressed in black. She also wore a shawl and walked with the aid of a stick. On Fridays my mother would keep an eye on the Logan between Garveross and Straid, and if she spotted her black shawl and white headscarf in the distance, she'd say, 'Granny Heekin is under sail today.'

When I was old enough, I began going over to Garveross to see her and Uncle Patrick. As a boy, I enjoyed going to Garveross because it gave me a sense of freedom. Neither Granny nor Uncle Patrick ever told me what I could or could not do. It was a little holiday from the regime at home, and it was an opportunity to cross two bridges and enjoy the music of flowing water. Passing the Straid houses on the way, I would often run into James Frank Nora who was related to my mother and always spoke to me in his gravelly voice. Once, on my way home, he gave me two big turnips and said, 'Tell your mother James Frank Nora sent her these.' They were lovely turnips with flesh almost the colour of orange peel, and next time he saw me he asked, 'What did your mother say about the turnips?'

'She said they were very good.'

'Didn't she say they were the best turnips she ever tasted?'

'No, she said they were very good.'

When I got home I told my mother about our conversation.

'You need to be quick for James Frank Nora. Next time tell him I never tasted anything like them. Let him make what he likes of that.'

The road between Straid and Garveross was pleasantly undulating with one or two twists to lend it interest. It ran alongside the river estuary on the left, and beyond the estuary lay a flat stretch of sand that was used as a football field when the tide was out. My mother told me that she could remember tides so high that they flowed across the road and into the adjacent fields. Always on the road to Garveross I kept an eye on Screig Beefan, a multicoloured crag that changed colour with the seasons and seemed to change in appearance as I approached it.

We could see Screig Beefan from our house in Killaned, but from there it seemed remote and unattainable. In outline it looked like an ancient motor car with Glen Head as the bonnet and the Tower as the radiator cap. At other times the patches of scree on its face took on the shapes of birds and animals, and as children we often argued about whether we were looking at a clocking hen or the head of a calf or wolf.

From Garveross Bridge, Screig Beefan seemed so close and overwhelming that I felt I could stretch out my hand and touch it. The colours that in the distance had looked pale or pastel-like now shone as bright as if nature had painted them that very minute. From where I stood it looked almost sheer, but I could tell that that was only an illusion. My mother had said that as a girl she knew a young man who'd climbed down from the top with a creel of turf on his back through the gully called the Chimney.

She had also told me about the Casán Ard, a pathway across the face of Screig Beefan running from east to west, which was used by men from Ballard coming to Garveross to fish. What she hadn't explained was why I could see the Tower from home but not from Garveross Bridge, where I was much closer to it. The vanishing Tower was a great source of mystery to me as a boy until my father told me that Killaned was higher up than Garveross. I couldn't see the Tower from the bridge simply because of the way it was set back, and because the curve of the mountain obscured it.

My grandmother died while I was at university but I still went to Garveross during the holidays to see Patrick and his wife Caitlín, who always made me welcome. When I was old enough Patrick took me fishing to Skelpoona, which was one of his favourite haunts. He was a skilled and patient fisherman who knew the best places for every wind and tide. He never used jigs, spoon-hooks or other shop lures, but relied entirely on the flies he himself tied from sheep's wool. He knew the Garveross coast from boyhood and he had the benefit of the lore and experience of previous generations of fishermen. As you might expect, he was a treasure house of information about every rock and cove, and the human significance, or indeed the funny side of a story, was never lost on him. His humour was celebratory, his gift being one of enhancement. If he found something amusing, he'd be sure to make it even more amusing in the retelling.

He also had an eye for eccentricity in human behaviour and an ear for the fortuitous phrase that revealed more than the speaker had intended. Looking back, I now realise that I learned more about life from him than I did from any of my professors. At a time when I tended to see things through the refracting window of literature, he taught me to observe with the naked eye and have confidence in the validity of my own experience. As I could not wait to find out what the future held in store for me, I used to ask him all sorts of impossible questions. Once I asked him how he'd sum up life. 'Sum up life!' he said. 'That's like trying to keep the tide out with a graip.' It was as near as he ever came to expressing irritation with me.

The first evening we went to Skelpoona he was sensible enough to say nothing at first and give me time to make my own mistakes. After half an hour he had caught two pollock and I had caught nothing. It was only then that he gave me a word of advice that seemed obvious enough but had the wisdom of long practice behind it.

'You're pulling into slack water,' he said. 'Always pull into a lively burn. If a fish is following the fly, it will rise in the burn, sometimes at the very last minute. Don't pull evenly. Give the rod the odd jerk. The fly shouldn't look dead in the water.'

This piece of advice made me realise that a fisherman is essentially an illusionist who, unlike a fowler or hunter, must perform his act without sight of his quarry. All he can see before him is an expanse of water, and he dare not admit to himself that it may be fishless. He needs patience and stamina to keep at it in less than perfect conditions and even when the take is poor. What holds his interest is that he does not know from one moment to the next when he'll make a strike. The thought kept me going. I developed a passionate interest in fishing, not just for the sport itself but for the wild, out of the way places I found myself visiting with my uncle.

The very names of the places were music to my ears: Sceilp Úna, An Clúidín, Poll a' Dubh-Lustraigh, Leic Aird Chúl na hUacha, Roisín Choimhthigh. They conjured up a world far removed from all the tedious routines of civilisation where I could be alone with rocks, sky and sea. Fishing in these places was essentially a solitary activity, a surrendering to an enclosed world of nature and its tranquillising sights and sounds, which demanded an emptying of the self and an escape from the restless, fault-finding mind. Sometimes Patrick and I would fish side by side for over an hour without exchanging as much as a word, each of us lost in the peace of slowly changing skies and the back-and-forth movement of windswept water. Sometimes I found myself on the edge of a trance, only to be awakened by the scream of a seagull wheeling or the sight of a cormorant flying low over the water to Doonalt.

My favourite places were Skelpoona and Poll a' Dubh-Lustraigh, two coves that are as different as chalk and cheese. Skelpoona, the more picturesque of the two, is open to the west, where it faces the long heave of the broad Atlantic, and is reasonably sheltered from north and south. Poll a' Dubh-Lustraigh, facing southwest, looks across directly at the Doonalt coast and is sheltered from the north and northwest. Narrower, more enclosed and secluded than Skelpoona, it is not the kind of place in which you would expect to find a tourist picnicking. To get to the fishing place, you climb down a steep bank and make your way between tall grey rocks to the edge of the water. The sound of the sea is quite different in both places. In Skelpoona the waves tend to wash with a fairly regular beat whereas in Poll a' Dubh-Lustraigh they often make a sudden plunging sound as if stumbling about blindly in a cave of echoes. If you are the type of person who is easily lulled by the polyphonic music of the sea, you would fall asleep sooner in Skelpoona. I never fell asleep in either place, but some of the happiest hours of my life have been spent in them. Whenever I went to them on my own, the outlandish shapes of cliff and cave mouth often inspired in me an eerie sense of desolation and sometimes a feeling of being in uncharted territory as light faded and darkness began to fall. At such moments I would have found it difficult to look all round and say, 'I know these cliffs. They are what they are, nothing more.'

One Sunday afternoon Patrick took his son Jamie and me to Carraig na nIolar under the Tower, which involved a tortuous climb down the cliff face to an anvil-like rock below, where we set about fishing byan or ballan with crab bait. The afternoon was gloriously serene with a light sea breeze to cool our faces. What struck me at once was the sheer breadth of the scene. It would require four eyes, two in front and one above each ear, to take it all in at a glance. Behind us was the towering cliff with a clutch of black rocks to the left and a gable-shaped sea stack to the right, while the Atlantic lay before us like an open prairie stretching to the bright horizon. Visually, it was so overpowering that the business of fishing seemed an unworthy preoccupation.

Another time Patrick and I went to the Círín on the Doonalt side of the bay to fish glassan or saithe. We left Garveross shortly after midnight and climbed down the bank in the dark, thinking that we might take up our positions before anyone else arrived. A few stars were trying to break through thin cloud, but I could barely make out the rock beneath my feet. When we had become accustomed to our surroundings, we began to fish in the belief that a glassan might spot a fly where a human eye would not.

'There's a man below on the neb,' Patrick said after a while.

I turned and looked but all I could see was a curtain of darkness. As the first shafts of dawn appeared in the sky to the east, we heard the flapping of a fish tail farther down the inlet.

'What did I tell you? He's caught one. We'll be in the thick of it before we know where we are.'

He hadn't quite finished the sentence before he had hooked a glassan and I had hooked another. I had never experienced such take. It was just a matter of casting, hooking, and unhooking. We kept at it as dawn spread across the sky and the outlines of the dark rocks around us became visible. I was so intent on fishing that I barely noticed the man on the neb, Roddy McGinley, a remote relation of my own. As soon as the sunlight hit the water, the glassan vanished. As Patrick said, we could spend the rest of the day without getting as much as a nibble. We couldn't complain, however. Our bags were so full that we had to split the catch and make two journeys up the bank to the top. Patrick had caught four score and I had caught just over two. Roddy didn't give us the satisfaction of counting his catch but to judge by the size of his bag, he must have caught about three score. I was surprised to find myself in third place. It seemed to me that I hadn't wasted a second. I could hardly believe that Patrick had caught two for every one of mine.

Patrick was an amusing and imaginative conversationalist. He had a good ear for dialogue, and in telling a story he had an unerring instinct for what to put in and what to leave out. Listening to him, I often felt that I could see the events taking place before my eyes, purely as a result of a single well-chosen word or phrase. He was never short of a subject, and no matter what subject I brought up, he was willing to talk about it. In conversation we both derived great pleasure from finding the right word to suit the occasion, and if we couldn't find a suitable word in English, we'd be sure to find an Irish alternative.

He used to read the odd book for relaxation after his day's work was done. He was particularly fond of books about the outdoor life, fishing and the sea. He was taken with the descriptions of fishing in Hemingway's short stories and novels but he always said that the book he enjoyed most was *Moby-Dick*. We were both captivated by Captain Ahab's ungovernable obsession with the white whale and the way its jaws had reaped away his leg 'as if it were no more than a blade of grass in the field'. We had many long discussions about Ahab on the way to and from fishing. However, I was much younger and less experienced than Patrick, and at seventeen I was impatient with Melville's long 'digressions': I simply wanted him to get on with the story. Nevertheless, the digressions provided us with much fascinating lore about whales. Melville is really a poet who chose to write novels and stories, and his book is full of haunting images that refuse to let go of the reader. 'Is it not curious,' he asks in a typical sentence, 'that so vast a being as the whale should see the world through so small an eye, and hear the thunder through an ear which is smaller than a hare's?'

What neither of us could understand was why a sperm whale's eyes are located at each side of its head corresponding to the position of the human ears. Does the whale therefore see two different pictures, one to the right and one to the left, while most animals, including humans, see only the view before them? As the whale can't see an object directly in front of him, we wondered if a courageous harpooner could row a small boat right up to its snout without being spotted by his quarry. We enjoyed speculating on what life would be like for humans if our eyes were positioned to the side of our heads above our ears. Would we learn to coordinate both views to form one picture in the mind, and what would we deduce from seeing two different views simultaneously?

Perhaps because I have revisited it many times since then, *Moby-Dick* has become one of my favourite novels, not least because there is no other novel remotely like it. It is a literary symphony, full of the most startling descriptions and wonderful metaphysical speculation. I shall never forget the image of the white whale surfacing with a 'tall but shattered pole of a recent lance' projecting from its back and a sea bird perched upon it. Perhaps the most memorable image of all is that of the *Pequod*, laden with fire on a dark night, looking like 'the material counterpart of her monomaniac commander's soul', as the harpooners stoke the flames and the whale oil bubbles in the cauldrons. No matter where I am as I reread *Moby-Dick*, I think of Garveross and the evenings Patrick and I spent fishing in Skelpoona.

Another of Patrick's favourite books was Hemingway's *The Old Man and the Sea*. For me the story of Santiago, the old fisherman who caught an 18-foot marlin only to have it destroyed by the voracious sharks of the Caribbean, represented man's unavailing struggle against nature, a struggle that must inevitably result in man's defeat. What caught Patrick's interest was the old man's courage, and what he said to himself alone in the boat with his mutilated fish: 'But man is not made for defeat. A man can be destroyed but not defeated.' We discussed the book many times on our fishing expeditions, comparing Santiago with Ahab and speculating on what they would have to say to each other if they met. Patrick reckoned that they were both hewn from the same rock, whereas I felt that Santiago would have seen Ahab as a madman. We both agreed on one thing: that we would never forget the old man's memory of lions in the evening playing like young cats on a beach in Africa.

The books that I read during the long summer holidays from boarding school and university have remained with me ever since. Some are now more than slightly foxed and some are falling apart from much rereading. No longer the books I first read, they seem to have grown in import with the years, keeping pace with the complications and changes in my own wayward life. I suppose that is one definition of a classic, a book that is with you always, a book that is forever new. Now I look at them on the shelf in my study and wonder what if anything they have in common: *Moby-Dick*, *Victory*, *The Sound and the Fury*, *The Return of the Native*. I am not a literary critic, nor is it my business to seek correspondences and abstract patterns. For me it is enough that these precious books have become part of my waking and dreaming life.

When I now go back to Glen on holiday, I make sure to go over to Skelpoona and sit on the slope above Leic na Mágach looking down. Usually, there is not a soul around to distract me. I look at the splintered shoulder of Glen Head to the right and the dark mouth of Úig a' Chogaidh to the left. I think mainly about the past, never about the present or future. On a good day I could spend hours there. Like a great medieval cathedral, it is a place of descending peace, of spiritual renewal, a place where the expectations and judgements of the go-getting world do not matter.

29

University

I put in some solid work for the Leaving Certificate during my final year at St Enda's because I knew that my only hope of escaping the teachers' training college was to win a university scholarship. After the exam I went home and waited. I helped my father with the mowing during the day and went fishing with my uncle in the evenings. I read little, pleased to be able to turn my back on books for a month or two. In early August I had a letter from the Department of Education letting me know that I had won a six-year scholarship to Galway University. It would pay £150 a year, which would cover the cost of lodgings and books with a few pounds left over for pocket money. I was overjoyed. I celebrated by sending off to Jonathan Cape for *The First Forty-Nine Stories* by Ernest Hemingway, a book that has remained with me ever since. It contains some of my favourite short stories, which I have read again and again over the years.

Before leaving home I had the benefit of a few words of advice from my father. First, he told me that he'd always stood on his own two feet and never owed any man a penny. Next, he told me not to trust appearances. Only he didn't put it like that. He said, '*Is iomaí curca aerach ur cheann gan staidéar*', which in English is to say that there's many a foolish head with a fancy hat. Lastly, he told me that Master Byrne, his old teacher, used to say, 'Beware the man of one book.' Then he smiled and said that when I came back I'd be able to tell him if old Master Byrne was right. I had no difficulty with the first two pieces of wisdom, but I was puzzled by the third. Surely, the whole point of going to university was to meet men of many books. Now, having spent the best part of my life working with university men of one fixed perspective, I think that the man of one book is all around us. Even some of the most intelligent men I know see life through a keyhole. They see whatever is set before them and simply lack the imagination to question the basis of their misplaced certitude.

I travelled to Galway by bus, and on a lovely October morning queued in the quad outside the Registrar's office in the company of the other freshers. When I had registered, a tall, distinguished-looking priest shook my hand in welcome. He had untidy white hair and black eyebrows with strong, craggy features as if his weathered head had been carved from a block of granite. I had seen pictures of him in the newspapers from time to time, and like most other students of that period I had learnt 'Valparaiso', one of his Irish poems, at school. He was Monsignor Pádraig de Brún, president of the university. I soon discovered that I would not be seeing much of him. The next time I met him formally was on conferring day three years later when he shook my hand again and presented me with my scroll.

Monsignor de Brún was a linguist and mathematician. A scholar to his fingertips, he seemed absorbed in his work to the exclusion of almost everything else. He carried a stick and walked with his eye on some invisible object in the far distance, as if he never noticed anyone or anything below eye-level. As you might expect, he was remote from the lives of us students. We were convinced that if ever he should notice one of us by some mischance, he would have no idea what to say.

We respected him as a scholar with an international reputation. He had translated Homer's *Odyssey* into Irish, and literary and scientific works from French, German and Latin. We saw him as a figure of legend, the kind of man who inspired anecdotes that reached us from the lips of the professors and lecturers. We did not greatly mind that some of them could have been apocryphal. Judged solely by what we knew of him, they all had the stamp of verisimilitude.

He had a name for pithy summation, and his reputed description of the Irish midlands as the Sodomy Belt gave rise to much speculation among the more imaginative of his students. To begin with we wondered if this particular *aperçu* was based on personal experience, if perhaps he'd been hearing confessions in Tullamore, Port Laoise or Abbeyleix. We had no way of checking its accuracy, since none of us had first-hand experience of the place. All we knew was that the midlands were flat farming country, noted above all else for its well-shaped heifers and bullocks. So what did he mean by sodomy? Was it bestiality with bullocks? In our eagerness to find an answer to the question, we overlooked the possibility that the description might have been made up by some mischievous student. We were too callow to know that Monsignor de Brún had the knack of inspiring a folklore and mythology all his own.

Having got over my encounter with the Monsignor, I went to my first English lecture, not knowing what to expect. I found myself listening to a short bald man of about sixty who looked rather crumpled and spoke in a deeply resonant voice that carried to the back of the room. At first sight he did not seem to be the kind of man whose soul was attuned to what I imagined must be the rarefied atmosphere on the higher slopes of Parnassus. He was Professor Jeremiah Murphy.

'To any action there is always an opposite and equal reaction,' he announced with an air of lofty seriousness. Next he told us that the reaction against classicism, which represents a preponderance of the intellectual, resulted in romanticism, which is largely a preponderance of the emotional. I thought I had misheard until I glanced at the notebook of the little nun who was sitting next to me and had taken down the sentence as spoken in her neat italic hand. When he added that a period of romanticism tends to follow a period of classicism and vice versa, I began to wonder if I had made a terrible mistake in choosing to read English. I hadn't heard anything quite so scientific, so cut and dried, from my English master in St Enda's.

The lecture that followed was discursive in the extreme, an excellent example of the Joycean stream of consciousness in academe. He glanced briefly at Greek tragedy, the GAA ban on soccer and rugby, the effect of the Elizabethan stage on the structure of Shakespeare's plays, the Irish Censorship Board, *Lyrical Ballads*, Milton's use of the caesura, mystery plays, morality plays, and the little-known fact that Irish writers who cross themselves rather than bless themselves are writing for the English market. He didn't go so far as to name names but I could tell from the glint in his eye that he had a few celebrated ones up his sleeve. By the end of the lecture I had learnt that Professor Murphy saw himself as a character. The air of seriousness with which he had begun his lecture was merely intended to deceive the uninitiated. Just as we all thought that he had run out of steam, he fired a parting shot that floored most of us. Almost as an afterthought he told us that the first principle of literary criticism is that nothing comes out of a work of art that hasn't gone into it, a truth he explained with the observation that 'more people never got off a train than had got on it'. Two serious-looking students in front of me looked doubtfully at each other, put down their pens, and closed their note-books. But I knew that I had at last found a teacher whose modes of reasoning I could appreciate. I was going to enjoy reading English. I was hooked.

On the way out of the lecture hall I spoke to a girl from Donegal, who told me that one such lecture was enough, and she was going to switch to French. I tried to persuade her to stay with Murphy, to make her see the comedian under the professorial gown, but she had already made up her mind. I do not know whether there were any other students at that lecture who felt the urge to switch to a safer subject. In the weeks that followed, how-ever, I got the impression that those of us who remained had come to appreciate our professor and were no longer merely reading a subject for an exam: we had joined a rather exclusive club as well.

Murphy was a Corkman who had spent the earlier part of his career teaching in secondary schools before becoming professor at Galway in 1933. His main aca-demic interest was Anglo-Saxon, and he had got his PhD for translating the *Anglo-Saxon Chronicle* into Munster Irish. He was not a brilliant scholar: he had done no orig-inal research and had published no substantial work of criticism. Instead he devoted his spare time to the College Boat Club, the Galway Literary Society, and Galway's Irish theatre *An Taibhdhearc*, for which he had written plays in Irish. Malicious rumour had it that he had been dropped from the cast on one occasion for failing to learn his lines.

I attended Murphy's lectures for three years with an increasing sense of amused disbelief. Even after three years his jokes had not begun to pall. Rather, they had a quality of absurdity that became funnier with familiarity. He obviously enjoyed teaching. He loved his audience, and we all felt affection for him, largely because we never knew what to expect next. One minute he would quote liberally to demonstrate how the variation of stress in the blank verse of *King Lear* contributes to the dramatic effect of the tragedy. A minute later would find him observing that the Shakespearean critic Edward Dowden, like Shakespeare himself, had the good fortune to go bald in the right place. If the more solemn students now and again longed for a mouthful of eager air from what Cyril Connolly called 'the chilly snows of Ben Leavis', they did not say so. We all joined in the general sense of amused appreciation and in the common desire to perfect our mimicry of Murphy's mannerisms and tricks of intonation.

Murphy confined himself mainly to Anglo-Saxon, Middle English, and English drama up to the time of Sheridan. He left poetry and the novel in the more conventional hands of his assistant Patrick Diskin, a tall, shy man in his early forties who, unlike Murphy, lectured from notes while smoking one cigarette after another. Diskin looked more literary than Murphy, and he contributed to journals such as *Notes and Queries*, his main interest being Anglo-Irish literature in the nineteenth and early twentieth centuries. In his lectures he kept strictly to the course, and for that reason his notes were much appreciated by those students who were reading English merely to pass their degree exams.

Diskin rarely revealed his own opinion of the texts that Murphy had decreed we should study. He saw himself as a dispassionate reporter on the continuing proceedings of a literary law court. His method was to give the conflicting arguments of different critics as they made the case for and against the defendant, being content to leave any summing-up or final judgment to us students. Some of us felt flattered while others appreciated his sense of delicacy, but, understandably perhaps, there were a few 'accountants' among us who would have valued a touch of Leavisian finality or at least something less indeterminate.

At all times I could see that Diskin was enjoying himself, though I suspected that he found his keenest enjoyment in what critics said about texts rather than in the texts themselves. Sometimes he would smile as he delivered a quotation, as if inviting us to acknowledge the absurdity of it all, or perhaps hinting at a literary jest that regrettably he could not share with us. I remember him looking out of the window on a gusty March morning, quoting from Wordsworth's 'Michael', "And never lifted up a single stone", then saying with a mysterious smile, 'Matthew Arnold praised that line.' I was half-expecting a counter-quote from some plebeian twentieth-century critic condemning Arnold as a silly old fart but none was forthcoming. I wondered if perhaps Diskin had in mind some bawdy literary joke that would have been inappropriate to share with the convent-educated ladies, and after the lecture I asked him for the reference so that I could look it up for myself. To my surprise he did not refer to his notes but quoted from memory the relevant sentence from Arnold's *Essays in Criticism*: "There is nothing subtle in it, no heightening, no study of poetic style, strictly so-called, at all; yet it is expression of the highest and most truly expressive kind."

It all sounded highly Arnoldian and I was none the wiser as to why he had smiled. I felt that I must be treading hallowed ground, or perhaps intruding on some private joke that had nothing to do with either Wordsworth or Arnold, and therefore none of my immediate business. I sensed that the house of literature is a house of many mansions and that having the entrée to one does not guarantee an entrée to any other. I noted that Diskin looked distinctly uncomfortable. Clearly, in my search for literary bawdy, I had taken a wrong turning. I decided not to trouble him again.

I was expected to read two subjects for my degree. The other subject I chose was Irish. At St Enda's I had an excellent teacher of Irish in Charlie Boyle. At the end of my four years there, I was a fluent Irish speaker and I was widely read in contemporary Irish literature. After such a beginning perhaps it is not surprising that I found the degree course in Irish at UCG uninspiring. The professors and lecturers were scholarly and serious about their subject, but their interest seemed to me to be entirely linguistic and philological as opposed to literary.

The course in Modern Irish consisted mainly of bardic syllabic poetry from the thirteenth to the seventeenth centuries. The accent was entirely on language, semantics and metrics, with little account taken of the historical conditions and the lives and personalities of the poets who produced the work. For all we gleaned from our professor, the works under consideration could have been written in the same period and by the same poet. After three years of study most graduates would not have recognised a poem by Gofraigh Fionn Ó Dálaigh (d.1387) from one by Tadhg Dall Ó hUiginn (d.1591) on internal evidence only.

Surprisingly, it was possible to get a degree in Irish without having a detailed knowledge of the work of any twentieth-century author, though there were several then alive and writing, including Máirtín Ó Cadhain, whose work would have richly merited sustained textual analysis and literary appraisal. Admittedly, we read some of Ó Cadhain's novels and short stories but not as works of literature. At all times the focus was on the language at its lexical, grammatical and semantic levels. As I look back, it now seems inexplicable that Ó Cadhain's major work *Cré na Cille*, published in 1948, was not among the texts that were considered by the professor of Modern Irish to merit closer analytical attention. Irish was being taught as a dead language like Latin, which seemed strange to me, since I had spent a large part of my life speaking it.

An important section of the course consisted of the study of Classical Old Irish and in particular the Ulster epic *Táin Bó Cuailnge* (Cattle Raid of Cooley), dating from the eighth century. It is a unique and archetypal literary work, from whose shadow many other works were later to crawl into the sunlight. Surprisingly, we did not study it as such. Instead we engaged in what seemed an arid exercise in semantics and philology. Judging solely by the tenor of the lectures I attended, I often felt that it had no more relevance to the Irish literature I knew than the *Ramayana* or the *Mahabharata*. Surprisingly, we learned little about early Irish lyric poetry, which contains some of the loveliest nature poetry I have come across in a lifetime of reading. I remember the Professor of Old Irish writing out a quatrain on the blackboard, which I give here with a translation that understandably fails to capture the complex music of the original:

Och, a *luin*, is *buide* duit
Cáit sa *muine* a *fuil* do net
A *díthreabaig* nad *clind cloc*
Is *bind boc síthamail t'fet*

Ah, blackbird, it is well for you
wherever in the thicket be your nest:
hermit that rings no bell,
sweet, soft, peaceful is your whistle

The subject spoke directly to the countryman in me, just as the imagery and beauty of language spoke to the student of literature, yet all our professor had to say was that it exemplified the triumph of rhyme over rhythm in the development of Old Irish poetry. I waited in vain for even one sentence that might consider why these ancient words ring so fresh and why the total effect is so unexpected, so arresting. Though Matthew Arnold can hardly be judged an authority on Old Irish, I found more intellectual sustenance in his *Study of Celtic Literature* than in all the lectures I attended in Galway on the subject. Our professors, alas, had got their doctorates for research work on source material, and were scholars rather than critics. They may have been skilled in collating and editing texts and in determining their provenance, but they seemed to me to have little instinct for the beauty of language or literary structure and evaluation.

At the end of my stint I realised that the knowledge I had gleaned from my Irish studies would only be of use if I were to follow in the footsteps of my professors and devote myself to research with a view to making a career in academia. I was no better equipped for creative work in the language or enjoyment of the works that were then being written and published. I could not help feeling that the time I had devoted to the study of Old Irish in particular could have been put to more creative use.

Still, I enjoyed my four years at university. After the confinement of boarding school, I gloried in the freedom of going here and there and skipping lectures I did not value. Contrary to my expectations, most of the lectures I attended were dull beyond belief, providing little in the way of intellectual enlargement. Our professors bombarded us with facts and little or no analysis to bind them together. Perhaps we students of the humanities were unlucky in our teachers, middle-aged men and women who were more noted for their mastery of historical vocabulary and its development than their intimacy with the world of ideas then current. The medical and science students were more fortunate. Some of their professors and lecturers were distinguished in their fields and more open to new thinking. Consequently, I found my mental awakening not in the lecture hall but in discussions with the medical and science students with whom I shared digs. Above all, I enjoyed their ribald humour and irreverent commentary on things I had hitherto seen as sacrosanct. If the purpose of a university is to encourage independence of thought and release young minds from the fetters of preconception, then our teachers failed us miserably. They themselves seemed dyed in the wool of convention and conformity. Intellectual daring was an alien concept in the ultra-Catholic Ireland of the 1950s.

That said, I suppose I should not complain. After all, I was among the privileged few. In the Ireland of that time a university education was open only to those whose parents could pay the fees and the cost of lodgings and subsistence. I was there because I was lucky enough to have won a scholarship, a fact that fostered an early sense of personal responsibility. I could not afford to indulge myself in the manner of the 'gentlemen students'. It was not a temptation I had to struggle hard to resist; I was a serious young man, resolute in the pursuit of knowledge for its own sake.

For me the most creative part of the university year was the long summer vacation. It was an opportunity to come down to earth, to talk to farmers and fishermen, and engage in the daily routine of work and leisure. Throughout my childhood much of the local life had remained a mystery to me, a matter of hints gleaned from snatches of adult conversations overheard. I had a vivid imagination, though: all I needed was one brick to build a castle. Much of the time my imaginings had been wide of the mark, a fact that was revealed to me in the next over-heard snatch of conversation. It all kept my mind from going stale, however, imagining and re-imagining and never arriving at a definitive picture.

The holidays from university provided an opportunity to complete the jigsaw. For the first few days at home I used to feel like a man with two heads: one stuffed with the local lore and the other with book learning that seemed far removed from the life around me. Talking to my neighbours, I would suppress my book learning and become one of them, but in my mind one question returned to haunt: which of the two was the real head? I would ask myself where my true centre lay, and invariably tell myself that it was to be found neither at home nor at university but on a continent I had yet to explore. My centre at that time was an Empty Quarter of featureless sand. I was camping here and there on the periphery, establishing makeshift stations to meet the requirements of the various situations in which I found myself. Nothing could be taken for granted; everything had to be thought out afresh. I was like a man who had been condemned to reinvent the wheel afresh every morning.

During the holidays Uncle Patrick was an unfailing source of reassuring normality. I was fond of him and admired in particular his self-possession and easygoing ways. I don't think I ever saw him flustered. He had all the gifts that I myself lacked. He was an amusing raconteur and a good singer, and, like my mother, he was utterly at ease in the world. Above all, he was good company, never short of a pithy comment or a story to enlarge an occasion. If he found me too serious, he pretended not to notice; and if he thought I was talking nonsense, he would be sure to cap my view with something even more out-landish and absurd. I realise now that he was at pains to make me see the funny side of life. When I told him one evening that the best view of Screig Beefan was the one from Ceann a' Deáin below his house, he thought for a moment and said, 'What do you think of when you look at it?'

'I think it might be about to say something.'

'Well, I've been looking at it for fifty years and it hasn't said a word to me yet. But if it did decide to speak, I think I'd listen.' He took off his cap, scratched his head, and laughed.

I knew what he meant. Screig Beefan has presence. It has authority, the gift of commanding attention. It is not to be cross-examined. When I told him that, he looked doubtful. 'Now, I think, you could be going a bit far,' he said. As I look back, I realise that talking and listening to my uncle was a vital part of my education. He was full of ideas and stories that were new to me. In talking to him I was matching my wit against his, and in listening to him I was immersing myself in the local culture and in things that seemed richer in interest than anything my professors had to tell me. My indebtedness to him did not become apparent to me until many years later when I began writing about the glen.

30

My Mother's Death

Towards the end of the 1957 summer term, as I was revising for the B.Comm degree exam, a car I thought I should recognise pulled up outside the window. Shortly after, a medical student with whom I shared lodgings came into the room and told me to brace myself for bad news.

'What's happened?' I asked.

'I'm sorry,' he said. 'It's your mother.'

He accompanied me out to the waiting car, which I recognised as my aunt's. In it were two men from Glen, one of whom was my mother's first cousin. Immediately I saw the look on his face, I knew that she was dead.

'She was taken to hospital last week,' he said. 'She didn't come through the operation.'

When I was home at Easter, she seemed her usual carefree and amusing self. In the weeks after I returned to university, however, she had complained of headaches and the doctor sent her to Dublin for tests. The consultant surgeon said that she had a brain tumour and he recommended an immediate operation.

I sat in the back of the car as we drove home through Tuam, Ballyhaunis, Charlestown, Tobercurry and Sligo. They were towns I had been through many times before. This time I was barely aware of them. Unseeingly, I looked out at fields, stone walls, farm buildings and hedges, and I listened from time to time to the muted conversation of my neighbours. I couldn't believe that my mother was dead. She was still quite young, only fifty-four, and she'd always seemed so full of life and fun. I was pleased that we didn't stop on the way. I simply wanted to get home.

The house was full of people who had come to offer their sympathy. The body arrived in a coffin and my father helped to carry it into the house for waking. He looked worn and abstracted, and he seemed to have aged in the month that had elapsed since Easter. While he shook my hand, we did not say much because words seemed alien and intrusive. For the first time in my life I felt sorry for him. I had never before seen him as yet another ordinary man with ordinary needs and feelings like myself.

I went into the bedroom where the coffin lay on the bed. On a small table a blessed candle burned on either side of a silver crucifix. I was alone in the room with my mother. She did not look like my mother, she looked more like a nun in a wimple because her black hair was covered where the surgeon had made an incision. I touched her cheek. It was firm and cold, the colour of a wax candle. I felt her foot through the shroud, seeking the bunion for confirmation. I bent down over the coffin and kissed her forehead. I couldn't remember ever having kissed her before.

People from all over the glen were coming and going. I met people I hadn't seen since before I went to boarding school. Some were practised at offering sympathy and uttering the right words and phrases. Others spoke with awkward gravity, as if acknowledging that silence would have suited best. That was also my feeling. I found that I had more in common with those who were tongue-tied. I went to bed at three and woke again before six. I had been dreaming of a summer day on the Brae as my father made hand-cocks and my mother gathered in the hay. It was a happy dream, full of warmth and sunlight. When I woke, I could not believe that the grey light of morning was real. My gut felt tightly knotted and there was a dull pain behind my eyes. I tried to recapture the day in my dream but that day and this most difficult of mornings were two separate worlds and there was no commuting between them.

After the funeral I went back to Galway to take the B.Comm exam. I did the papers on economics, banking and accountancy with all the personal involvement of a robot. I was surprised when I got a first but it gave me no pleasure. I felt that someone else had done the papers on my behalf. I went home for the summer to help my father on the farm and to prepare for the B.A. degree exam in September. Though there were seven of us, counting my father and Auntie Kate, the house seemed empty and cheerless. The only time I felt at ease was working out of doors.

The June weather was fine, and my father and I spent the days on the bog stacking turf. I gathered the dry sods in heaps with a wheelbarrow while my father did the building. He worked solidly, pausing only now and again to charge and light his pipe. When each stack was finished, we cut scraws and placed them on top to keep out the rain. We also placed scraws at the corners as a protection against scratching sheep. When we talked, it was mainly about the work, though work was not on our minds. We had our midday meal at one. I had bread and cheese. My father who didn't eat cheese had two hard-boiled eggs instead. When my mother was alive, she used to bring us a lunch of fish and potatoes. One day, as we ate, I looked over my shoulder, remembering how her dark head was the first thing to appear as she came up the slope.

'You'd think you should see her forehead rising above Ailt a' Mhianaigh,' my father said.

'Curiously, I was thinking the same thing.'

'There was nothing any of us could do for her,' he said half to himself. 'The surgeon said that if she had come out of the operation alive, she would have been a vegetable. It was a cruel sentence. Maybe it's as well this way.'

'She was looking fine when I was home for Easter.'

'She had splitting headaches. She didn't want anyone to tell you because of your exams. Strangely, she never looked better, she was putting on weight.'

There were so many questions I wanted to ask him. Had they known each other as children at Cashel School? Had they been going out together before she went to America? What did she look like when she came back? I was about to speak but I couldn't find the right words to begin.

'If tomorrow is good, we'll finish the stacking,' he said.

The moment had passed. We had finished eating. He was filling his pipe and I did not wish to intrude on his grief. Things were difficult enough for him without subjecting him to unnecessary cross-examination.

Halfway through the afternoon I walked down within sight of a little corner of shimmering sea and the white lighthouse of Rathlin O'Birne Island in the distance. I sat on the heathery slope looking down at the water of the lough below and across at blue-grey Slieve League in the distance, rising solidly behind a brownish green hillock. I wondered if there was any point from which you could look at the twin loughs simultaneously as they were separated by a rocky height. The more easterly of the two was called Loch an Óir (the Loch of Gold) and the other Loch an Airgid (the Loch of Silver). When I was a boy, my father told me that the Vikings had dumped their gold in Loch an Óir and their silver in Loch an Airgid while fleeing from the Irish to their ships in Doonalt. I had asked him if anyone had ever tried to recover the treasure, thinking that he might have another story to tell.

'You'd be a long time searching,' was his laconic reply.

Fond of these loughs, I rarely missed an opportunity of going down the slope to have a look at them. I particularly liked to watch wild duck feeding and the wind ruffling the surface of the water. On rough days I would walk round the edge, listening to the fitful music of the waves plopping against the shore. Today there was no wind and no wild duck either. My father must have taken my mother to see these loughs when she first came to Killaned, but she'd never said anything about them. She'd never talked about nature or scenery, though she must have seen plenty of it as a girl growing up in Garveross. She derived her enjoyment in life from observing and listening to people and from recounting what they had to say. I walked back up the slope to where my father was putting the finishing touches to a stack, which looked as if it had been built not from turf but from real bricks.

'You went sight-seeing?' he smiled.

'I went down to the loughs, thinking I might see trout feeding.'

'And did you?'

'Nothing doing. Not a ripple.'

'I could have told you that, if you'd said where you were going.'

'It wouldn't have mattered. I went for the walk there and back.'

That was typical of my father. He was not a man who wasted time on entertainment, particularly if there was work to be done.

When we'd finished the last stack, he went round the others to make sure the mountain sheep had not disturbed his handiwork. The bog looked clean and tidy. Where there had been a sea of black footings, there was now an uncluttered expanse with not a clod to be seen on the ground. The turf stacks looked like artefacts from a long-forgotten civilisation, and the bog face, bearing the marks of the slane, could have been a frieze of ogamic inscriptions. Everything was as it should be. I was reminded of Swift's definition of style. 'Proper words in proper places.' What we had created was in its own way as stylish.

'It will do,' my father said. 'Now we can forget all about it until next year.'

I could see that he was pleased. There was nothing he liked better than work done to perfection.

After the turf stacking we had a few weeks of relaxation before it was time to sharpen our scythes for the harvest. I didn't spend the days in idleness, and devoted the afternoons to study in the bedroom where no one came to disturb me. But I wasn't in a mood for study. Even poems, plays and novels I knew I should enjoy had lost their savour. I remember rereading Vanbrugh's *The Relapse* and thinking that both Lord Foppington and Sir Tunbelly Clumsey were monstrously tedious creations. The only subject I could study with any enthusiasm was Anglo-Saxon, because the worlds of *Beowulf* and the *Chronicle* had no associations with any world I had known or was ever likely to. Perhaps it is not surprising that Anglo-Saxon turned out to be my best paper when I came to sit the exam.

Whenever the weather was fine, I went fishing with Uncle Patrick in the evenings. If I'd read a good play or novel during the day, I'd tell him the story, and sometimes I would try to embellish it, if only to keep the spark of imagination from dying. More often than not he'd have something pungent or amusing to say, and for that I was grateful because it helped me to keep things in perspective. Most evenings I'd come home with at least one pollock, and my sister Tina would cook it for supper. It was the best way to eat fish, cooked within a few hours of being caught, while it still retained its delicate flavour.

One evening in early September I went over to Garveross only to find that Patrick had gone to a wake. I took my fishing rod from under the eave and set off along the road alone. Normally, Patrick would decide where we should go, having considered the state of the tide and the way the wind was blowing. On this particular evening the tide was turning to fill and there was a stiff breeze from the north. I thought I might do worse than try for a pollock from Leic na Mágach in Skelpoona. It was easy to get to, and with cliffs on both sides it was a delightful place to spend the few hours left before sunset.

I fished steadily for an hour, using the tail of a fresh eel as a lure, without attracting as much as a nibble. Next I tried a homemade fly but it didn't make a ha'porth of difference. It was as if the sea was fishless and I was slashing empty water. There was still time to go to another rock, possibly Poll a' Dubh-Lustraigh, which was more sequestered, but I was reluctant to leave Skelpoona as it was Patrick's favourite cove and I was half-expecting him to join me there. Looking around, it occurred to me that I was in a place of familial significance. My mother had known these rocks and coves as a girl. Her father and grandfather had fished thousands of times from the rock on which I was standing. It was a place of pilgrimage that had been sanctified by long frequentation, a place in which men fished sometimes for the pot and sometimes for the pure pleasure of being there.

As I fished, I kept an eye on the shoulder of Glen Head on my right, a rough-edged cliff of jagged rock that formed a bold outline against the sky in the west. One rock in particular, the Cloch Mhór, caught my eye. It seemed to be perched precariously on the slope of the bluff as if a child could dislodge it with one finger. The sun was hidden from view and the clouds in the west had taken on a golden tinge at the edges. When I looked again at the Cloch Mhór, I felt that I was seeing it for the first time. The whole cliff looked closer, larger and more formidable, each rock and stone rising out of its side with exaggerated definition, as if bathed in otherworldly light. I couldn't make out the direction the light was coming from — for all I knew it could have been coming from inside the cliff itself. It was as if I had been granted a vision of a universe in which even inanimate objects glowed with some arcane significance I could not begin to understand.

While I was still wondering what trick of science had caused this extraordinary transfiguration, the rod came alive in my hand. I was stuck in a pollock, and it went straight down, seeking the wrack at the base of the rock. I kept an even pressure on the line and watched the fish's strongly resisting rise to the surface. It was a good-sized pollock that seemed to have taken on the dark colour of the wrack itself. The hook was buried deep in its gullet and it took me at least a minute to dislodge it.

When I had finally put the flapping fish in my bag, I straightened and looked up at the cliff face only to find that it had reverted to its familiar, everyday self, and the clouds in the west had lost their golden tinge. The moment had fled while my back was turned, and I was left wondering what would have happened if the pollock had not taken my fly. I had been in Skelpoona many times but I had never before experienced such a moment of intensity and light, and I felt saddened by the thought that I might never experience it again. I kept looking at the cliff face, willing the moment of heightened sensation to return but it was not for me to command. With a disquieting sense of flatness and regret at being back in the world of everyday reality, I cast the line once again, hoping that another stray pollock might come in with the filling tide. I remained on the rock until dusk had fallen and I could barely see the movement of the white fly in the water. By the time I got back, Patrick had returned from the wake.

'How many did you catch?' he asked knowingly.

'One good-sized pollock.'

'Did any get away?'

'No, but I saw the strangest sunset ever in Skelpoona. It seemed to light up the rocks and it didn't cast any shadows.'

'It's a great place for sunsets. I must have seen hundreds and I never saw two that looked the same.'

I thought about describing this particular sunset just to find out if he'd ever seen anything like it but I was reluctant to make a fool of myself. How could I explain that I had been caught up in a world I had not seen before; it was not the sort of thing that words could convey with any accuracy, more like a reflection of a state of mind, a subjective experience on which it would be folly to dwell too closely. Alone on the way home, I leaned over the Minister's Bridge and looked down into the river. In the dark I could not see the water but I could hear it, and I began thinking about my mother. She had died before I'd had a chance to get to know her properly. There were a thousand things I'd never know, but now it seemed to me that I should be grateful for the things I did know because they were things I could build on. I took a deep breath, sensing that I was enclosed in the scent of the river. For the first time since her death I felt at peace.

31

The Job Problem

I graduated in the autumn of 1957 and immediately found myself wondering what to do next. Advertised jobs were few and far between in the Ireland of that time. The only job I seemed to be qualified for was teaching, and that was the last thing I wanted to do. Thus I began applying for trainee jobs in business while trying to work out how I could convince a practical businessman that a bookish theorist might be of some use to him. A job that attracted me most was one with a Galway merchant. If I got it, I could stay on in Galway and perhaps do a post-graduate course in my spare time.

I prepared for the interview by polishing my shoes and brushing my only suit. I was shown into a dusky room in which a tall, gaunt man sat behind a cluttered desk with a reading lamp at his elbow. I found my chair uncomfortable, which made me wonder if perhaps it was meant for mortification rather than relaxation. Instinctively, I drew it closer to the desk, into the circle of light. The interviewer had a long face, straight, thin lips and a sandy-red smudge for a moustache. Placing his pipe in a polished wood ashtray, he told me that he was looking for a graduate who would do a bit of everything at first and in time get to know the business from bottom to top with a view to succeeding him as sales manager. Good people were hard to find, he said. He had had thirty odd applications, not counting those from time-wasters who were only chancing their arm. Out of the thirty, he was seeing six of the most promising candidates. I assumed that this was his way of telling me that jobs didn't grow on trees.

'We sell timber among other things. When you think of timber, what comes to mind?' He picked up a pen. As he began doodling, I wondered if he was trying to distract me.

'Trees.' I resisted the temptation to quote Long John Silver's 'Shiver my timbers!'

'Anything else?'

'A timber yard,' I replied truthfully and hopefully.

'If you were asked by a customer to explain the difference between hardwood and softwood, what would you say?'

'One is hard and the other is soft,' I said, realising too late that it must be a trick question.

'That's what most people think. Balsa is a hardwood but it's softer than pitch-pine.'

'The hardwoods are heavier, perhaps?'

'No, the difference depends on the tree. Hardwoods are deciduous and softwoods are evergreen. Ah, the world of timber is fascinating. I've been buying and selling timber since I was seventeen, and it was only last week that I came across my first piece of vinhatico. There, have a look at it. Do you think you could sell it to a man who was bent on buying mahogany?'

'I'm sure I could.' I ran my forefinger over the roey grain. 'If I knew enough about both woods, I think I could convince him of the superiority of either for whatever purpose.'

'Knowledge, I'll grant you, has its uses. It might help you to know that vinhatico is also called Brazilian or yellow mahogany.'

Smiling, he retrieved the cube and replaced it in his desk drawer, making me wonder if he was playing a game of cat and mouse with me.

'What is your great ambition in life?' He began toying with the stem of his pipe.

'I'd like a career in business. That's why I took a degree in commerce.' I met his hooded gaze, hoping that he wouldn't see through my barefaced lie.

'You've also got a degree in literature. It's an odd combination.' There was a note of suspicion, or perhaps incomprehension, in his voice.

'I thought a literary degree might help me write better business letters,' I said lamely.

'Very good. When you looked at that piece of vinhatico, what was uppermost in your mind?'

Was this another trick question? Somehow I felt that everything depended on my answer. 'The colour and feel of it,' I replied.

'An artistic answer. You're not a poet by any chance?'

'No,' I replied truthfully.

'You didn't have a desire to sell vinhatico?'

'Not yet. It's something I'd obviously have, if I got the job.'

'I'll let you in on a secret. We've never sold any vinhatico here.'

He smiled again as he leant back in his chair and began telling me about the history of the company. As he spoke, his tongue clacked drily. After a few minutes I came to the conclusion that he loved to hear himself talk. I asked three or four routine questions about the job in order to give him ample opportunity to indulge his personality. Then I decided to say no more in case he might get the impression that it was I who was interviewing him. Finally, he got to his feet and extended a hand across the desk.

'You'll be hearing from us within a week.' His moustache spread thinly as he smiled.

Excited, I walked back to my lodgings. It was my first interview for a job, my first foray into the world of commerce. It didn't seem too daunting. After the idiosyncrasies of Professor Murphy's Middle English lectures, it was just staggeringly banal. I remembered that 'wood' as an adjective in Shakespeare meant 'mad', a thought that pleased me. I began thinking of the other wood, trying to conjure up literary associations. I came up with several about woods and trees but not one about wood itself. As I walked up Dominic Street, a string of words, precious as emeralds, dropped into my mind:

> *Under the greenwood tree*
> *Who loves to lie with me,*
> *And turn his merry note*
> *Unto the sweet bird's throat,*
> *Come hither, come hither, come hither…*

For a reason I could not explain, I had formed the impression that I was a strong candidate for the job. Goodbye Shakespeare. Goodbye Thomas Hardy. I saw the future, and it was timber-framed. I went back to Glen in high hopes and waited.

As we were gathering hay for a tramp-cock, my father asked me what I was planning to do with my life. I told him that I had applied for a job with a firm in Galway, and that I was waiting to hear from them. He pursed his lips and leaned on his hayfork, a sure sign that I'd said something very odd indeed.

'What would you be doing?'

'For the first six months I'd be on the road, getting to know about selling timber. After that I'd be given training for a job in management.'

'You went to a great deal of trouble in that case,' he said. 'You don't need a first-class degree to peddle wood.'

I couldn't help laughing. As my father had put it, 'peddling wood' sounded quite ridiculous.

'I've got to start somewhere,' I said.

'What are your friends doing about jobs?'

'Most of them are planning to teach when they get their teaching diploma.'

'At least teaching is reliable,' he said slowly.

I could see that he was puzzled and somewhat disappointed. I didn't tell him about vinhatico in case he should think me cuckoo. Neither did I tell him that, if he must know the truth, I didn't want a job, that what I really wanted was to spend my life reading great literature and possibly writing the odd slim volume here and there. He'd probably have told me that what I needed was a month or two rowing up and down the bay, fishing lobsters in wet weather in order to clear my mind of cobwebs. But he didn't have to say it. He had the knack of making me think his thoughts, so we built our tramp-cock and said no more.

A few days later I had a letter from the Galway merchant saying that he had offered the job to another applicant and thanking me profusely for my interest in the company. I waited for a few weeks, thinking that there might be other opportunities. My father was glad of the help. I thought I'd stay on until he had made the haystack, as I hadn't been home for 'the day of the stack' since I went to St Enda's seven years before.

Haymaking, more than any other work, depended on the weather. In a good summer it was a pleasure. In a wet one it was a depressing and heartbreaking experience. Understandably, haystack day was a special day, the culmination of two or three months of effort. Four or five neighbours would come to give a hand, each with his particular skills. Two would build while others forked. One would trim the loose hay and give the stack its final shape. There would be jokes, stories and light-hearted conversation, a drink before dinner and again before tea in the evening. It was all very relaxing and enjoyable, a day out of the usual run of days, a day for the whole townland.

In the weeks since I had come home, the weather had been showery and uncertain. My father listened to the forecast every night on the radio, as he waited for a suitable day. At last the forecast for the following morning was good but rain was expected in the afternoon. He said that we wouldn't go to bed, that we'd make a start on the stack as soon as the moon got up. We had our supper and every now and then he would go out to look at the sky. At last he came in and said that the clouds had cleared.

It was a night of moonlight and starlight with no breeze stirring. The neighbours' houses were in darkness. The only lights in the glen were the village streetlights and they seemed far away. My father had already prepared the stile of the stack by putting down a layer of dry heather. Next he shook some hay over the heather and trampled it. We took the ropes off the tramp-cocks in the haggard and started building. My father was in his element. He left me on the ground to pitch up the hay with a fork, which required more elbow grease than skill. It was pleasant work, all the more enjoyable since we were doing it in the middle of the night with everyone else in dreamland. Now and again he would ask me whether the stack was heavy on one side and I would rake down the loose hay while he waited. When he had reached the widest part, the *sceimheal* as we called it, I put up the ladder and he climbed down to have a look at his handiwork.

In the east the rim of a reddish sun had sliced through the haze over the hills. It was a lovely dawn, one that I shall always remember. In spite of the redness that is the shepherd's warning, it seemed to promise nothing but good weather. A wisp of grey smoke rose and curled over Paddy Johnny's chimney.

'The early birds are stirring,' my father said.

'Strange how we never heard the real birds and dawn chorus,' I remarked.

'I'm sure there was one. We were just too busy to notice.'

Paddy Johnny came out and stood in his doorway. He took off his cap and scratched his head, as if he couldn't believe his eyes. I suppose it was an unexpected sight, a haystack already half-made at six-thirty in the morning.

'It won't rain today,' my father said. 'We don't have to rush, we'll have breakfast now.'

When we'd eaten, I said to him that the two of us would easily finish the work before noon.

'Enough is enough. We won't overdo it,' he said. 'I'll ask a few of the neighbours to give us a hand with the thatching and roping.'

I couldn't help smiling, as I realised what was on his mind. The two of us could easily have finished it, but that was not what mattered. According to the time-honoured custom, the making of the stack was an occasion for the neighbours as well. It was a communal rite, and my father was not a man to break an ancient custom.

After a while two or three neighbours came, and within two hours the stack was finished.

'You must have been up early,' one of them said.

'Earlier than usual,' my father replied. 'I was half-expecting rain in the afternoon.'

It was to be my last haystack. A week later I went back to Galway because by then it had become apparent to me that it was the sensible thing to do. My scholarship, which was for six years, had another three to run. I had decided to start reading for an MA in English and at the same time take the Higher Diploma in Education, which would enable me to take up secondary teaching, if all else should fail.

After two or three chats with Professor Murphy I found myself working on a thesis concerning the humour of Henry Fielding while attending the H Dip lectures on the side. I had come to feel that, if nothing else, another year at university would give me time to think and possibly sort myself out. As it happened, I didn't enjoy myself as much as I had expected. My mother's death was still on my mind. No matter what I did, it was there in the background like low cloud pressing down.

To escape from myself I tried to make Fielding's preoccupations my own. My previous acquaintance with his work was through two of his novels, *Joseph Andrews* and *Tom Jones*, which I had greatly enjoyed for their sharp satire and robust humour. Now I found myself getting to grips with an extensive oeuvre, including plays, pamphlets and journalism, much of which related to what I saw as the ephemeral issues of his time. After six months I had come to realise that what I sought from literature would not be found in research and scholarship where I would be tied to one period or subject. Instead I would read whatever took my fancy, taking on a mixed cargo in every port with a view to becoming a writer myself.

By the time the summer term came round, however, I could no longer put off thinking about what I should do to keep myself. Some of my fellow students who were taking the H Dip in Ed had already got teaching jobs lined up for the beginning of the next school year, which was only three months away. A bright and lively girl whom I admired was going to teach with nuns in a convent school in a small midland town. Another was going to teach in Tullamore, which was noted more for its 'dew' than its cultural activities. It all seemed such a waste of intellect and talent, yet no one complained about the enormous littleness of life. I couldn't help feeling that I was out of step with everyone else — that perhaps I ought to think again. What I could not see at the time was that my study of literature had fostered expectations about life and my place in it that had no immediate hope of fulfilment.

After sitting the H Dip exam I went home for the summer. I mooned around the farm, wondering what I should do. Intoxicated by the ideal of self-cultivation, I was still reluctant to contemplate anything as mundane as teaching. I had become so intoxicated by the rarefied air on the higher slopes of Parnassus — my head stuffed with the plays of Marlowe, Shakespeare and Webster; the poetry of Chaucer, Milton, Wordsworth, Keats and Tennyson; and the novels of Jane Austen, Dickens, George Eliot and Thomas Hardy — that the foothills held no attraction. I told myself that the plays of Synge and O'Casey were seriously flawed, and that Joyce's *Ulysses* was grossly overrated, a mere omnium-gatherum of literary baubles. Nourished at university on a diet of prescriptive criticism, I was blind to the myriad possibilities cast up by the somersaulting imagination; the innumerable ways of seeing, feeling and thinking; and the manifold forms that artistic expression can take. Instead, I had become a willing victim of misplaced academic certitude.

To pass the time on wet days when I couldn't do any farm work, I began writing short stories. I gave what I thought was the best of them to my uncle, just to see what he'd say. He didn't take my efforts as seriously as I had hoped and told me that they weren't as good as the

Hemingway stories I had just lent him. I took his casual comment as serious criticism. I knew that I couldn't stay at home for the winter, sponging off my father and my aunt and writing short stories that would never see the light of day. There was nothing for it but to start looking for a job in teaching.

32

Teaching

My first two years as a secondary teacher were spent in a new school in Gweedore in the Donegal Gaeltacht. Gweedore is no more than fifty miles from Glen, yet no two parishes in the same county could be more dissimilar. Whereas Glen is a kind of womb enclosed between mountains, Gweedore is open country dominated by Errigal, a granite peak of classical beauty, whose scored sides on a clear day can be seen for miles from every direction. At that time Gweedore looked more prosperous than Glen. The bigger and better-appointed houses were mainly slate-roofed, whereas most of the Glen cottages were thatched. The Gweedore people were also more outward looking, possibly because they'd been exposed to more outside influences. But in spite of a long tradition of travelling to and from Scotland for seasonal work, they had kept their culture and traditions largely intact. Irish was the spoken language in most houses and also the language used in shops and pubs, the first places where you'd expect English to have made inroads. I couldn't help being impressed at finding a place in my own county so different from the place in which I was born.

I found myself working with two other teachers, the headmaster Father Hugo Bonar and Charlie Boyle, who had been my Irish teacher in St Enda's only four years before. As the school was new there were only two classes, and my job was to teach Irish, English and Commerce to both. I liked the school and the pupils and I got on well with Father Bonar and Charlie Boyle, whose reminiscences about St Enda's I was able to share. In my first year my annual salary was £220. Fortunately, frugal living was not new to me; at university I had got by on a scholarship of £150 a year. By comparison £220 seemed to promise opportunities for all kinds of excess. I was soon to discover, however, that £18 6s 8d a month didn't go very far. It was just enough to pay for bed and board, a daily newspaper, a book or two a month, and two ounces of pipe tobacco a week.

As classes finished at three in the afternoon, I had a lot of spare time on my hands. Like many a schoolmaster before me, I thought I might write a short story or two and thus painlessly embark on a literary career. The most promising short story I wrote was entitled 'An Obstinate Bird'. It concerned a poor widow who was fattening a goose for Christmas to celebrate the expected return of her only son from Australia. As she had barely enough food for herself, she collected scraps of all kinds from the neighbours, but no matter what she fed the goose, it refused to put on weight. As the weeks went by, she became worried in case it might not make a decent meal for two. In desperation she denied herself her daily bowl of porridge in order to feed a cup of oatmeal to the goose, but whenever she lifted the miserable bird in her hands, it felt as light as ever. As a last resort she brought it into the house and put it under a creel by the fire where it could enjoy the warmth of the kitchen, but still it refused to mend. Christmas Eve came and her son had not arrived. Ever since she had brought the bird into the house, she felt as close to it as if it were a child of her own. Now she told herself that perhaps it was a good thing her son had not returned, because she would not have had the heart to kill the treasured bird. For her Christmas dinner she made a bowl of porridge with her last cup of the oatmeal and shared it with the goose.

On Boxing Day the goose stretched out its neck and died, leaving the poor widow distraught. All afternoon she sat fondling her dead companion and stroking its smooth neck feathers. In the evening she dug a hole in the garden and buried the unfortunate creature, after which she took to her bed. A few days later her son returned from Australia. He found her in a fever and unable to speak. He sent for the doctor, but by the time he arrived the poor woman had died. 'She was fattening a goose for Christmas,' the doctor said. 'She wouldn't listen to common sense. She fed the bird the food she herself should have eaten. She died of malnutrition or sheer good nature, depending on how you look at it.'

I was so pleased with my story that I sent it off to *The London Magazine* and waited eagerly for the editor's congratulatory letter and cheque. Two months passed but neither letter nor cheque had arrived. Then one day my short story came back in the post with a note saying that ever since Liam O'Flaherty wrote 'The Fairy Goose', everyone in Ireland seemed to be writing stories about old women and their geese. However, if I should care to submit a factual or amusing piece on the fattening of geese for Christmas, the editor might consider it for publication in due season. That put a serious damper on my literary dreams. I was sufficiently young to have grand ambitions, and the suggestion that I might sit down and write a factual article, even an amusing one, I took as an affront to my literary dexterity. In fact, the idea of writing such an article horrified me. It smacked of journalism, and I had read somewhere that a famous critic had dismissed journalism as literature in a hurry. I wasn't in any hurry, and telling myself that I could afford to bide my time, I tore the offending letter in two and lit my pipe with it.

After a few days, however, I simmered down a bit, and when I reread my tale I had to admit that if I hadn't read O'Flaherty's story, I would probably never have written it. Next time, I told myself, I would write something that had grown out of my own experience as opposed to another writer's. Unfortunately, my experience of life was limited to having grown up on a farm and being educated at boarding school and university. I hadn't fought in a war, I hadn't fished marlin, and I hadn't been to Africa on safari. Compared with the life of action led by the young Hemingway, my experience of the world seemed thin and insubstantial. However, when I thought of Jane Austen and the "two inches of ivory" on which she worked, I took heart again. In my innocence I told myself that what I needed was a keener awareness of literary technique, something I could acquire from a serious immersion in the best contemporary literary criticism. At university I had been a diligent student and I would become one again in my spare time. Just as some people live to eat, I would read to write. The idea appealed to me — an opportunity to resume my literary studies from where I had left off without having to worry about deadlines or exams.

I began borrowing books from the Central Library for Students in Dublin, which came to me through the post. I remember reading LA Marchand's weighty biography of Byron, whose *Don Juan* had made me laugh out loud. Having already read Leavis and Henry James on the novel for my degree exam, I now felt that deeper immersion in 'the common pursuit of true judgment' might not go amiss and so I borrowed critical works by I A Richards, Yvor Winters, G Wilson Knight, Cleanth Brookes and Lionel Trilling in the hope that some of their analytical acuity might rub off on me. What I had yet to learn, however, was that criticism is one thing and literary creativity something else, and that only one or two novelists have ever managed to excel in both.

One of my regrets while at university was that I didn't have enough time to read widely in contemporary fiction. Now I would do just that, and in case I should miss anything that was worthwhile in the contemporary canon, I took out subscriptions to *The Times Literary Supplement* and *The New Statesman*, the back half of which was given over to book reviews at the time. As the best novels reviewed were not available in Ireland, having failed to meet the exacting literary standards of the Irish Censorship Board, I ordered them direct from Blackwell's in Oxford. They came in the post in sober-looking brown parcels embellished with the Blackwell logo. And they always seemed to get through the Irish Customs without a hitch, a fact I attributed to Blackwell's unimpeachable reputation as purveyors of scholarly works.

I have fond recollections of my time in Gweedore. One of my most vivid memories concerns a visit to Ards Friary on a Saturday evening in May 1960. When a friend mentioned that he was going to Confession with the Franciscans in Ards, I asked if I could come along, seeing it as a good opportunity to fulfil my 'Easter duty'. At that time the Franciscans resided in Ards House, once the rather grand home of an English family. As we entered the grounds, I found myself trying to deduce something of the history of the place from the tall trees that lined each side of the drive. It was a scene that suggested a prosperous past and a more leisured life than any I had known.

Now it offered the kind of serenity in which a friar might walk up and down in contemplation as he read the office of the day.

Entering the oratory, we were met by the uplifting scent of burnt incense. The altar was arranged for Mass and the evening light filtered gently through stained-glass windows. In a bench by the confessional four or five people knelt in prayer. Somewhere behind us a clock chimed the half-hour, accentuating a silence that seemed eternal. It seemed to me to be the kind of place in which prayer might come easily, a place of silence broken only now and again by the sibilant whisperings of penitents and their confessor. I knelt for five or ten minutes and thought about my life and its shortcomings. Then I listened to the Franciscan's words of advice and encouragement, words that he had repeated many times but sounded freshly coined for the occasion.

We had planned to take the Dunlewy road home but somewhere along the way we took a wrong turning and found ourselves at the foot of Muckish Mountain without a house in sight. We tried again, and soon fetched up in an expanse of black turf-cuttings and bleached stumps of bog-oak. As we went back on our tracks, the light began to fade from gold to purple in the west and a dark purple mist descended on the hilltops. It seemed to me that we were on a spiritual quest in uncharted territory, a primeval continent predating doubt and despair. At last we found the Dunlewy road that runs over the moorland behind Errigal, a conical mountain whose noble solidity and uncompromising austerity only reinforced my sense of the numinous. Now the landscape before my eyes seemed to represent a world of illusory appearances, while hidden somewhere in this unaccustomed light was a true world that could be mine if only I had the art and perception to explore it.

'Ards is a peaceful place,' I said to my companion when we'd passed Dunlewy. 'Is that why you go there?'

'I go because it isn't on the doorstep. And no matter how many times I go, I always find a different Franciscan. They never look at you. They could just be talking to themselves.'

'Most of the time, maybe they are,' I replied. 'I liked the oratory, though. It's so different from any chapel I've ever been in.'

'It was once a ballroom, you know. Under the English.'

I imagined the walls ringing with careless laughter, and the smiles of young ladies outshining the glow of the candelabras. Somehow I preferred to think of it as a peaceful oratory and I made up my mind to go back one day. As things turned out, I never did see Ards House again. Some years later I read that it had been demolished and a new friary built in its place, but the memory of that evening and our journey back to Derrybeg will always remain with me as one of the rare otherworldly experiences of my life.

After two years of country living and intensive reading, I felt that it was time for a change. I spent a further two years teaching, one in Dublin and one in Mullingar. I enjoyed the social life of Dublin, though teaching in the city was more demanding than teaching in the country. There were stacks of essays to be corrected each week and the pupils were not as eager to learn. Trying to teach them Irish, a compulsory subject and a dying language, was a thankless task. Most of the Irish books on the course concerned rural living, which was far removed from the personal experience of city children. Not surprisingly, some of them saw Irish as the language of the bogman and the culchie, and in their superior wisdom resented having to learn it.

The drudgery of the work sapped my energy, and I had little inclination to persist in my attempts at writing in the evenings. Most of the other teachers were older than me. They had little interest in books, theatre or cinema. They had more or less given up serious reading, even in their subjects. One day I had a vision of myself in twenty years' time going home in the evening with a briefcase of uncorrected essays, resigned to a life devoid of intellectual challenge. It was not an inspiring prospect.

Dublin revealed different facets of life from the ones I had known in the country. I particularly remember an encounter with a young barrister, to whom a friend from UCG introduced me. I was shy and callow, while he was worldly wise and socially sophisticated in a way I could never hope to be. When I began telling him about an Ibsen play I had just seen at the Eblana, he told me that he had no desire to go to the theatre because his clients provided him with all the drama he needed. 'In fact,' he said, 'the stories I hear at briefings trump Dickens at his most phantasmagorical.' As he began telling me enthusiastically about his career and ambitions, I asked him what kept him going from day to day. He looked at me uncomprehendingly and explained that what kept him going was simply wondering what might happen next. 'Just think, I have no idea of where I shall be in five years' time,' he said. 'Anything can happen, and isn't that enough?'

He was thinking of his brilliant career, of course, whereas here was I at twenty-four trapped in a nondescript job from which I could see no escape. I happened to be reading *Middlemarch* at the time, and the thought occurred to me that while he found his excitement in wondering what was in store for himself, I found mine in wondering what fate George Eliot had in store for Dorothea, Will Ladislaw, Mr Casaubon and Dr Lydgate. I drew some comfort from the thought that I'd rather be an ill-paid, ill-regarded teacher than a successful barrister who could not see beyond his own career. I wouldn't dream of drawing any general conclusion about barristers from our encounter but I can still recall his well-fed face and how he looked and sounded. He was the first well-heeled, middle-class Irishman I had met, and our mercifully brief conversation left me with an unaccustomed sense of defilement that made me wish I had not met him.

During my year in Mullingar, I finally became convinced that teaching was not for me. In the short dark days of early January 1962, I was overtaken by a malaise of the will unlike anything I had experienced before. I would wake up in the morning and close my eyes again to shut out the grey light of day. It was as if I had despaired of my life and could not begin to imagine a way of changing it. At first I put it down to living inland. In Glen, Galway and Gweedore I could get the tang of the sea in the air I breathed. Even during my year in Dublin, where I lived in Sandymount, I could go for a walk on the strand whenever the fancy took me. Here in Mullingar I was over fifty miles from the smell of saltwater. There were fresh-water lakes but they were a poor substitute for the Atlantic and mountain tarns of home.

I struggled through the days, not caring much how they began or ended. I was living in slack water, a salmon trapped in a pool, waiting for a high tide that would provide a means of escape. It was a feature of my malaise that I was convinced that only an outside agency, a kind of *deus ex machina*, could provide a solution. In the hope of relieving the tedium, I went to a dance in Tullamore where I met a girl whom I knew in Galway and who was now teaching in the town. I could not help being struck by the change in her. When I first knew her, she was all abloom. Now, only four years later, she seemed to have already lost her freshness. The sheen had gone from her hair and her skin looked pale and dry. I asked her what she thought of Tullamore. She smiled at what she saw as a naïve question and told me that she was going to teach in Italy next year to escape the stifling boredom of small-town life in Ireland.

'You could get a job in Dublin,' I said.

'Italy is warmer. Besides, I prefer Italians to Dubs.'

We talked about our four years in Galway and how far away they now seemed.

'We started out with such high hopes,' she said. 'In the staff room yesterday one of the other teachers remarked that she felt like a character in a Chekhov play. She made me laugh. I had never before thought of comparing life in the Irish midlands with that on a Russian estate in the nineteenth century.'

On the way home I kept thinking about our conversation. Quite possibly it was she herself who felt like a Chekhov character, though she didn't dream of Moscow but of Venice, Florence or Rome. I told myself that it was time I began dreaming to some purpose. It was after midnight and bitterly cold. Looking out at the gleaming frost on the road and the low drifts of crawling fog, I realised that on no account must I spend another winter here.

I went home for the Easter holidays and gave my father a hand with the turf-cutting. The old bog on top of the hill was cut out, so he had opened a new bog in Loughunsha on the main road to Carrick, which was convenient for getting the turf home by tractor. As we reached the bog on the first morning, a damp mist lay over the moor. We were expecting a day of dreary mizzle, but then around noon the sun burned its way through the cloud, the mist cleared, larks began singing, and the workers on the other bogs became visible. Plumes of blue smoke rose over the moor, as men lit fires to cook their midday meal, and the lough in the hollow below mirrored the pure blue of the sky. We sat down for lunch and talked about this and that.

'Do you ever think about your life when you're out here on your own?' I asked after we'd eaten.

'Only when I can't help it,' he smiled.

'And have you come to any conclusion?'

'Things went against me. I never had any luck in life. I hope you have more.'

'You did well, given the lack of opportunity.'

'That sums it up. Lack of opportunity. You're lucky. You live in a different world.'

'I think you're right, though. No matter what the opportunity, you need luck to go with it. Some have more luck than they deserve.'

'I don't envy them. I got what I worked for and no more. I have no one to thank but myself.'

'Well, you did your best for all of us.'

'I'm pleased you think so. It's what I was trying to do.'

It's the nearest I ever came to finding out what he thought about his life. He saw it as a struggle against the odds, and he wasn't unduly perturbed by the thought that he'd got no more than he'd worked for. If there were men who did better, he did not envy them. He saw life as an uphill trudge to the top, which you reach only at the last gasp. I told him the story of Sisyphus who was condemned to roll a stone up a hill without respite. Every time he reached the top, the stone would roll back down and he would have to start again from the bottom.

'No, it isn't that bad,' he said. 'Hope and good humour keep us going. Without them, we'd be lost.'

It was the beginning of a week of lovely April weather. We cut a year's supply of turf in four days and carried two tractor loads of the previous year's turf to the roadside. I never felt stronger or better and I envied my father his life of physical labour. To me it seemed more creative than the work I was paid to do.

One evening after we'd eaten, I sat at the kitchen table writing up my diary for the day.

'What are you writing?' he asked, as he puffed at his pipe in the corner.

'A few lines about what we did today.'

'It was like any other day except you were home.'

'For me it was different. I made a discovery that may surprise you. Turf-cutting is more enjoyable than teaching.'

'Why do you say that?'

'At the end of the day there's something to show for your labour, something you can actually see. Teaching dozy pupils is a fruitless task. It's like preaching to the tide, trying to convince it to turn.'

'Maybe you're too impatient. Any tide will turn by itself if you give it time.'

'I'd rather cut turf.'

'Turf-cutting is in your blood. This time we were lucky, the weather was with us. You might change your tune after one or two good wettings. I've had hundreds in my time.'

At that moment what I most desired was to live in Glen and support myself on writing. I could cut my own turf, grow my own potatoes and vegetables, and do a spot of fishing for the pot. I could live on next to nothing. After all I had managed to live in Gweedore on £220 a year. In my enthusiasm I wrote it all down and even did some rough accounting. Yet as I read over what I'd written, I realised that it was a pipe-dream. I didn't tear out the page, though. I put away the book for another day, telling myself that in time life would provide an answer.

As I look through my diary now, I am surprised at the things I left out and the things I chose to record. What interested me then is not what interests me now. I was impatient and hungry for experience: a caterpillar feasting on a single leaf of a single tree, and I could see only one leaf at a time. I had no idea of what the tree looked like, and no idea of the relationship between leaf, twig, branch and trunk, not to mention the all-important roots. I would need to become a butterfly before I could size up the tree from a distance and its place in the wider landscape. Truly, our past selves are strangers. More disappointingly, they are unknowable strangers who can no longer speak to us across the dividing years where they stand mute and defenceless in the face of our uncomprehending censure.

Feeling fit and strong, I went back for the summer term to Mullingar, where I was in the habit of going for a walk along the canal after school. I liked being close to water, and, since I couldn't have the sea, I took the view that stagnant water would have to serve my purpose. On my walk one afternoon I heard what sounded like a metallic whine to my left. Looking up, I saw four white swans flying low over the canal, their bent wings beating slowly, their long straight necks extended. I was thrilled by their sudden appearance, which I saw as some kind of omen. They had passed so close to me that they seemed to shake the stillness of the air. They were easily counted. Only four, not Yeats's nine-and-fifty. After all, the century was older and further removed from the days of high romance. I turned and watched as they descended and then seemed to ski on the water, their rigid thighs moulded by the breeze. I walked on, wondering if the figure four could have any significance. Unlike fifty-nine, it was not a prime number, nor was it a magical one. Still, there were four seasons, and in the legend of the Children of Lir there were four swans, not three or five. It used to be one of my favourite stories, and now on my walk I recounted it to myself, almost as an act of consolation.

Lir, a deity of the Tuatha Dé Danann, married Aeb who bore him four children, a girl named Fionuala and three boys, Hugh, Conn and Fiachra. Sadly, Aeb died in childbirth and Lir married her sister Aoife, who remained childless. After a time she became so jealous of Lir's love of his children that she took them to Lough Derravaragh in Co Westmeath and transformed them by sorcery into four white swans, condemning them to spend three hundred years on Lough Derravaragh, three hundred years on the Sea of Moyle between Ireland and Scotland, and a further three hundred years on the Atlantic off Erris on the rough coast of Mayo. For her evil deed, Aoife's father transformed her into a demon of the air and condemned her to roam among the clouds forever.

These swans, as you might expect, were no ordinary swans. Possessing the power of human speech, they sang the loveliest of songs, and people came from near and far to hear their music. After three hundred years of relative peace among their admirers on Lough Derravaragh, they took wing to the angry waters of the Sea of Moyle where they endured storm, loneliness and terrible hardship, while Fionuala protected her brothers from winter frosts with her feathers.

Finally, the time came for them to begin the last three hundred years of their sentence off the coast of Mayo, where they suffered even greater hardship. By the time they had completed their term, the country had been converted to Christianity. For the first time the swans heard a hermit's bell for matins. They were startled by this alien sound but, when the singing of matins was over, they themselves began their lovely song. The hermit was enchanted by their music and he instructed them in the new religion.

At that time there lived a princess in Munster who was betrothed to a chieftain from Connacht. Having heard of the singing swans in his province, she begged him to give them to her as a wedding present. He seized them by force and took them to his princess. As soon as she laid eyes on them, their lovely plumage fell off, revealing four wizened and hoary human beings.

'Lay us in one grave,' Fionuala implored. 'Place Conn on my right hand, Fiachra on my left, and Hugh before my face, for that is how we were when I sheltered them on winter nights on the Sea of Moyle.'

As I went over the story, it seemed to me that my instinct as a boy was right — that it is a beautiful and tender tale of transformation, which speaks of the mysterious relationship between human life and the world of nature. I too had had my Lough Derravaragh, my Sea of Moyle, and finally my Erris, and with any luck I might be given time to sing a song or two before being transformed into a hoary old man. I was so engrossed in my search for symbolism that I had not noticed how the sky had darkened in the east. I had turned and headed back towards the town, still thinking of the Children of Lir, when I spotted the four swans on a stretch of the canal about fifty yards ahead. I sharpened my pace, wondering how close I'd get before they took off again. They were feeding, dipping their beaks and curved necks as if nothing mattered except the business of gobbling. Except for one, which floated listlessly with a black web projecting from beneath her trailing wing. Now and again she would propel herself along with a vigorous stroke of her other foot. Then, before I could get any closer, they took off, rising from the water with raised wings, then running on the surface as their wings began to flap. As they passed overhead with long necks outstretched, again I heard the dry metallic whine. Yet what impressed me most was the sheer effort of their ascent. The water seemed like treacle holding them back, and their bodies looked too heavy even for their powerful wings. Somehow it seemed to me to be a prefiguring of what I myself must do. Rise from the stagnant water that held me prisoner, and take glorious wing in a less destructive element. Their example was the only *deus ex machina* I could expect.

Ireland is a small and intimate country. Wherever I went, I kept meeting people I knew. I met them on trains, buses, and in the street. I particularly enjoyed meeting old acquaintances from Galway University because we seemed to pick up immediately from where we'd left off some years before. It was as if we had shared something unique, as if we belonged to a secret society with its own codes and passwords. Talking to them, I could see that they suffered from the debilitating intellectual isolation that afflicted my own life. Everyone with a capacity for taking honest thought could speak only of the terrible flatness of life in Ireland.

In those four years I met only one Galway graduate who was happy in his work. He had read physics and chemistry and was teaching general science in a school in Dublin. He began telling me about the joys of introducing young minds to the worlds of Newton, Faraday and Humphry Davy. When I told him that the only thing I knew about Sir Humphry Davy was that he abominated gravy and lived in the odium of having discovered sodium, he said that *au contraire* Sir Humphry was better known for having invented a safety lamp for miners, which was called the Davy lamp to this day. That more or less ended our conversation, and as we parted I wondered if the key to human happiness might be the study of physics and chemistry to first-degree level only.

At the same time, our conversation about Sir Humphry made me realise that I was not a born teacher. I was still trying to educate myself rather than anyone else. As a student I had a passion for learning, whereas most of my pupils resented having to come to school. They had no interest in books, and teaching them filled me with a sense of futility. In moments of despair I reminded myself that they were all future citizens, and that some of them might become community leaders and even occupy responsible positions in government. In that event, as I saw it, there could be no hope for the country. I foresaw a bleak and depressing future for all of us, reminiscent of what Tolstoy had seen in nineteenth-century Russia: 'Whenever I enter a school and see a multitude of children...I am seized with restlessness and terror, as though I saw people drowning.'

The 1950s and early 1960s in Ireland was a time of much dancing and little sex. The contraceptive pill had yet to come, and a young man inclined to take a chance would consider himself lucky if he found a like-minded girl. That said, the life-denying priests ruled the roost, and most young girls listened to them. Luckily, we were not lacking in imagination and in the invention of substitute activities to make up for straightforward lovemaking. Frottage and masturbation were common. The phrase 'a rub of the relic' may say something about the kind of sex that was prevalent among the young at the time. Of course, there was the occasional carefree girl, and here and there an accommodating landlady or widow. I once heard a man who thought of himself as a scholar argue that the phrase 'a rub of the relic' referred to obliging widows, and was really a corruption of 'a rub of the relict'. What every young man longed for was a girl who would go the distance but only when it was safe to do so. Nurses, it was felt, knew precisely what they were about and were in great demand among men with an eye to serious business.

Meanwhile, the priests ranted from their pulpits about so-called sins of impurity. In their obsession with sex, they had invented a rich and specialised vocabulary to label every act that a red-blooded young man and woman might get up to — heavy petting, improper kissing, immodest touching, close dancing, and promiscuous dancing (whatever that was). To judge by their sermons, you'd think we all lived in a pleasure dome of sexual abandon, whereas in truth there was no scarcer commodity than straightforward, honest-to-goodness sex. Like everyone else, the priests had a vivid imagination, and at times I felt that they had foreseen and classified every conceivable sexual manoeuvre, had anticipated the very acme of sensuality, so that no further refinements could be invented. How could we have guessed that within a generation the floodgates would burst open and the prurient clergy and their taxonomical morality would be swept away?

In confession priests were merciless in their probing. They cross-questioned with the forensic fervour of prosecuting counsel in order to establish the exact nature and degree of the 'transgression': of which there were venial sins and mortal sins, sins of commission and sins of omission. Or, above all, the dreaded sin of emission. From hearing thousands of confessions, they were experts on the sin of Onan, as they were inclined to call it. Onan deliberately spilled his seed on the ground, but for the Irish clergy spilling it by accident while courting a girl was even worse.

Ireland at that time was an intellectual backwater in the grip of pampered, self-important bishops and conservative politicians who were little better than the bishops' lackeys. As such, the very air I breathed seemed to lack oxygen. Again and again it was brought home to me that I simply had to get out. I did not, however, fancy going to America. As most of my leisure reading had centred on my study of English literature, increasingly my thoughts turned towards London. I knew from previous visits that it was a metropolis of infinite variety that spelt freedom from petty constraints, a place where I could lose myself happily and indulge my interests in modern literature, drama and cinema. Still, I was reluctant to make a move. Like most of my colleagues, I was so wedded to the familiar that nothing short of a revelation would force me to turn my back on the comforts of a safe job with a secure pension. Yet the revelation, when it came, was not of the Damascene kind. In fact, it could hardly have been more homely and pedestrian.

On one of my trips up to Dublin that spring to see a girlfriend who lived in Glenageary, I overheard a comment that stayed with me. A middle-aged man and a middle-aged woman were sitting in front of me on the bus. The woman, I remember, was wearing a tartan headscarf, and the man a brown felt hat of the kind I associated with the turf. They had been talking to each other in whispers when suddenly the woman lashed out in a strong, declarative voice, 'It doesn't have to be like this.' Quick as a flash, the man responded, 'We can't change things now, not at our age.' I had no idea what they were talking about. Nevertheless, I repeated the woman's words to myself, realising that I was still young and that my life did not have to follow a predetermined course. Ever since I left university, my life had been flat and featureless. The best that could be said for it was that it was cosy and unchallenging, drifting from one day to the next without any sense of direction. Teaching was taking up all my energy, and I was spending the evenings drinking with my male friends in pubs. It doesn't have to be like this, I kept telling myself, but whenever I thought of change I was reminded of a line from Horace beloved of the classics master at my school: *Caelum non animum mutant qui trans mare currunt* — they change their clime, not their frame of mind, who rush across the sea.

When June came, however, I said, 'To hell with Horace.' Like many a restless Irishman before me, I took the boat from Dun Laoghaire to Holyhead. It was a lovely evening, the sky clear, the sea calm. I spent half an hour on deck looking back at the widening wake, as Howth Head receded into the distance. Then I went to the bar and found myself sitting near a table at which two priests and two middle-aged men were playing poker. One of the priests, who was bald and smooth-faced, kept mopping his forehead with a white handkerchief. The other was tall and spare with a thin neck and hollow cheeks. In looks at least he would have made an excellent Don Quixote. Now and again one of the men would go up to the bar and come back with two whiskies and two brandies. They attracted my attention because in those days Irish priests did their drinking in private. These two were probably emigrants like most of the other passengers, or perhaps they had simply left the restrictions of the Island of Plaster Saints behind in Dun Laoghaire.

We arrived in Holyhead some time after midnight. The train to Euston was packed with young men and women returning to London after their annual holiday. I found a corner seat in a compartment carriage and closed my eyes. By the time we had passed Chester most of my companions were asleep. Some time in the small hours I thought I might stretch my legs, and I struck up a conversation with a young Connemara man who was sitting in the corridor on a battered suitcase secured with a piece of string. He was freckled and sun-tanned with sandy-red hair, and he looked the picture of physical fitness. I could imagine him mowing an acre of ground with a scythe in a day and feeling none the worse for the labour.

'Where do you work?' I asked.

'In London,' he said. Then as an afterthought, he added, 'In the tunnels.'

'Tunnelling must be heavy work.'

'It pays well. I'll only do it as long as I have to.'

'What do you think of London?'

'It's noisy and smelly. I spent the last fortnight fishing from a currach to get the poison out of my system.'

He asked me what I did for a living. I told him that I'd been teaching and that I was going to England to find something better to do.

'Lots of teachers come over for the summer. Some of them work on the buildings. They must be mad.'

'I'm here to stay,' I said.

'You're mad, too, chucking in a cushy job like teaching. If I could get work in Ireland, I wouldn't come over here.'

'You don't like England, then?'

'*Talamh gan trócaire*. Land without mercy.' He raised his head and laughed. It was a proud and scornful laugh, the laugh of a man who did not seek mercy.

I stood by the open window, listening to the grinding and hammering of steel on steel and enjoying the rush of the cool night air on my face. I asked myself if the Connemara man was right. I was leaving a secure job with a good pension, but my mind was not on pensions. Instead I felt like an escaped prisoner about to start a new life. I didn't know why I felt so confident because the £140 in my wallet was the sum total of my worldly wealth, apart from the books I had left behind in Mullingar. I had no ties; I had not told anyone of my plans because I didn't have any plans. I would find out in time what was in store for me. It was a great feeling, the sense of having thrown off the shackles that had been holding me down, of being open to whatever should come along. For the first time since leaving university I felt carefree and fully alive.

33

The End of Killaned as Home

I arrived at Euston station early in the morning of Derby day, June 1962, and in the afternoon I found myself among a group of excitable men gathered outside a shop window watching the race on television. It was the most extraordinary Derby in living memory. Seven horses, among them the favourite, fell six furlongs from the end, leaving a rank outsider, an Irish colt named Larkspur, to win at twenty-two to one. Though I hadn't backed him, I couldn't help feeling that his good luck might bode a change of fortune for me as well.

Not being one of nature's optimists, I kept thinking of the Connemara man's description of England as 'a land without mercy'. Had he been reading too much Irish history or was his opinion based on bitter experience? Perhaps he was merely referring to the merciless heat of the London pavements in June. I recalled the afternoon I had seen the swans on the canal in Mullingar. It was enough to make me realise that there was no going back.

The following day I bought a copy of *The Times* and answered an advertisement for an assistant editor. Within a month I had a job in book publishing, doing stimulating editorial work among lively colleagues of my own age. I remained in London for the rest of my working life with the exception of a year spent on secondment in Australia in 1965-66.

A few months before I went to Australia, I met Kathleen Cuddy who came from outside Mountrath in County Laois, deep in the Irish midlands. At the time I had no thought of marriage, nor of the kind of girl I should like to marry, but within ten minutes of meeting Kathleen I realised that here was a girl I must see again. She was different from the other girls I'd been meeting; talking to her gave me an unaccustomed sense of completion. It was as if I'd been at war with myself and had unexpectedly found peace and resolution. When I asked her if Monsignor de Brún had been justified in calling the Irish midlands the Sodomy Belt, she told me that she'd been educated by nuns who had less skill than priests in such matters. She was good-looking, lively and amusing. We shared an irreverent sense of humour. Meeting her in London was like stumbling on a dear and familiar face in a jungle clearing.

Though we had both been brought up in the country, our childhood experiences were different. Kathleen was brought up on a sizable farm, where farming methods and even the terminology of farming differed from those of my experience. She told me about the joys of picking fraochans or bilberries and wild raspberries, and the fun she and the other children had on threshing day. She knew all about milking time and bringing home the cows in the evening. Whenever we met, we compared memories of the past. Before too long we were seeing each other nearly every day, but things didn't go smoothly for us. Kathleen had to go back to Ireland for family reasons, and my job took me to Australia. During my year in Sydney we carried on our conversation entirely by airmail. When we met again on my return, I felt that we had known each other all our lives. We got married in 1967 and settled in Petts Wood in Kent, where we still live. Our son Myles was born in 1970.

For a long time we went back to Ireland for a fortnight every year to see friends and parents. Now when I think of a time of quiet happiness, I think of summer holidays in the Irish midlands with Kathleen's family. I think of straight lanes, high hedges, flat fields, cattle grazing, birds singing, insects buzzing, and the burgeoning stillness of long afternoons. From time to time the hum of a tractor or car might do brief violence to the ear, only to be followed by another silence even deeper than the first. It seemed to me then that this life had been going on since time itself began, and that it would continue until the final extinction of the sun. It gave me a sense of permanence at the centre of change, and a yearning for constancy in the world of fickleness in which I had chosen to live.

I would go for long walks on my own while Kathleen cooked dinner and talked to her mother, and I would find myself comparing life in the midlands with the life I knew in Donegal. Whereas I had a sense of possession in places like Skelpoona in Glen, of treading in the footsteps of my ancestors, in the midlands I would always remain an outsider. I would be moved by a sense of incomprehension in the face of otherness, by a sense of mystery, the mystery of a place with the power to haunt. In London the midlands would still lurk at the back of my mind, nagging and beckoning, as if trying to tease me into an understanding that by birth and nature I was incapable of achieving. The thing that I sought from this strangest of places always seemed to be round the next corner, behind the next hedge, or eternally on the far side of Slieve Bloom.

At other times the midlands would fill me with a sense of warm envelopment, of being a thousand miles from every source of disquiet and irritation. I remember driving to Mountrath with Kathleen one summer afternoon and going into Jim Murphy's pub for a pint of Guinness while she went shopping. It was a quiet time. Everyone was at work. I was the only customer. Murphy pulled my pint and went to the window as he waited for the head to form. He stood with his back to the whiskey bottles, peering over the frosted glass partition at cars and tractors coming and going in the square. And all the time he kept up a lively commentary, like a card player who tells jokes while studying his hand and never misses a trick. I couldn't see the square from where I was sitting, and I couldn't help wondering if perhaps something of great moment was going on outside.

'What's happening?' I said finally, worried in case he'd forgotten to top my pint.

'Nothing ever happens,' he smiled. 'And isn't that the beauty of it.'

Only then did I realise that I'd committed a cardinal sin, that of impatient expectation. Murphy topped my pint and returned to his post by the window, still regaling me with stories about the changes that had taken place in the town since we were home the previous summer. Needless to say, they were insignificant changes, which I wouldn't have noticed if he hadn't reminded me.

As I took my first sip of the day, it seemed to me that I had discovered the secret at the heart of heaven — being told by someone else that nothing is happening, that there is no longer any trauma, and no longer any need for journalists. Nothing to report, even at second- or third-hand. I envisaged myself returning to Mountrath in my eighties to find Murphy still at his station, still looking out at the old familiar square. Alas, it was not to be. A summer or two later I came back to find that he had gone the way of all humankind. The pub was boarded up; his pale, untroubled face no longer at the window looking out.

After a week with Kathleen's people, we'd go north to Donegal to see my father and my aunt. During our stay, my father would spend the time being good-humoured and amusing. He was fond of Kathleen and she of him. They both loved making fun of each other. Only now and again, sometimes in the midst of mirth, would I catch a glimpse of the submerged man, the man beneath the wave. At such times my heart would go out to him and I would seem to take on some of the burden of his solitude, having become aware of another man, a private man whom I would never reach. If I tried to probe by means of a direct question, he would fob me off with an innocuous generalisation, which only underlined his essential reticence and a remoteness that may have been born of disappointed ambitions. Whether the ambitions were for himself or for his family, I do not know. Most of the time these thoughts did not trouble me. He was my father, and over the years I had learnt to enjoy his company and to accept him as he was. His desire to preserve the mystery of his life and the tenor of his innermost thoughts were matters for himself alone.

'What do you think about now that your work is done?' I once asked him over a drink.

'There's nothing to think about. No family to rear. No hay or turf to save. No cow, no bother. No early rising.' He looked at me and smiled to let me know that he was joking.

'Don't you ever think back to when you were young?' I was trying to establish if all old men live in the past. He paused for a moment, wondering if I were being serious.

'When I was young, I didn't know I was young. I could overtake a wether on the run and think nothing of it. Now I can't walk to Cashel without wishing Cashel was in Killaned.'

He was putting me off again but still I persisted.

'If you don't think about the past, what do you think of?'

'People who think about the past are lucky. I think about today and tomorrow. And then another tomorrow. I suppose you could say I think about the future.'

I realised that I'd pushed him far enough. He'd said as much as he was willing to say and I admired him for it.

For a long time he used to go down the field to visit Andy Gillespie in the evenings. He and Andy grew up together. Their farms were next to each other, and, as young men, they both played on the first Gaelic football team in Glen. Later, they fished from the same boat. It was only natural that in old age they should keep their friendship in good repair. With Andy he would go over old times and discuss the local news. They would watch television for an hour and laugh at the follies of the great world. They were mainly interested in the news and, of course, the weather forecast. Sometimes they'd watch a documentary or a programme of light entertainment but they rarely watched old films, which surprised me. I remember one evening while on holiday finding them both with eyes glued to the television as a troupe of high kicking dancing girls flashed their knickers.

'Those girls know how to shake a leg,' my father said.

'Do you think they could shake hay?' Andy wondered.

'They wouldn't just shake it, they'd roll in it.'

My father enjoyed good health for most of his life. Apart from the odd bout of lumbago, he rarely suffered from anything more serious than the common cold. As he grew older, he used to complain of 'pains in the bones'. He suffered from corns, which made walking difficult. In his early eighties he stopped going down to Andy's, and he stopped going to Cashel to meet his friends in the pub. He became more detached, more introspective. I could tell that he was beginning to lose interest in the world.

Whenever we came home to see him, he'd make an effort to be his old amusing self. He'd tell the yarns I enjoyed hearing and he'd be sure to salt his conversation with his customary sayings. In order to get him out of the house for a change, we used to take him on trips to Carrick, Killybegs and Donegal Town. Though he had Auntie Kate for company, I sometimes got the impression that he felt lonely. My sister Bernadette used to come to see him once or twice a week, but he saw the rest of us only rarely. Tina and I lived in England, Peter Joseph lived in Germany and Mary had gone to America. I sometimes wondered if he regretted having advised us all to 'get out while you're still young'. And I could see that gradually he was beginning to feel his age. At one time he used to say half-jokingly that he would live to a hundred. When I reminded him that he still had seventeen years to go, he shook his head and said, 'Seventeen years? It's a long time.'

'How do you feel?' I asked.

'Tired. I've never felt so tired in all my life.'

I knew then that he had given up his ambition to be a centenarian. Even now in my seventies, I have an instinctive understanding of how he must have felt.

He died in February 1986 at the age of eighty-three. Bernadette had already phoned me to say that he was feeling poorly. Though I knew that he had high blood pressure, I told myself that his illness couldn't be serious. He was made of tougher fibre than the rest of us. He would be there in Killaned to greet us whenever we came home on holiday for many years to come. My refusal to believe the worst was an indication of how much he meant to me, and perhaps a foolish reluctance to admit to myself that his life must end.

I went home for the wake and funeral. The house was full of friends and neighbours who had come to offer sympathy, using well-worn phrases that I had heard and had uttered myself on similar occasions many times before. In everything that was said there was a sense of completion, of finality. People recalled when they last spoke to him, what he looked like, and what he'd said. Neighbours who'd dropped in to see him before he died said that he hadn't lost his sense of humour. To me it all sounded unreal: I was finding it difficult to accept the fact that he had gone. At times I felt that it was someone else, not my father, who had died.

He was laid out in a coffin in his bedroom, where I sought in the lineaments of his face some vestige of the man I knew. But the man I knew wasn't there. His face had an expression I had never seen before, or perhaps it was the absence of anything personal in the expression that made me understand for the first time the true meaning of the word 'remains'. I looked then at his hands, which I knew so well. They were cold to the touch but otherwise they had not changed. Only the face spoke of absence, of the extinction of the spark that had made him such a vital presence. I thought of the passionate interest he took in mowing and turf-cutting, of his love of a job well done. Work seemed to me to have given purpose and substance to his life. Yet in conversation he would always dismiss it. 'There's nothing to it,' he would say. 'Who would spend his life slaving, if he had something better to do?'

In order to be alone with my thoughts for half an hour, I went out the Line for a walk. I hadn't been home in February for over twenty years, yet everything was as I remembered it at that time of year, the day dry, windless and cold, the fields closely cropped by sheep, the hills a washed-out greenish brown. Grey and solid, the rocks on the hillsides stood out like misshapen monsters that had been frozen in their posture for all eternity. When I had passed the rock we called the Caiseal Ard, I was out of sight of the Killaned houses, but I continued walking until I reached the S-bend in the road and stood looking down on Cashel village.

I recalled that the Line was the road my father walked many years ago on the night he went out to Daniel's for a pup and came back saying that there were 'openings' in the sky. I remembered how he used to fear wind from the direction of the Caiseal Ard during winter, and how he used to secure the thatch with extra ropes whenever a southeaster threatened. Then he would lie in bed listening to the couples and rafters creaking, and he would get up at dawn to see if any storm damage had been done. Everywhere I looked had associations with the living past. He had spent his life among these rocks and hills. He knew no other life and for the most part he was content, neither envying nor emulating any other man. Above all he had known unity of experience, which was something I often longed for and would never achieve.

In his heyday he had been a difficult man to please. Only two of our neighbours lived up to his exacting standards. The rest were 'slovenly workers' or just 'bone idle' and therefore not to be taken seriously. Whereas he himself expected to be taken seriously. He wouldn't even discuss the weather with a man whose opinion he did not value. For all that, I never once heard him say a harsh word to my mother. There were no arguments in our house but there were sermons aplenty because there was nothing he liked better than laying down the law for us children. Though he may have thought the world of us, it was not in his nature to show it. It did not take us long to learn how to please him, which was simply to do as we were told. He probably did not mean to be harsh. As he saw it, he was only making sure that we didn't grow up into what he would term 'useless articles'. In his middle years he seemed to become aware of his limitations as a father. When one of my sisters got married, he remarked with a glint of humour that though he'd brought up three daughters, he'd never once kissed any of them. Cheekily, I asked him if his remark had been prompted by the type of men they had chosen to be kissed by. He ran his fingers through his white hair and laughed. Too late, he had seen the absurdity of it all.

The day after the funeral I went through his 'papers', which he kept in a small brown attaché case. It contained mainly official documents in brown envelopes — birth certificates, marriage certificates, rate demand notes, notices about seed potatoes, and a press cutting about W T Cosgrave, one of the few politicians he respected. There was nothing of a personal nature, no notes or letters that might have shed light on his inner life. At the bottom of the case was a girlie magazine I'd brought him as a joke many years before. He'd looked briefly at the pictures of naked ladies and said, 'Nothing I haven't seen before. Next time bring me a big rubber doll.' Then he laughed and said, 'If Mary Kate saw this, she'd have a fit.' That was what I liked about him, his essential innocence coupled with a determination never to show surprise.

After the funeral I went down to Garveross to see Uncle Patrick and his wife Caitlín. We talked about my father, recalling the ups and downs of his life. He had been unlucky in losing his wife so young, but he didn't allow himself to dwell on misfortune. He soon immersed himself again in the work of the farm, in keeping everything shipshape and tidy about the house.

'It's just as well he loved his work,' I said. 'It kept his mind off other things.'

'His father was the same,' Patrick said. 'He worked so hard that he looked old before his time. He was barely sixty when he died.'

I was interested to hear about my grandfather because my father had never told me anything about him. Patrick said that he was a silent man. He rarely spoke, and when he did he uttered no more than one or two words at a time.

'You could rely on your father,' Patrick said finally. 'When he said he'd do something, it was already as good as done.'

It wasn't a bad epitaph. It was also something I'd often heard said about Patrick himself. Talking to him about my father's life helped me to come to terms with his death, but for a long time afterwards I felt that a piece of my own life was missing, like a chunk of a cliff that had fallen into the sea. For a reason I could not understand I felt vulnerable and exposed, as if I were standing on a high plateau at the mercy of winds that blew from the east one moment and from the west the next. Unwittingly, I had been jolted into an awareness of my own mortality.

My mother's death had affected me differently. It had left me with a burden of guilt, which I sought to rationalise. I suppose I blamed myself for having taken her presence so much for granted. I had always been more concerned with pleasing my father. For the last seven years of her life I saw her only while I was home on holiday from boarding school and university, and even then I did not talk to her much. I spent the days working with my father in the fields.

After his death I thought of the conversations we used to have as we worked, and of all the conversations we didn't have and now would never have. There were so many things I wanted to ask him now that he had gone. A friend who had lost his father at an early age said to me that I was lucky to have had him for so long, but the truth of the matter is that the loss of a parent at any age is a turning point in one's life. It is a door through which we go and there is no going back into the room we've left. It is the end of something, and it brings in its train a sense of diminishment and dislocation. It forces us into scrutinising our own life, seeking to distinguish between what is genuine and true and what is not.

I am pleased that I enjoyed a good relationship with my father, a relationship that had its roots in farm work done together. Cutting or stacking turf on the bog, we would spend a whole day side by side, absorbed in the work, hardly aware of each other. Eventually, one of us would say something that would spark an animated conversation lasting twenty minutes or more. Then there would be another silence for perhaps an hour, of which neither of us would be fully conscious. It was as if our conversation sprang naturally out of the ground we stood on. Each of us was alone with his thoughts, and if we uttered a thought now and again, it was only our way of thinking aloud or perhaps our way of talking to ourselves. For all I know we may have stumbled on the condition to which all relaxed conversation aspires.

My aunt was unable to go to church for my father's funeral. She was weak and feeble, confined to bed. Now there was no one to look after her, and she was unable to look after herself. Reluctantly but resignedly, she went into a nursing home in Sligo where she spent what remained of her days. Whenever I visited her, she would talk of my father and 'the house in Killaned'. She and he had been together since childhood. 'Why wasn't I called first?' she would ask again and again, as if I should know the answer.

She would have neither radio nor television in her room. Wanting nothing more than to be quiet, she spent her waking hours saying her prayers. The last time I went to see her she spoke of herding cows for her father as a young girl. She was not given to reminiscing, nor had she ever spoken of her childhood before. She died in August 1987 at the age of eighty-nine. I was saddened to think that she had to spend the last year of her life away from what she called 'the house in Killaned'. She would have been happier at home among her own things and among the people she knew. Though she was well looked after by the nuns in Sligo, she found what comfort she enjoyed in her religious belief and unquestioning faith in God. Her life ended quietly and painlessly, which was fitting because she was a quiet person who never sought to give pain to anyone.

My uncle Patrick died in January 1994 at the age of eighty-five. Even as a boy, I had seen him as a solid and unchanging presence. He had an instinctive understanding of children and young people; he knew how to enter into their sense of fun. Never patronising, he always listened to what I had to say, even at a time when it did not make a great deal of sense. After reaching manhood, I discovered that we shared a quirky sense of humour and an appreciation of things that did not conform to common expectation. He had a lively imagination and a keen eye for human foible. He taught me to find interest and amusement in seemingly mundane situations and especially in conversations in which the speakers unintentionally divulge their innermost thoughts. In his later years I would phone him from Kent and tell him about something that had tickled my fancy. Most people are fairly predictable in their reactions but Patrick always had an original comment up his sleeve, and no matter how hard I tried, I could never predict what it might be. Even today, when I come across something out of the ordinary in my reading, I say to myself, 'Patrick Heekin would have enjoyed this,' and more often than not I can think of no one else with whom to share my pleasure.

A few years ago, as I read Pierre Loti's *Iceland Fisherman* for the first time, I could not help thinking of Patrick and wishing he were alive to enjoy this fateful story of Breton fishermen with its unforgettable evocation of perilous coasts, unpredictable winds, thick fogs, and the myriad moods of the sea. He wouldn't have been slow to make comparisons with the Glen coast and the lives of the local fishermen he knew so well, thus deepening and enlarging my enjoyment of the book and his own. One of the reasons I enjoyed talking to him about novels we both had read was that I always learned something new about the glen as well as gaining a different perspective on the story.

Shortly after my aunt's death, Kathleen and I went back to Glen to visit the house in Killaned. My aunt's armchair and the sofa on which my father used to doze were still there. All that was missing was the life the house once knew. Kathleen put on the kettle and made tea. We sat in the kitchen looking out at Screig Beefan and across the field to Jamie Boyle's, remembering the meals we'd had at the little table and talking about how things used to be. After a while Kathleen went out to the garden, leaving me alone in the house. I opened one or two drawers and found some old postcards I'd sent from Rome, Canton, Bangkok and other places I'd visited years before. There was a smell of mildew in Auntie Kate's room and the range in which my father always kept a roaring fire was cold. The day was calm. There was not a sound within or without and I found myself quoting lines from Thomas Hardy:

> *But the rapt silence of an empty house*
> *Where oneself was born,*
> *Dwelt, held carouse*
> *With friends, is of all silences most forlorn.*

My father had left the house and farm to all five of us, thinking that we might enjoy it as a holiday home. Sadly, we are not a harmonious family. We find it difficult to agree on the simplest thing. In belonging to all five of us, the house belonged to none of us. It soon fell into disrepair. Rising damp and woodworm did for the woodwork. What was once a snug and warm cottage became an empty shell. It was the end of Killaned as home.

34

Home But Not Home

In September 2003 Kathleen and I went back to Kil-laned for a holiday. We rented a cottage about two hundred yards from the house where I was born, so I was living as close to home as I am ever likely to get. It is strange how different two adjacent places can be, especially when you can't see one from the other. The view from the front windows was different from the one to which I had been accustomed as a boy. I grew up looking out on the blank end-wall of McGlinchey's house whereas now I saw before me a steep bank of grey rocks with grassy ledges where ewes and lambs were grazing. White sheep, green grass, and grey drystone walls: a comforting scene that awakened sleeping memories.

The sounds were also different from those I grew up with. Now in bed at night I listened to the music of the wind in the overhead electric cables, a continuous whine that rose and fell but never seemed to die away, whereas the sound I remembered from childhood was the moaning of the wind in the chimney, threatening to drown out its hiss and whistle in the thatch of the eaves.

On my first morning I looked out of the bedroom window at Screig Beefan and the north side of the Glen. To the west I could see a corner of the bay and the terraced waves breaking over the Oitir as well as the black rocks of the Garveross coast. After breakfast I went for a walk on Killaned hill. I looked down on new lookalike bungalows that could have been designed by one madly obsessive brain. There were houses in hollows and houses on slopes commanding magnificent views of shore and sea, and houses in places that were once a jumble of tortured and twisted rock. The bungalows stood out against the austere landscape, providing sharp contrasts of form and colour, unlike the old thatched cottages which sprang as naturally as a tree out of the land itself.

Turning to the hill behind me, I could not but be aware of how small the once towering rocks now looked. In childhood I climbed them with difficulty, as if I were no bigger than a tortoise. There were rocks on every side — rocks perched precariously on slopes, grey rocks with sharp, severe faces, rocks smothered in moss and lichen. I sought out a flat bed-like rock with the names of former neighbours carved on it. Most were now dead, and those who weren't had left to make a life elsewhere. I thought of Oisín who returned from the Land of Youth, only to find his old comrades in arms gone to a happier hunting ground. My own situation was not dissimilar; of the older generation whose conversation I used to enjoy, only three were left, all of them close to eighty.

On the way back I called in to see Johnny Gillespie, an old neighbour of mine who never left Killaned. He is seven years older than I, but Kathleen says he looks five years younger, which Johnny puts down to 'the strong sea air'. He still has a lively and inventive mind, and he is blest with a prodigious memory. He can recall in detail everything he has seen, and every story and saying he has ever heard. He is thoughtful as well. As I take my leave, he gives me a bag of black turf 'to keep the fire going' until I have time to go to the shop.

In the afternoon I went down to Gannew to see Conn O'Gara and his wife Una. At that time Conn was almost eighty, but he still went out in his boat in the summer months to fish cod, mackerel, pollock and anything else that came his way. He would spend the winter months in his loom-house weaving rugs with highly complex patterns, which he sold to tourists from countries the world over. As I expected, he is still an incisive and combative conversationalist. Talking to him is an enlivening experience; he keeps switching from English to Irish and back again with the speed of a shuttle. He talks in anecdotes, which is his way of commenting obliquely on whatever I say. The only proper and courteous response to this method of discourse is to tell another story as a comment on his. He would see it as a failure of the imagination if I resorted to the adversarial methods of argument adopted by pundits and politicians in their verbal battles on radio and television. Talking to Conn becomes a covert battle of wits and a test of my powers of impromptu invention. His conversation has years of tradition behind it, and is not the kind of conversation to be found among the fast-fun-seeking young.

The following day we visited my sister Bernadette in Clogher, a townland at the foot of Slieve League on the way to Carrick. As we talked, I realised what a trickster memory can be, suppressing some things and conflating others. Our memories were not so much contradictory as variously selective. We remembered different conversations, different incidents, and different facets of the same events. To complicate matters, I am six years older than my sister. I could remember things that happened before she was born and she could remember things that happened while I was away at boarding school and university. Talking to her, I was reminded again and again of my mother. Bernadette is the only one of us who has inherited her sense of fun and gift for mimicry.

In the afternoon the three of us visited the family home in Killaned to celebrate Bernadette's sixtieth birthday. Though the day was mild, the house felt cold. In every room was a pervasive smell of mould and damp. Kathleen made tea and Bernadette produced some digestive biscuits to remind me of those Auntie Kate used to keep hidden in her bureau. In the field below the house three rams were grazing. As we walked down the slope we call the Brae, the rams lifted their heads and stared at us inquisitively. They looked quite docile but with the approach of the ramming season in six weeks' time they would take on a more belligerent character.

For me the Brae had become a place of special familial significance. My grandfather and great-grandfather mowed it, and my father and I had mowed it. I can never walk it without listening for footfalls other than my own. As I paused at the places my father used to build his haycocks, I found myself reciting a few lines from Pope:

> *Happy the man, whose wish and care*
> *A few paternal acres bound,*
> *Content to breathe his native air*
> *In his own ground.*

I had to travel a long way to discover the force and truth of those simple lines. It was no comfort to recall that Pope was only twelve when he wrote them.

I unhasped the barn door, bending low to enter. On an unmortared wall hung my father's farming implements. Two scythes and two turf-spades, his and mine, caught my eye. I took down my father's turf-spade, the one with the polished horn, and went through the motions of cutting and casting. Then I tried out his scythe, which was hung just right for me, since we were both almost the same height. Next I took down a large wooden needle called a *snáthadán*, with which he used to mend nets and knit covers for lobster creels. He himself had carved it, I remember, from a piece of cast-in hardwood. As I turned it over in my hand, I decided to take it back to Kent and hang it on the wall of my study so that I could look at it from time to time while writing or listening to music. In vain I was seeking the key to an elusive past that continued to resonate in my mind like a bell that had just been rung.

Like all who return after a lengthy absence, I was keenly aware of the changes that had taken place. When I was growing up, Glen was a tightly woven, homogeneous community. Most families had lived in the parish for generations; only a handful of surnames came from outside. Now there were scores of new families and new surnames, making Glen a more complex and less cohesive community. The old ethos of 'we're all in the same boat' was dying out; the days of the *meitheal*, of neighbours helping each other with major farming tasks, were over. Now there was a greater desire for personal privacy, a greater readiness to mind one's own business and let other people mind theirs. No one yet quite subscribed to the philosophy of 'devil take the hindmost' but in time that, too, will come.

The fields of the small farms also looked different. There was no one shaking hay. There were no trampcocks and no haystacks. The handful of farmers who still raised cattle made grass silage for winter feed. The land was being used mainly to grow potatoes and vegetables for home consumption, and as pasture for sheep. Consequently, there was no longer much need for the ancient and honourable scythe. Within a generation or two, it would become a forgotten implement. The same was true of the slane or turf-spade. Those who still 'saved' their own turf had them cut by machine. The slane and the scythe were destined to go the way of the flail and the quern stone before them — ending up as quaint exhibits in McDyer's folk museum.

In meeting and talking to people, I found, unsurprisingly, that I had more to say to those of my own generation, who hadn't changed much since I first knew them. They might be more prosperous than their parents but they still lived by the same beliefs and shared the same mores. The younger generation inhabited a different world, a rural version of the life lived in Sligo, Galway, Cork, or any other large provincial town. Children of the television era, they were tuned into the latest pop culture. They were energetic, uninhibited, and independent. They had cast off the shackles of religion; they would not be told by anyone, parent, priest, or politician, how to live their lives.

Judging by appearances, Glen seemed to have found the prosperity that McDyer sought for it over fifty years ago. The new houses looked spick and span, and everyone had money to spend. More pupils were going to secondary school, technical college and university, and there was a thriving Irish college for those who wished to learn the native language. Though I should have been impressed by all this purposeful activity, I couldn't conceal from myself the feeling that prosperity had been bought at a price. In my conversations with elderly people I soon discovered that I was not alone in my judgement.

Those who remembered Glen in the 1930s and 1940s spoke of the younger generation with a mixture of amusement and puzzlement. While they admired their independence of spirit and their impatience with shibboleths and outmoded practices, they questioned their unthinking appetite for the good things of life and their desire to live for the day without a thought for tomorrow. Though no one wished to return to the bad old days of scraping and scrimping and forelock-tugging deference to so-called superiors, I found a willingness to wonder if in the rush to modernise, too much of the traditional way of life had been sacrificed. As one neighbour put it, 'the water that went under the bridge carried off more than garbage.' I wondered if that was his way of saying that the baby had gone out with the bath water.

A few days later on my way to Garveross I passed a field where one of my old school friends was mowing with a scythe. He was brown as a hazelnut from sun and wind, and his hair had gone white. By his style of mowing I could tell that he was no longer loose-limbed. I climbed in over the ditch and asked him if I could try my hand. With a smile he handed me the scythe and watched critically as I mowed a swathe. I told him that I just wanted to remind myself of the rhythm of the work and the swish of the blade in the falling grass.

'You've still got the gait,' he conceded, 'but could you last out till nightfall?'

I told him that I'd rather not try. I picked up the whetstone and with a few rubs sweetened the dull blade before mowing another swathe. This time the scythe felt lighter and the blade went through the grass with a lilt. At least I hadn't lost my edge.

'We're all in the same boat,' he said as I handed him back his scythe. 'Two or three hours are more than enough for me now.'

We talked about old times for a while. When I asked him what he thought of the mad cavortings of the Celtic Tiger, he wiped the blade with a handful of grass and looked at me quizzically.

'He's a bit like Santa Claus. He doesn't come to everyone.' 'Like any tiger, he may be a bit elusive,' I suggested.

'No, he isn't elusive but he's choosy. He's fond of business people and property dealers. He spends most of his time in the big towns.'

'Well, as far as I can see, he's paid more than one visit to Glen. He's finally banished the wolf from the door.'

'The Tiger is a stranger here. The wolf isn't. Mark my word, we haven't seen the last of him.'

At the time I thought it a defeatist thing to say. Neither of us knew then that in less than six years the Tiger would have caught pneumonia and the wolf would be back at the door.

I left him to his gloomy prognostications and continued on my journey. Pausing on the Minister's Bridge to look upriver, I told myself that the past was dead and that no earthly power could resurrect it. If a scythe couldn't resurrect it for me, nothing could. Not even an oatmeal farl. The heart, alas, grows old, and younger hearts were now enjoying their own unique version of our yesterdays.

I looked across at inscrutable Screig Beefan and told myself that history in its quirky way had amply rewarded McDyer for his self-mythologising. Since his death in 1987 his reputation in the folk memory had swelled and burgeoned. I wasn't in the least surprised to hear one of his more simple-minded disciples suggest that the ancient glen of Colmcille be renamed GlenMcDyer, while an even more excitable acolyte wondered piously if there might be some possibility of beatification leading ultimately to canonisation. McDyer, who was not the most modest of men, would have gloried in the thought. As one of his less excitable admirers, I like to think that in heaven he has at last found a role worthy of his talents, perhaps conducting a choir of angelic beauties singing hymns *a cappella* or assisting St Peter at the pearly gates as a strong-armed chucker-out. The former role would gladden his lively eye for the female form and the latter would surely flatter his sense of self-importance.

Towards the end of our holiday, I visited the old bog at the top of the hill, just to see if anything had changed. The weathered stumps of bog oak looked whiter than I remembered. The raised beds of vanished turf-stacks were still there, and so was the footbridge of bog oak, stones, scraws and heather my father had built over the little stream. It was the only evidence of his handiwork that remained, and in time, I knew, that would also disappear. As I stood on the footbridge looking round the featureless bog-land, I recalled Longfellow's disenchanted view of the fate of all human artefacts:

> *Behind us in our path we cast*
> *The broken potsherds of the past,*
> *And all are ground to dust at last.*

I tell myself that what applies to my father's handiwork applies equally to my own handful of novels, and somehow I know that it does not matter, that my personal satisfaction lies not in the hope of their survival but in the rare sense of freedom I had in their creation.

Looking round the denuded moorland, I found myself yearning for a time long past, a time when my grandfather and great-grandfather worked here. Over the years Glen and I had changed, and in changing we had not kept in step. To be myself and to fulfil the needs of my nature, I had to carve out a path that led me farther and farther from the place where I was born. For that, I could hardly blame myself, if only because I had little choice in the matter. Neither do I deprecate the changes that have taken place in the glen itself. Nothing that lives stands still. Life is a dance leading ultimately to the dance for which there is no word in English. Our lives are built on sand, on misunderstandings and misconceptions, and even our most precious memories of childhood glow and flicker with our moods. But whether or not they are true to the past, they are part of our waking and dreaming hours; they are imbued with their own unique reality. The paradise we most yearn for is the paradise we have lost, the paradise that is no longer there to receive us.

I walked down the slope overlooking Loch an Airgid and rested on a clump of heather. It seemed to me that I was talking to my father, both of us remembering how it used to be. We didn't seem to be talking about anything in particular. Our conversation meandered without benefit of logic along the avenues of memory and random association. He asked me what I'd learnt from life and I said, 'Next to nothing.' That seemed to please him, final summation being foreign to us both. We talked about 'next to nothing' for an hour or so, and I felt at the end that we'd talked about everything. If someone had asked me what we'd been talking about, I would have said truthfully that I lacked the words to translate it. That was my father, the last of a tribe. There was no one left who could make his kind of conversation.

I looked at the grey water before me. Near a patch of weed at the far end a solitary bird with a curved neck and dark plumage was facing into the breeze. She was sitting perfectly still, neither feeding nor paddling, just holding her position in the current with an occasional stroke of her webs. I watched her for a good hour, seeking to match her attitude of relaxed vigilance, and during that time she neither changed her position nor looked to left nor right. I was hoping that she might be joined by a flight of duck or, better still, a swan or two, but no other bird came near. She had the lough to herself as I had the mountain to myself. We were both alone, and I did not know what to call her. She was the colour of a cormorant, yet she didn't have a cormorant's neck and shoulders. The cormorant is a nervous bird, forever on the alert, while this bird seemed quietly contented, even a shade phlegmatic. Suddenly she raised herself and for a moment seemed to stand stock still on the water. Then she settled down again, resuming her lonely vigil, looking westwards straight into the breeze. I told myself that she was an odd bird, a solitary bird, *éan corr, éan cuideáin* or *éan scoite*, as we say in Irish. The longer I looked at her, the greater affinity I felt with her. I got to my feet and began walking slowly towards her, just as I once walked towards the crane on Loch an Óir as a boy. I reached the near shore but still she made no move. I began walking slowly round the lough to the far shore but my bird remained majestically unaware of my approach, lost in contemplation of the water beneath her crop. Then with a raucously contemptuous cry that startled me, she rose and turned, making straight for Loch Abha on the way to Slieve League.

I stood on the shore, looking out on the empty water. Even my solitary companion had gone; I was alone. I had come back in search of the sacred places of my boyhood, and this was one of them. Here the past was all around me: in the lisping of lough water and in the hiss of the wind in the heather. It was here in the heavy scent of the spongy bog-land, in the reflected grey of the sky, and in the ghost-voices of another time. I closed my eyes and instead of voices heard the drumming of the wind in my ear. I searched my mind for a word but no word came. The past was a mystery that words could not make known.

I couldn't ask for a more peaceful scene. It seemed to me to be the kind of place where one day I might find a last resting place. I would ask to have my ashes scattered on this unfrequented water under the indifferent gaze of Slieve League. In this bare windswept hollow there was no possibility of ceremony or charade. There were few colours, apart from washed-out greens and browns. It was a place far removed from the meretricious glitter of the cities in which I had lived. There was no place like it. Other parts of Glen might suffer transformation but Loch an Airgid — the Lough of Silver — would surely remain itself.

Glossary of Place Names

Most of the Glen place names are in Irish or are transliterations of the Irish, e.g. Beefan for the Irish *Biofán* and Garveross for the Irish *Garbhros*. Folklore has it that Beefan and Garveross were once a single farm owned by a family that lived in Garveross. The younger son asked the father to give him the northern end of the farm. The father said, '*Gabh anonn is bí fann,*' (Go over and be weak and destitute), which is how Biofán got its name! I don't know if that is the real derivation of *Biofán* but it's the best explanation I've heard.

Many of the Irish place names have survived in the dative case. I've never heard any fisherman refer to a rock called 'Leac Ard'. Among the locals at least, the old dative Leic Aird is the form that has survived. Some Irish place names are so old that their meaning has become obscure, perhaps because they are corruptions of words no longer in use. I have not included any of those in this necessarily brief glossary.

Ailt a' Mhianaigh: *Ailt ⟩Alt*, cliff or hillock. The hillock of the mineral ore.
Áit Dhomhnaill Bhuí: sallow or yellow-skinned Donal's place or field.

Caiseal Ard: the high stone fort or rock.

Carraig na nIolar: the rock of the eagles.

Carraig na Saíán: the rock of the young glassan or coal-fish.

Casán Ard: *casán ›cosán*, path. The high path.

Ceann a' Deáin: the head of the sea channel (at low tide).

Círín: crest or ridge.

Cloch Mhór: big stone.

Clúidín: diminutive of *clúid*, nook or corner. The small nook.

Corr-Mhalaigh: uneven, humpy hillside.

Cúl a' Gharraí: the back of the garden.

Garbhros: rough promontory.

Garraí na hEorna: the barley garden.

Leachtaí: plural of *leacht*, slab or pile of stones.

Leargain na Saortha: the height or slope of the craftsmen.

Leic Aird Chúl na hÚacha: leic ›leac, flagstone or slab. The high slab behind the caves.

Leic na Mágach: the slab of the pollock.

Log na dTrúan: hollow of miserable people or animals.

Logán: little hollow.

Oileán na gCapall: the island of the horses.

Páirc a' Mhíodúin: the meadow park.

Píosa Neddy: Neddy's piece or field.

Poll a' Dubh-Lustraigh: The inlet of the black seaweed.

Roisín Coimhthigh: *roisín*, diminutive of *ros*, headland. Peculiar little headland.

Sceilp Úna: *sceilp* › *scealp* or *scailp*, crevice or large rock. Una's large rock. Refers to the Carraig Mhór, a large rock in the inlet.

Spinc: a high, pointed rock.

Tóin a' Foinse: the bottom of the spring or fountain.
Tor a' Chreasaigh: *Tor*, tall rock or sea-stack. The belted sea-stack. Refers to its layers of rock that look like belts.
Úig a' Chogaidh: the war cave.